L.M. MONTGOMERY'S RAINBOW VALLEYS

L.M. Montgomery's Rainbow Valleys

The Ontario Years, 1911–1942

Edited by Rita Bode and Lesley D. Clement

McGill-Queen's University Press
Montreal & Kingston • London • Chicago

© McGill-Queen's University Press 2015

ISBN 978-0-7735-4574-8 (cloth)
ISBN 978-0-7735-4575-5 (paper)
ISBN 978-0-7735-9738-9 (ePDF)
ISBN 978-0-7735-9739-6 (ePUB)

Legal deposit fourth quarter 2015
Bibliothèque nationale du Québec

Printed in Canada on acid-free paper that is 100% ancient forest free (100% post-consumer recycled), processed chlorine free

This book has been published with the help of a grant from the Canadian Federation for the Humanities and Social Sciences, through the Awards to Scholarly Publications Program, using funds provided by the Social Sciences and Humanities Research Council of Canada. Funding has also been received from the Symons Trust Fund for Canadian Studies.

McGill-Queen's University Press acknowledges the support of the Canada Council for the Arts for our publishing program. We also acknowledge the financial support of the Government of Canada through the Canada Book Fund for our publishing activities.

Library and Archives Canada Cataloguing in Publication

L.M. Montgomery's rainbow valleys : the Ontario years, 1911–1942 / edited by Rita Bode and Lesley D. Clement.

Includes bibliographical references and index.
Issued in print and electronic formats.
ISBN 978-0-7735-4574-8 (bound).–ISBN 978-0-7735-4575-5 (paperback).--ISBN 978-0-7735-9738-9 (ePDF).–ISBN 978-0-7735-9739-6 (ePUB)

1. Montgomery, L. M. (Lucy Maud), 1874–1942–Homes and haunts–Ontario. 2. Novelists, Canadian (English)–Homes and haunts–Ontario. 3. Novelists, Canadian (English)–20th century–Biography. 4. Canadian fiction (English)–20th century–History and criticism. 5. Ontario–Intellectual life–20th century. I. Bode, Rita, 1950–, editor II. Clement, Lesley D. (Lesley Diana), 1951–, author, editor III. Title: Rainbow valleys.

PS8526.O55Z928 2015   C813'.52   C2015-904167-8
                                  C2015-904168-6

To Ella, Emily, and Evie,
a new generation of Montgomery readers

Contents

Illustrations / xi
Acknowledgments / xiii
Introduction / 3
RITA BODE AND LESLEY D. CLEMENT

Prologue

1 Leaskdale: L.M. Montgomery's Rainbow Valley / 21
ELIZABETH WATERSTON

A New Home in Leaskdale: War and Religion

2 "To the Memory of": Leaskdale and Loss in the Great War / 35
MARY BETH CAVERT

3 "Being a Christian" and a Presbyterian in Leaskdale / 54
MARGARET STEFFLER

The Changing World of Women: Mother, Daughter, Friend

4 "A Gift for Friendship": Revolutionary Friendship in *Anne of the Island* and *The Blue Castle* / 77
LAURA M. ROBINSON

5 The New Mother at Home: Montgomery's Literary Explorations of Motherhood / 91
CAROLINE E. JONES

Shadows in Rainbow Valley: Loss and Grief

6 The Shadow on the House of Dreams: Montgomery's Re-Visioning of Anne / 113
WILLIAM V. THOMPSON

7 "My Pen Shall Heal, Not Hurt": Writing as Therapy in *Rilla of Ingleside* and *The Blythes Are Quoted* / 131
MELANIE J. FISHBANE

Interlude

L.M.M. / 147
KATHERINE CAMERON

A Sense of Place: Reading and Writing

8 Old Years and Old Books: Montgomery's Ontario Reading and Self-Fashioning / 151
EMILY WOSTER

9 (Re)Locating Montgomery: Prince Edward Island Romance to Southern Ontario Gothic / 166
NATALIE FOREST

Travels to Muskoka: Commodification and Tourism

10 Propriety and the Proprietary: The Commodification of Health and Nature in *The Blue Castle* / 187
E. HOLLY PIKE

11 Bala and *The Blue Castle*: The "Spirit of Muskoka" and the Tourist Gaze / 203
LINDA RODENBURG

Life in Toronto: Professional and Cultural Links

12 Advocating for Authors and Battling Critics in Toronto: Montgomery and the Canadian Authors Association / 223
KATE SUTHERLAND

13 Toronto's Cultural Scene: Tonic or Toxin for a Sagged Soul? / 238
LESLEY D. CLEMENT

Epilogue

14 Dear Grandmother Maud on the Road to Heaven / 263
KATE MACDONALD BUTLER

Appendix

Montgomery's Ontario Legacies: A Community Presence in the Twenty-First Century / 275
RITA BODE AND LESLEY D. CLEMENT WITH THE ASSISTANCE OF KRISTINA ELDRIDGE AND CHLOE VERNER

Notes / 281
Bibliography / 305
Contributors / 317
Index / 323

Illustrations

Montgomery's photographs (indicated by an asterisk) are used by permission of the L.M. Montgomery Collection, Archival and Special Collections, University of Guelph Library.

1.1 Three good pals* / 22
1.2 On the lawn one summer day* / 23
1.3 Corn roast with Chester, Stuart, and Montgomery (1922)* / 27
1.4 Leaskdale swimming hole with Chester and Stuart (1925)* / 27
1.5 Halloween mask (1922)* / 28
1.6 Chester and Stuart at water pump* / 28
1.7 Cover for first edition of *Rainbow Valley* (Maria Louise Kirk, illustrator) / 29
1.8 Chester's first picnic (1914)* / 32
2.1 Three Leaskdale First World War soldiers / 36
2.2 Leaskdale allotment map / 37
2.3 Montgomery, Frede, Ewan, and Chester in the Leaskdale dining room* / 47
2.4 Frede's room, Leaskdale manse / 48
2.5 Cameron MacFarlane* / 51
2.6 Good Fairy, Leaskdale manse* / 52
5.1 Mother and child: Chester and Montgomery* / 96
10.1 Dreaming, Bala* / 199
11.1 Montgomery on veranda of Roselawn, Bala* / 205
13.1 Dorothy Stevens, "The Whirlpool of King and Yonge" / 240
14.1 Stuart's graduation, University of Toronto (1940)* / 266

Acknowledgments

L.M. Montgomery's Rainbow Valleys: The Ontario Years, 1911–1942 has been a collaborative effort at every turn. From the beginnings of the project on a co-editing model, through the generous efforts of our contributors to work with us and each other, to the helpful guidance of McGill-Queen's University Press, a sense of mutual support has consistently informed the creation and production of this volume.

We are grateful to the institutions and individuals who have helped to bring the chapters into their present form. Among them, we would like to mention a few specifically: Elizabeth Epperly, Benjamin Lefebvre, Jean Mitchell, and Mary Rubio for their encouragement and useful advice at various stages of the project; Christy Woster for providing the cover image of the first edition of *Rainbow Valley*; Sally Keefe-Cohen and the Heirs of L.M. Montgomery for their professionalism and interest; the helpful staff at the Archival and Special Collections, University of Guelph, and at the Ontario Archives; the Lucy Maud Montgomery Society of Ontario and its members, especially its leadership; McGill-Queen's University Press's astute anonymous readers, support staff, and production team; and editor Mark Abley, from whose wisdom and intellectual generosity we have benefited greatly.

We thank the Symons Trust Fund in Canadian Studies at Trent University for their generous support of this project through an award in aid of publication.

This book has been published with the help of a grant from the Federation for the Humanities and Social Sciences, through the Awards to Scholarly Publications Program, using funds provided by the Social Sciences and Humanities Research Council of Canada. We gratefully acknowledge this publication support.

ACKNOWLEDGMENTS

We thank our colleagues and friends at Trent and Lakehead for their contributions to an environment that supports and stimulates intellectual endeavour. We thank other friends, some of whom are also family members, for support of various kinds. In particular, Rita thanks Brian O'Byrne, Adam O'Byrne, and Julia O'Byrne; Lesley thanks the Ottawa Clements as well as Julian Clement and Alexandra Clement-McNamara.

PERMISSIONS

Material written by L.M. Montgomery is excerpted with the permission of Heirs of L.M. Montgomery Inc. *L.M. Montgomery*, *Emily of New Moon*, *The Story Girl*, and *Blue Castle* are trademarks of Heirs of L.M. Montgomery Inc. and are used with permission.

Anne of Green Gables, *Rainbow Valley*, *Rilla of Ingleside*, and other indicia of "Anne" are trademarks and/or Canadian official marks of the Anne of Green Gables Licensing Authority Inc. and are used with permission.

Permission for photographs from L.M. Montgomery Collection, Archival and Special Collections, University of Guelph Library.

The interview in chapter two appears with permission of Jack Hutton, Bala's Museum with Memories of Lucy Maud Montgomery.

A composite of images of Goldwin Lapp, Robert Brooks, and Morley Shier was acquired from the Uxbridge Historical Museum and provided by the Canadian Virtual War Memorial Photo Collection, Veterans Affairs Canada (Shier).

Permission from Allan McGillivray, *Decades of Harvest* (Uxbridge: Scott History Committee, 1986) for images of two 1895 maps of the township.

Katherine Cameron's "L.M.M." appears by permission of Oolichan Books.

Interviews appearing in the appendix appear with permissions of Kathy Wasylenky, Melanie Whitfield, and Tess Dempster.

L.M. MONTGOMERY'S RAINBOW VALLEYS

Introduction

RITA BODE AND LESLEY D. CLEMENT

On 28 January 1912, after a ten-month silence, L.M. Montgomery once again took up her journal writing. Much had changed since her last entry of "Saturday, Mar. 4, 1911 Cavendish, P.E.I." Under the January date, as before, she added her place of residence. Her first comment is her response to seeing "The Manse, Leaskdale, Ont." on the page before her: "I look at the above entry," she writes, "rather stupidly, since I have written it down. It seems unreal."[1] The feeling of dissociation in her words conveys a profound sense of the disruption that would continue to characterize the Ontario years, from 1911 through to her death in April 1942.

Montgomery copied into her January journal entry brief passages from a notebook of occasional jottings made throughout the "past strange year," but mostly, the long January account is a retrospective record of life-altering events. Not unexpectedly, she movingly recounts her grandmother's final illness, death, and funeral; perhaps more of a surprise are the muted and ambivalent words with which she describes her marriage, after a five-year-long engagement, to the Reverend Ewan Macdonald, asserting her "*despair*" at her loss of freedom, but also her contentment. The most enduring sense of troubling change, however, comes through her keen awareness of physical displacement; for Montgomery, dislocation carried the deeply painful effects of emotional severance. She recalls her "dear old room" in her grandmother's house, declaring, "I loved that little room more than I ever loved another place on earth – and more than I shall ever love any place." In her explanation for the lapse in her journal writing, she equates the loss of human life through death with the loss of place: "I long shrank from the pain I knew would be attendant upon the writing of grandmother's death and leaving Cavendish." Thinking back to the previous June, as she was preparing for her marriage to Ewan in a fortnight and also parting from her cousin Bertie McIntyre, who was going on holidays, she recalls feeling "that I could *not* endure any further rending of old ties." She wonders, more mournfully than happily, "Could all that a new life had to offer me compensate for the things the old life took in its going?"[2] Such an open-ended question eludes answer. Montgomery's new life would come to mean many things, but perhaps most significantly it meant the permanent move to Ontario where she would spend almost half her lifetime. It proved to be an eventful half, reflecting the vicissitudes of the first four decades of the twentieth century that buffeted and buoyed her in both her personal and professional life.

When late in September 1911 Montgomery returned to Canada as Mrs Ewan Macdonald following her trans-Atlantic honeymoon, she did not go to Prince Edward Island. Instead, after stops in Toronto and Uxbridge, she and Ewan travelled to Leaskdale, the small rural Ontario community in Durham County approximately seventy kilometres northeast of Toronto. For the previous two years, Ewan had held a position as the minister of St Paul's Presbyterian Church in Leaskdale, with responsibility also for the Presbyterian parish in the nearby community of Zephyr, ten kilometres to the northwest. After spending almost thirty-seven years of her life on her beloved Island, Montgomery felt "discouraged, heartsick and homesick" on first arriving in Ontario with its "starless darkness" that seemed "merely one long *blot* of wet shadow." Before long, however, she was revelling in the region's beauty, in its "October sunshine and crimson maples, with snug, prosperous farmsteads."[3] These extremes suggest the beginnings of a pattern that for the next thirty years, until her death, would inform Montgomery's attempts to make Ontario her home.

Two more moves would interrupt – and disrupt – Montgomery's Ontario life. After fifteen years in Leaskdale, Ewan received the call to the two-point charge of Presbyterian churches in Norval and Union (just east of Glen Williams) in Halton County, about one hundred kilometres southwest of Leaskdale. Montgomery felt regret at leaving the community where her two sons, Chester and Stuart, had been born in 1912 and 1915, but also excitement over the new opportunities the move presented, especially since Norval, fifty kilometres from Toronto, was much more accessible to the world of publishing, friends, and cultural activities. Although she had owned a car since May 1918, she had never learned to drive. Now she would no longer be dependent on Ewan (and eventually Chester) to drive her but instead could take the high-speed radial train. In just over an hour, she could travel from Norval either northwest to Guelph or southeast to Lambton Mills, on the western edge of Toronto at the intersection of Dundas Street and the Humber River. Alternatively, she could alight at any of the one hundred stops along the seventy-four kilometre Toronto–Guelph Interurban line.[4]

Initially, one of the appealing features of Leaskdale for Montgomery had been that it was "*so* small – only about ten or twelve houses – that it is almost as good as the pure country," as she writes in her journal. But she was disappointed in the manse, "built of white brick in the ugly 'L' design so common among country houses," and even more disappointed that it had "no bathroom or toilet."[5] In addition to its proximity to Toronto, Norval promised the physical comforts for which she longed. Ewan's position there meant "a nice manse with electric light and bathroom," all features that appealed to Montgomery in her multiple roles as minister's wife, mother and homemaker, and professional writer. Yet, despite these attractions, she laments the departure: "My home that I have loved. And I must leave it." She details her loss: "Oh, how I hate the thought of leaving! And the thought of new places and people ... The beautiful woods behind Mr Leask's, the leaf-hung corner of the side-road, the lovely hill field beyond with the elms on its crest. I love these things and grieve to leave them. But what has been my life but a succession of leaving things I loved?"[6]

The final Ontario move was even more disruptive. In 1935, seven years before her death, Montgomery bought her first house, on Riverside Drive next to the Humber River in what was then the village of Swansea. Today, Swansea is the part of Toronto just south of vibrant Bloor Street Village and west of the High Park area. Montgomery had low hopes of finding anything to her liking in the city, but when the realtor, Mr Lepage, drove her and Ewan along Riverside Drive in early March, she saw "a new house with a 'for sale' placard on the lawn" that she "liked the look of ... at first sight." Her journal entry continues: "I think it was when I saw the ravine I knew I must have the house."[7] Montgomery's heartfelt reaction to the Riverside environment appears through Jane of *Jane of Lantern Hill* who finds in "the new Lakeside development on the banks of the Humber" "a pretty country village" featuring "hills and ravines with ferns and wild columbines growing in them and rivers and trees ... the green fire of willows, the great clouds of oaks, the plumes of pines and, not far away, the blue mist that was Lake Ontario."[8]

Despite the misunderstandings that led the Macdonalds to leave Norval more willingly than they might otherwise have done, despite the "worries over Chester" that had "darkened" their final years there, and despite the welcome anticipation of furnishing the new house, "Journey's End," and her joy in its woods and vistas, Montgomery acknowledges that she had "put deep roots into the Norval life and it was absolute anguish to be uprooted." As with her departure from Leaskdale, her words recall her feelings on leaving Cavendish almost a quarter of a century earlier. She vacillates between feeling "an exile" in Toronto and the sense that Journey's End is "home,"[9] an ambivalence that characterizes her Ontario years from beginning to end.

Years have a tendency to overlap through memory, but Mary Rubio's biography, *Lucy Maud Montgomery: The Gift of Wings*, provides a telling insight into the significance of the Ontario years for Montgomery scholarship. Rubio devotes one section of approximately 125 pages to Prince Edward Island, while the Ontario period takes up three sections of about 400 pages. The challenges, gratifications, and responsibilities of Montgomery's Ontario years were more than most people experience in a lifetime. Ewan's illness took a great toll on her. Her sensibilities and needs and her great creative drive made their own relentless demands. Montgomery's life was complicated, but she was also a complex person, multi-faceted, gifted, and highly productive. In Ontario, she raised a family; she fulfilled the duties of a minister's wife by contributing substantially to community life through parish work; she maintained her relationships with friends, neighbours, and rela-

Introduction

tives in reciprocal visits, often extended, and written correspondence; she participated in professional organizations that advocated for copyright protection and recognition of Canadian literature. Most significantly for Montgomery scholarship, she wrote fiction that confirmed her place, established by the early *Anne* novels, in not just Canadian letters but world literature.

L.M. Montgomery's Rainbow Valleys takes a new direction in Montgomery studies by shifting the focus away from Prince Edward Island to Ontario with its new associations and influences for the years that Montgomery lived in Leaskdale (1911–26), Norval (1926–35), and Toronto (1935–42), and vacationed in Bala (1922). Its title alludes to the title of the author's 1919 novel, set in the years immediately preceding the First World War, and anticipates a number of related themes explored throughout the chapters as they apply to both Montgomery's life and literary output: geographical features of the landscapes with which she engages, the social and economic shifts of the first four decades of the twentieth century, her ever-changing moods and states of mind, and the personal and professional highs and lows of her life during her Ontario residency as she sought to establish a new home and carve out new writing spaces. Home and belonging are themes that have been addressed in much Montgomery scholarship within its Prince Edward Island context; however, the Ontario years generate a new urgency because of Montgomery's keen sense of displacement in time and place. Although it is clear that in the decade before her death she became increasingly disillusioned, perhaps even pathologically depressed, there is no consensus on whether, even during her earlier years, she lived primarily under the rainbows or in the valleys. This critical debate is established immediately in the first three chapters of this volume, from the tensions "between valleys of depression and rainbow-coloured affirmations" that Elizabeth Waterston outlines in chapter 1, through Mary Beth Cavert's contention in chapter 2 that the Leaskdale years "were rich in joy and sorrow" despite the manse being "the memory-filled home that summoned her deepest grief," to Margaret Steffler's conclusion in chapter 3 that, for complex reasons involving loss and the manipulation of memory, "Montgomery was never fully at home in Ontario."[10] Seemingly contradictory conclusions such as these which the volume's chapters sometimes draw provide telling insights into Montgomery's tumultuous inner life as she negotiated personal and global events. These early chapters also establish a paradigm for the interconnections among the volume's chapters; drawing on a body of mutual references, they nonetheless approach Montgomery's experience and work from different perspectives that create a dialogue or, more accurately, a developing and expanding conversation about central scholarly questions concerning Montgomery's Ontario years.

The organization of the volume's content, framed by a prologue and epilogue and with a poetic interlude, reflects another motif that the chapters reveal: the extent to which Montgomery's life-writings, and indeed her life, were a consequence of self-fashioning and self-dramatization. The sense of displacement and the need for self-fashioning are directly related to the rapidly changing world of Montgomery's Ontario period, which is bookended by two world wars and characterized by increasing commercialization and commodification of values and even people, changing tastes in literature, and the struggles among those empowered with developing and promoting the direction that Canadian literature would take.

Studies of the familial, cultural, historical, and geographical associations and influences on Montgomery's writings of the Prince Edward Island years are productive, abundant, and ongoing. The importance of Ontario has not been ignored in Montgomery scholarship, especially in the work that invokes her journals, but it is rarely the focus of study and most often receives only limited acknowledgment. In one of her notebook jottings during her year of journal silence, Montgomery records, on 23 May 1911, her mingled joy and anxiety on receiving her copy of the newly published *The Story Girl*. "I wrote it in my dear old room [at Cavendish]," she recounts, "where I shall never sit and hold pen more." She then continues, "I have been haunted, ever since leaving home, with a nasty obsession that I can never write again."[11] Her sense that these feelings are "foolish" turned out to be true because the Ontario years became her most prolific. In addition to numerous poems[12] and short stories, she added six books to her *Anne* series, four while in Leaskdale – *Anne of the Island* (1915), *Anne's House of Dreams* (1917), *Rainbow Valley* (1919), and *Rilla of Ingle-*

side (1921) – followed by two others while she was living in Toronto, *Anne of Windy Poplars* (1936) and *Anne of Ingleside* (1939). Early in her residence in Leaskdale, she produced *The Golden Road* (1913), a sequel to *The Story Girl*. In Leaskdale, she also created Emily and the three novels in which Emily is the heroine – *Emily of New Moon* (1923), *Emily Climbs* (1925), and *Emily's Quest* (1927) – and *The Blue Castle* (1926), the one novel set entirely outside of Prince Edward Island, in which she gratified her imaginative responses to Muskoka. Also in Leaskdale, she recopied her PEI journals and produced her autographical work, *The Alpine Path* (1917). Two further novels written in these years would not be published until later: *Magic for Marigold* (1929) and *A Tangled Web* (1931).

In Norval, she wrote the two *Pat* novels, *Pat of Silver Bush* (1933) and *Mistress Pat* (1935), the latter published a few months after her move to Toronto. She used her new city as a partial setting for *Jane of Lantern Hill* (1937), moving her heroine between the two provinces that informed her own life so strongly. Unsurprisingly, the happy ending of *Jane of Lantern Hill*, with Jane's reunited family, involves plans for "winters in Toronto … summers at Lantern Hill."[13] Finally, there is the posthumously published *The Road to Yesterday* (1974), which Benjamin Lefebvre has edited, restoring the deleted sections, as *The Blythes Are Quoted* (2009). The chapters in this volume examine the literature that Montgomery produced during her Ontario years within their Ontario context, reflecting the complexity of her psyche, her life, and the period.

This volume begins with a prologue by Waterston (chapter 1) that discusses Montgomery's *Rainbow Valley* as a novel capturing in its plot and characterization, its images and themes, "valleys of depression and rainbow-coloured affirmations," which, as mentioned above, reflect the personal and professional changes Montgomery was undergoing in the early Leaskdale years and anticipate the contours of her life thereafter. As Waterston states, "The intriguing new title with its double references to physical elements of sky and earth promises a new emphasis on place rather than person."[14] The first paired chapters, Cavert's "'To the Memory of': Leaskdale and Loss in the Great War" (chapter 2) and Steffler's "'Being a Christian' and a Presbyterian in Leaskdale" (chapter 3), examine two topics – war and religion – that disrupted the lives of those living in even such a small community as Leaskdale and that entered into Montgomery's fiction and life-writing as she struggled with an unsettling sense of displacement in Ontario. Cavert contextualizes these disruptions in the interconnected stories of those to whom Montgomery dedicated *Rainbow Valley* and *Rilla of Ingleside*: three young men from Leaskdale who lost their lives in the Canadian war efforts of the First World War, and Montgomery's cousin and best friend, Frederica Campbell (Frede), who died in the influenza pandemic of 1919. Steffler, in turn, explores Montgomery's articulations of a deep aversion to the "oppressive religion" that she associated with Presbyterian doctrines, an aversion that she could not keep out of her responses to Ewan's melancholia. Through Montgomery's contemporary and retrospective entries in the Leaskdale journals, "the recopying of the diaries of the PEI years, and the composition of the first *Emily* novel – all written out of the Leaskdale manse," Steffler traces "the complex impact of religion" that followed Montgomery from her PEI childhood into her Ontario adulthood.[15]

In the next section, on the changing roles of women, Laura Robinson and Caroline Jones explore some of the shifts, both societal and personal, that affected Montgomery's attempts to fulfil an already demanding range of female expectations, as well as her fictional strategies in depicting both the obstacles and gratifications of women's circumstances. Robinson's "'A Gift for Friendship': Revolutionary Friendship in *Anne of the Island* and *The Blue Castle*" (chapter 4) focuses on the two novels that frame the Leaskdale years to show how Montgomery accommodates her depictions of female friendships to align with changing mores that saw same-sex relationships as increasingly suspect, while at the same time finding subtle ways to problematize the heterosexual happy marriage plot as women's ultimate fulfilment. Jones in "The New Mother at Home: Montgomery's Literary Explorations of New Motherhood" (chapter 5), explores Montgomery's "complex engagements with literary motherhood over the course of her actual motherhood," which allow her not only to position herself as daughter to her own lost mother but also "to reflect upon – and construct – herself as mother in varying phases of her own and her sons' lives."[16]

Introduction

While loss and grief enter into most of the volume's discussions, William Thompson's and Melanie Fishbane's perspectives make Montgomery's anguish their central focus, exploring various ways in which her deep sorrows over personal loss and global strife emerge in her art. In chapter 6, as the title "The Shadow on the House of Dreams: Montgomery's Re-Visioning of Anne" indicates, Thompson examines how Montgomery's growing sense of a darkening world marks "a change in the fictional life of Anne" most clearly evidenced in the two *Anne* books, *Anne's House of Dreams* and *Rilla of Ingleside*, appearing in the immediate aftermath of the Great War. In arguing moreover that these two novels "best represent the intersection of Montgomery's public and private lives," Thompson invokes the writer's consciousness of the need to create a persona "appropriate for public consumption" as revealed in her autobiographical work, *The Alpine Path*. The relationship between the journals and her other writings, Thompson suggests, is ultimately less a "divide" than a "point of connection in understanding."[17] Fishbane, in chapter 7, "'My Pen Shall Heal, Not Hurt': Writing as Therapy in *Rilla of Ingleside* and *The Blythes Are Quoted*," approaches Montgomery's grief from the perspective of the practising artist, raising questions about the extent to which writing is therapeutic and also addressing the role that suffering plays in creativity, as manifested in both the writer's life and literature. These and other chapters suggest that the interplay among the journals, the life that those journals record, and Montgomery's fictions is endlessly layered, nuanced, and intricate, their boundaries dissolving and reshaping into newer manifestations of both Montgomery and her characters.

Katherine Cameron's poem, "L.M.M.," provides a brief interlude midway through the volume. Her poetic tribute to Montgomery, with its suggestions of the inner life masked by Montgomery's public persona, stands as a transition between the previous chapters' discussions of anguish to the following chapters' focus on literary inspiration, connections, and influences.

While places, people, and meaningful occupations and roles inform Montgomery's search for a sense of belonging during her Ontario years, her intense, enduring involvement with literature, as witnessed in the extensive markings in her books now housed at the University of Guelph

Library's Archival and Special Collections, help her make significant transitions between past, present, and future times and places, personally and culturally. In the next section, "A Sense of Place: Reading and Writing," Emily Woster's and Natalie Forest's respective chapters foreground the importance of Montgomery's active engagement with books, both as reader and writer. Reading and rereading, and writing and rewriting, create productive cycles for Montgomery the author but also offer intricate crossings in which singular intents grow into multifaceted productions of both the self and her literary output. Drawing on theories of women's autobiography, memoir, and reading practices, Woster, in "Old Years and Old Books: Montgomery's Ontario Reading and Self-Fashioning" (chapter 8), focuses on Montgomery's "textual occupations" to argue that her "Ontario reading records, separate from and enfolded in her journals, can be read as an autobiographical act, one facet of her complex, layered self-definition." In the next chapter, "(Re)Locating Montgomery: Prince Edward Island Romance to Southern Ontario Gothic" (chapter 9), Forest turns her attention to Montgomery's increasingly nuanced readings of place each time she revisits the Island and returns to Ontario. Memories, distant and recent, begin to collude and destabilize a sense of reality of which she had once felt sure. Building on previous studies that engage Freud's concept of the uncanny in interpreting Montgomery's work, Forest suggests that Montgomery's "real life, as she presents it in her journals, is as 'rich' in the uncanny as her fiction," thus circumventing Freud's privileging of the fictional uncanny as more intense.[18] Forest situates the *Emily* books and several of the short stories associated with them as developments in a literary tradition that Timothy Findley would later designate as Southern Ontario Gothic and that align Montgomery with the shadowy spaces of Alice Munro's small-town environments.

Montgomery's remarkable ability for full and intense experience could never be limited to a singular interest, and her engagement with the natural world was as central to her emotional and intellectual core as was her life in books. The chapters in the next section, "Travels to Muskoka: Commodification and Tourism," engage Montgomery's discovery of what Rubio designates as northern Ontario's "lake district"[19] and her subsequent explorations of it in *The Blue Castle*, her one novel set entirely in Ontario. Vacationing with her family in Bala in the summer of 1922, Montgomery revelled in the waters, the woods, and the "cool silence ... the gods of the wild wood welcomed back their own," she writes in her journal.[20] Although long valued for its vivid descriptions of nature's beauty, Montgomery's Muskoka novel, as Holly Pike and Linda Rodenburg both suggest, nonetheless challenges the expected approaches to nature through the kinds of appreciation evoked. Both chapters suggest the importance for Montgomery of accessing nature and place on the heroine's and her creator's own terms. She seems deliberately to resist separating the effects of nature and culture in her quest to bring happiness to her heroine, Valancy Stirling, who, at the novel's opening, would appear among all of Montgomery's female protagonists to be the least likely to achieve fulfilment. In "Propriety and the Proprietary: The Commodification of Health and Nature in *The Blue Castle*" (chapter 10), Pike acknowledges Montgomery's Romantic belief in the restorative powers of the natural world but also looks to the influences that the region's developing tourism in the first decades of the twentieth century exerts on her representation of Valancy's struggles to find her place in both the natural and social orders. Pike contends that Montgomery allows the "culturally and commercially mediated experience of Muskoka" marketed by the "emerging tourist industry ... as a healthy lifestyle destination" to facilitate Valancy's movement toward "the freedom, health, and happiness that, despite her being surrounded by Muskoka's natural environs her whole life, were previously inaccessible to her."[21] Rodenburg's chapter, "Bala and *The Blue Castle*: The 'Spirit of Muskoka' and the Tourist Gaze" (chapter 11), more directly contextualizes Montgomery's stay in Muskoka as a tourist experience through frameworks provided by contemporary theories on tourism and travel. In interweaving Montgomery's account of her stay in Bala with the novel that this travel inspired and with the experience of contemporary Montgomery-related tourist sites, Rodenburg explores the possible ways in which visitors to the Bala Museum are called upon to move beyond the stance of "passive museum-goer or recreational tourist ... to recreate actively the story of Montgomery in Muskoka," a re-creation that positions the tourists' "critical imaginings at the centre of ... [their] own integrated counter-text."[22]

Muskoka enchanted Montgomery, but her Ontario locations also facilitated other forms of respite that soothed, stimulated, and challenged her in different ways. The volume's final section, "Life in Toronto: Professional and Cultural Links," turns to exploring the opportunities afforded by proximity to Toronto's amenities of her Ontario residences in Leaskdale, Norval, and Swansea. The chapters in this section show that the Montgomery who embraced the natural world with so much genuine pleasure and appreciation was also eager to engage actively in professional meetings and public speaking, to attend exhibitions, theatre, and moving pictures, and to disburse her money sometimes too liberally at Toronto's large department stores. When leaving Norval, moreover, she looked towards Toronto for her "Journey's End." In "Advocating for Authors and Battling Critics in Toronto: Montgomery and the Canadian Authors Association" (chapter 12), Kate Sutherland examines Montgomery's adaptation of the executive skills that stood her so well as a minister's wife and contributor to the parish community to a range of significant initiatives in the promotion of Canadian letters and authors. She traces Montgomery's involvement with and contribution to the Canadian Authors Association (CAA) to analyze the complicated gender politics of a Canadian literary scene attempting to position itself as realist and modernist at the expense of the popular and sentimental literature that Montgomery's work represented. Sutherland suggests the close links between the history of the CAA and the direction of Montgomery's late career. In the next chapter, "Toronto's Cultural Scene: Tonic or Toxin for a Sagged Soul?" (chapter 13), Lesley Clement approaches Montgomery's urban experience as a final expression of the significant conflicts that informed much of her life. Clement examines the "irremediable tension" between Montgomery's attraction to Toronto, with its cultural environment, community of writers, and affirmation of her status as a successful author, and "her growing consciousness of herself as a consumer product." In recounting Montgomery's attendance at and reaction to various theatrical productions and other cultural events, Clement investigates the toxic effects of Montgomery's celebrity status when celebrity "depends on exhibiting only those personae that the public is willing to consume."[23] She argues that Montgomery's engagement with theatrical productions, most notably G.B. Shaw's *Saint Joan*, turns her from the self-fashioning that her journals regularly evince to self-dramatization in which she emerges at the centre of a tragic narrative that both sustains and dooms her.

The volume's epilogue, "Dear Grandmother Maud on the Road to Heaven" (chapter 14), is Kate Macdonald Butler's letter to her famous grandmother whom she never knew in person but initially came to know well through her father's memories and stories of growing up in Leaskdale and Norval and then attending the University of Toronto. Butler's own memories include her father "poring over the contents" of the journals, "these old, worn, rather shabby, black ledgers," and sometimes reading aloud from them to Kate and her brothers, who "could see and hear from his voice how important these journals were to him." Montgomery's reputation and writings, as Butler details, remain an important family legacy and responsibility, to be treated, as her father treated them, with "respect."[24] Her speculations about what Montgomery's responses might be to the global and wired world of the twenty-first century remind us that, although rooted firmly in place – whether Prince Edward Island or Ontario – readers' and critics' responses to Montgomery's creative imagination have been transcending boundaries of multiple kinds for over a century.

An appendix traces briefly, as its title "Montgomery's Ontario Legacies: A Community Presence in the Twenty-First Century" suggests, Montgomery's enduring and vibrant place in Ontario through public spaces, performances, museums, and educational sites. An interview with executive members of the Lucy Maud Montgomery Society of Ontario, conducted with the help of university students Kristina Eldridge and Chloe Verner, details the origins and continued growth of the society and shows the commitment of its members, all volunteers, to establishing a concrete and physical presence for Montgomery in Ontario. The Leaskdale manse, which the society has restored, and the Historic Church, which it maintains, provide a historical, educational site enabling visitors – actual and virtual – to envision the Ontario minister's wife and mother as an active community member and as the creative artist who retreated daily into the ground-floor front room to write.

In Lefebvre's introduction to the first volume of the *L.M. Montgomery Reader*, which assembles neglected writings by and about Montgomery from the publication of *Anne of Green Gables* to a few years beyond her death, he observes: "What I have found over the course of this research is that, even under the guise of absolute frankness, her journals and letters rarely tell the whole story."[25] Montgomery's lifewriting and the life on which it is based, her fiction, both long and short, her poems, and her commentary and opinion pieces are all parts of the story, and their intricate interlaying itself, as Montgomery scholarship amply illustrates, creates another narrative. By directing the critical gaze on Montgomery's Ontario experience, the chapters in *L.M. Montgomery's Rainbow Valleys* begin to tell the Ontario story. They provide a new locus from which to approach Montgomery's work, finding in Ontario an inspirational centre that informs both her life and art. The volume's explorations build on, extend, and modify old stories and tell new ones. We anticipate, moreover, that these chapters will also provide the "spade work" (one of Montgomery's favourite terms) for future directions in Montgomery scholarship. The multiple shadows of the Ontario years associate her fiction with the dark strain evident in the work of other Canadian writers, suggesting that there may be a firmer place for her writings, one that until recently has largely eluded her, in the nation's literary canon. This dark strain, furthermore, associates her with a female literary tradition beyond nation. Montgomery's literary relationship to British and American writers of the nineteenth and early twentieth centuries, especially women authors, has received notice but little analysis. Her ready engagements with Ontario's landscapes and urbanscapes are promising for reassessments of her work in the context of environmental studies that might newly illuminate her relationship to nature by repositioning her relations to a Romantic tradition and to those of her Canadian contemporaries known for their nature writing and paying due attention to her enduring interest in built environments. Ontario facilitated Montgomery's interests in dramatic performances, visual arts and media, and photography, both as observer and practitioner, which invite further inquiries into their alignment with her own literary art. Montgomery's scrapbooks, with the newspaper clippings and other artifacts

Introduction

that capture the debates leading to the formation of the United Church in 1925, the financial vicissitudes of the 1920s and 1930s, and the calls for and responses to women suffrage, are still untapped resources. They also provide an intimate portrait of Montgomery and her Ontario neighbours agonizing over every defeat and celebrating every victory of the two world wars that frame this period. There are, indeed, many Montgomery stories left to tell.

Ontario recognized Montgomery's accomplishments from the outset. When she arrived in Leaskdale, the *Uxbridge Journal* showed its awareness that the minister's new wife was also the "famous 'L.M. Montgomery,'" describing Mrs Macdonald as both "gifted and charming."[26] The Ontario appreciation never waned even as it shared the "beloved writer," as the *Aurora Era* deems her in 1940, with the wider reading world.[27] On Friday, 25 April 1942, the *Globe and Mail*'s obituary on Montgomery notes that many of her "more than a score of books ... have been translated into Polish, French, Swedish, Dutch and Spanish. Many have been published in Braille." It lists her many "honors": "She was made an officer of the Order of the British Empire in 1935 and became a Fellow of the Royal Society of Arts and a member of the Artistes' Institute of France, the Canadian Authors Association and the Canadian Women's Press Club."[28] The L.M. Montgomery who made her final journey back to Cavendish for burial and memorialization in 1942 was a very different writer and woman from the one who had left there in 1911. This volume's chapters, in exploring these intervening years in Ontario, aim for an increased understanding of that difference.

Prologue

I
Leaskdale: L.M. Montgomery's Rainbow Valley

ELIZABETH WATERSTON

With her genius for choosing effective titles, L.M. Montgomery called the novel that caught the essence of her life in Leaskdale *Rainbow Valley*. The two words in the title have biblical connotations. They recall the rainbow of hope that God sent to the world after the flood, as well as the valley of the shadow of death that psalmist David had to walk through. Later poets have reused these natural symbols of high moments of joy and low moments of sorrow: William Wordsworth cries, "My heart leaps up when I behold / The rainbow in the sky!" while folksingers moan, "Down in the valley, the valley so low / Hang your head over, hear the wind blow."

In 1917–18, as Montgomery worked in the Leaskdale manse composing her new novel, her mind and heart and imagination swung between valleys of depression and rainbow-coloured affirmations. She exposed this alternation directly in her journal: on 20 April 1918 she wrote, "This has been a hellish week of ups-and-downs."[1] At the same time, she explored it obliquely through plot and characterization in *Rainbow Valley*. In her journal, she focused explicitly on her husband, her children, the ongoing world war, the position of women, and the seasonal shifts in the local landscape. Through fictional symbols, the novel discloses her secret hopes and fears about all these aspects of her current life.

Rainbow Valley focuses at the outset on a Presbyterian minister. In her earlier works, Montgomery had portrayed clergymen, some of them rather ridiculous, as in *The Story Girl*, some of them menacing. But never had she placed a minister in a central position in one of her novels. Now, writing in Leaskdale, she could paint a subtle, ambiguous, full-length portrait of a minister – because she was married to one. She could imagine the Reverend John Meredith as a dominant figure in a church-centred village because she was living in such a setting now as the minister's wife.

In her early years in Leaskdale, Montgomery, as Mrs Ewan Macdonald, played the traditional role of the minister's wife. She was relatively happy in that role. Her continued success as a respected and popular author eased some of the financial difficulties of her marriage. Before his nervous breakdown in 1919, Ewan was lovable enough to let her sympathize with the isolation and loneliness of a small-town minister. She inserted family photographs from 1917 into her journals that show a smiling Ewan interacting with his sons and captioned the pictures "Three good pals" and "On the lawn one summer day."[2]

1.1 *Opposite* Three good pals

1.2 *Above* On the lawn one summer day

In *Rainbow Valley*, John Meredith is treated with great sympathy as a very lonely man. Like Ewan, he is well educated; a university degree plus two years at a theological college have given him familiarity with Greek and Hebrew as well as Latin, depth of church history, and Bible interpretation – all guaranteed to separate such a learned man from the hard-working, hard-handed farmers and housewives in his spiritual care. Both the real and the fictional minister are watched warily and incessantly by their congregations. Unlike Ewan, the Reverend Mr Meredith has lost his beloved wife, but in both cases, the minister is suffering from mild depression, walking in the deep valley known in that time as "melancholia."

For Ewan, real life provided no relief from his vale of sorrows, but in fiction, Montgomery can raise a rainbow for his sad counterpart. In the imaginary parish into which John Meredith has moved, a gentle, pretty woman will appear. They will gradually find pleasure in quiet conversations. He will fall into the habit of going to meet her at sunset by the spring in Rainbow Valley. Eventually she will marry him and become a mother for his children.

Like the eventually happy fictional minister, the children in *Rainbow Valley* both reveal and conceal Montgomery's increasing concerns over her own two sons. Mr Meredith's children have been sorely neglected. Rapt in thought about a "new book which was setting the theological world by the ears," he has not noticed that his children are badly dressed and badly fed.[3] The whimsy and warmth of child life presented in earlier novels such as *Anne of Green Gables* and *The Story Girl* give way here to a more ambivalent picture. Montgomery's life in Leaskdale had enlarged her own vision of childhood. She now had new experiences to draw on, as minister's wife in charge of adolescent groups, as a helpmate who had learned surprising facts about every family in Ewan's charge, and as mother of growing boys. She writes in her journal, for example, about Chester, "a big, sturdy fellow," but adds that "he has been a rather difficult child to manage – he is so determined and so full of ebullient energy."[4]

Chester and his younger brother, Stuart, also faced special problems as children of the manse, like Jerry, Faith, Una, and Carl Meredith in *Rainbow Valley*. Montgomery knew that such children, like her young sons, would always be watched and also set apart from the village children already at work in the fields. For the fictional children, however, she could provide a refuge in the friendliness of the sons and daughters of Anne and Gilbert Blythe.

Yet her experience of village life also impelled her to add darker shadows to childhood life in the valley. A malicious force enters in the form of Mary Vance. Manipulative and warped by early experiences, given to lying and trouble-making, Mary plays a role somewhat like that of Josie Pye in *Anne of Green Gables*. Mary Vance, however, is much more complex than any Pye. Her sly gossip shadows the innocence of the Meredith children, and her spite adversely affects the lives of the young Blythes.

But there is an even darker shadow in this story of childhood, a consequence of Montgomery's intense response to the darkness of her times. These boys and girls share a destiny of doom. Anyone reading *Rainbow Valley* when it first appeared in 1919 would know that the boys – Jem and Walter, Jerry and Carl – are of a generation soon to be decimated. The dedication of the book continues to remind readers of that shadow. The young men named on that first page, all victims of the First World War, had been boys in the Sunday school or adolescents in the Young People's Association when Montgomery first assumed her role as minister's wife in Leaskdale. Now, as she wrote *Rainbow Valley*, they were gone, killed in the war. A journal entry written 22 January 1917 catches the immediate sombre response to the death of one of these young men: "This morning word was 'phoned over that Goldwin Lapp had been killed at the front … He has been in the trenches for a year and four months and went through the Somme offensive without a scratch. Poor boy! We drove over to Lapps' this afternoon. It was bitterly cold and the roads were dreadful. And it was a heart-breaking errand. But is not life a heart-break these days? It seems to me that the very soul of the universe must ache with anguish."[5] Because of that sense of the times, Montgomery gives to Anne's poetic young son Walter a fey sense of impending death. She assigns to him the kind of horrifying prophetic dream of war that she herself experienced and recorded in her journal: "Last night I dreamed again. I stood on a plain in France. It was sunset and the red light streamed over the plain. I held in my arms a man whom I knew, in some inexplicable way, to be dying. He leaned against me, his back and head against my breast. I could not see his face. Then he died, slipped from my grasp, and fell to the ground."[6]

Montgomery breaks up the shadow of doom in the valley, however, by offering two individual stories of the potential force of childhood. In chapter 12, Faith – faith, not piety – bursts into the church and harangues the parishioners for their hypocrisy. She throws her heresy at the shocked churchgoers, passionate in defence of honesty and love and charity and selflessness in the face of a congregation that seems lacking in all these virtues. Gentle, romantic, needy Una shows those same virtues of selflessness and charity and bravery. In chapter 34, she trudges up a steep dark hill to face a woman she has feared. For young readers, feisty Faith and courageous Una bring reassurance: a child can charge against the menacing walls of adulthood.

Montgomery's early years of motherhood offered similar flashes of happiness. Her boys sharing their evanescent joys could lift her darkened spirits. Happy family times, such as a delightful afternoon when "not only did the minister's son go paddling but the minister's wife went too" – and as the accompanying photograph and other photographs from this period attest[7] – revived rainbow memories of her own early years.

In this novel, however, as in all her recent work, Montgomery had already slipped away from the child-centred stories that had made her so famous. *Anne of the Island* (1915) features college-age young women; *Anne's House of Dreams* (1917) is dominated by Anne's early motherhood and the trauma of a miserable marriage for her friend Leslie Moore. *Rainbow Valley* still rings at times with the familiar Montgomery gaiety. The children's happiness draws on the pleasures of life in Leaskdale, which the novelist genuinely enjoyed. It also revives the cheerfulness of some of Montgomery's memories of her own early years in Cavendish, preserved in the journals she could still consult. The more recent pages of the journal, however, focused on more adult emotions. The war-torn world, even in a village like Leaskdale, posed new questions about the status and role of women in society. Montgomery notes the day that Ontario women are accorded

1.3 *Top* Corn roast with Chester, Stuart, and Montgomery (1922)

1.4 *Bottom* Leaskdale swimming hole with Chester and Stuart (1925)

1.5 *Above*
Halloween mask
(1922)

1.6 *Right*
Chester and Stuart
at water pump

1.7 Cover for first edition of *Rainbow Valley*

the vote.⁸ This becomes the third theme of *Rainbow Valley*. In spite of the known appeal of a Montgomery book for child readers, the very cover of the first edition of *Rainbow Valley* signals this shift. It pictures a sunset moment when a slender woman goes alone down into a darkening valley.

Rainbow Valley presents several adult women, differentiated from each other in nature and experience: dreamy Anne and sensible Susan Baker; competent Miss Cornelia, accepting responsibility for raising Mary Vance, and feckless Aunt Martha, leaving the Meredith children their own dubious devices; gentle Rosemary West, dreaming of love, and her clever, domineering sister, Ellen, mocking male power. Rosemary and Ellen, bound together in their house on the hill by an old fateful vow, present a fairy-tale duo. These pairings of unlike women reflect the duality of Montgomery's own life. Her position in Leaskdale intensified the pull between her ambitious, creative intellect and the traditional expectation that a woman should be "the angel in the house."

In many ways life in Leaskdale made it easier for Montgomery to satisfy the urge to write. There was no demanding grandmother, no dread of childless spinsterhood, and no mockery of the artist's métier by a farming/fishing village and a bunch of sneering Simpsons. Maud Montgomery Macdonald had status now; the village knew she was a writer and admired her work. In larger communities, such as nearby Uxbridge, people respected her ability to continue writing while maintaining traditional domestic and pastoral roles.

It was increasingly difficult, however, for the minister's wife to find time to write, what with Young People's meetings and the Women's Mission Society's need to be led in prayer, and the little boys who did not like to see a door locked against them, and the self-absorbed husband who wandered in to explain again about his sense of sin and worthlessness. Furthermore, the war had added to the weight of traditional female roles the new demands to rally the Red Cross workers, to cope with food shortages, to comfort the bereaved.

Montgomery concocts a happy ending for at least two of her women characters. Ellen West's chauvinistic suitor renews his courtship and is accepted on feminist terms; Rosemary West, recognizing the needs of Mr Meredith's daughters, drifts down to Rainbow Valley to accept his offer of love and marriage.

As to her own marriage, no romantic glaze can hide Montgomery's recognition of its base not in romantic passion but in societal security. "I was never in love with Ewan," she writes in her journal, "never have been in love with him. But I was – have been – and am, very fond of him ... Life has not been – can never be – what I once hoped it would be in my girlhood dreams."[9] The honest, pained recognition of the difference between "life" and "dreams" marks her enlarged vision of the duality of woman's experience. The happy ending confirms the generally upward tone of Montgomery's sense of women's lives in the mid-war years. When so many men left the village to join up or to work in city factories, Leaskdale became a world of women rising to new challenges. In her own life in those years, Montgomery was filling contradictory female roles: writer and wife, mother of little boys and speaker to Toronto authors' groups, Uxbridge literary star and swabber of the barn. She was on the whole happy with the current status of women (she was not a supporter of women's suffrage) and with her own status.

Notably, although *Rainbow Valley* involves so many female characters, not one of them is central enough to establish her name in the novel's title. Earlier book titles named a person and set her in a physical environment: Anne – in Green Gables, of Avonlea, of the Island, in her House of Dreams; Kilmeny of the Orchard; Emily, Pat, Marigold, and Jane, each in her special place in a book's title. The intriguing new title with its double references to physical elements of sky and earth promises a new emphasis on place rather than person.

The poet whose heart leapt up at the rainbow intoned more generally, "Nature never yet betrayed the heart that loved her." By 1917–18, Montgomery's heart had opened fully to the landscape around the little Ontario village of Leaskdale. In Cavendish, the picturesque landscape had run toward the vastness of the sea. In Leaskdale, there was no such orientation. This rural village nestled in a rolling, undramatic land of small hills and shallow valleys. Montgomery, who had always been a walker, could slip out her front door and cross to the narrow dirt road running up past the Leask homestead toward the old sawmill. To her right, at the top of the hill, the mill brook ran, like the brook in her fictional world sparkling "with amber waters," running quietly between wild cherry trees, violets and daisies in summer, or ferns and goldenrod and asters in fall, and trilliums in spring.[10] In July 1917 she planned a picnic for Chester "in the woods up the old mill-race" – a favourite retreat, as revealed by her description and photograph of Chester's first picnic on 24 May 1914 – and shortly thereafter she recorded an evening when, with Bertie McIntyre, she took "a most memorable and glorious walk at sunset ... up the north hill."[11] She was enabled to create a secret place where children could play games and tell stories and enjoy picnics of fish caught in the amber stream. Here Rosemary, edging toward middle age, could accept an unworldly minister as a possible husband. This valley would be a haven from a grown-up world, with rainbow colours of laughter, fantasy, outrageous impudence, and happy comradeship, but tinted with presentiments of doom. A writer could escape from "life" into "dream" here. Returning from this place of quiet natural beauty, she could put into memorable words her new vision of the pathos of religious ministry, the complexity of joys and troubles in children's experience, the unavoidable consequences of war, and the wide range of women's lives.

1.8 Chester's first picnic (1914)

A New Home in Leaskdale: War and Religion

2

"To the Memory of": Leaskdale and Loss in the Great War

MARY BETH CAVERT

Whether pointing to loved ones or inspirational ties, book dedications are a public declaration of an important relationship. Dedications can be decoded to reveal latent stories behind a few inscribed words. L.M. Montgomery's "To the Memory of" always carries deep meaning. Montgomery wrote twenty-one books into which she inserted dedications to people (or pets) who enhanced her personal or creative life and to places that inspired her.

Two of these dedications are connected to the years Montgomery lived in Leaskdale, Ontario, preceding, during, and following the First World War. Her two Ontario-related dedications are in *Rainbow Valley* (1919) and its sequel, *Rilla of Ingleside* (1921). *Rainbow Valley* spotlights three young men from her husband's, Reverend Ewan Macdonald's, congregations who perished while serving in Canada's forces in Europe between 1917 and 1918: "To the memory of Goldwin Lapp, Robert Brookes, and Morley Shier, who made the supreme sacrifice that the happy valleys of their home land might be kept sacred from the ravage of the invader."[1] *Rilla of Ingleside* is dedicated to Montgomery's cousin (known as Frede): "To the memory of FREDERICA CAMPBELL MACFARLANE who went away from me when the dawn broke on January 25th, 1919 – a true friend, a rare personality, a loyal and courageous soul." The dedication of *Rainbow Valley* is the only one Montgomery ever made to people whom she knew after 1904 and after she became famous. However, these dedications are not simply memorials to those who served and died or whom she loved and mourned; they are also invitations to unearth the interconnected stories of those whom Montgomery urges us to remember.[2]

To THE MEMORY OF
GOLDWIN LAPP, ROBERT BROOKES AND MORLEY SHIER

WHO MADE THE SUPREME SACRIFICE
THAT THE HAPPY VALLEYS OF THEIR HOME LAND
MIGHT BE KEPT SACRED FROM
THE RAVAGE OF THE INVADER

2.1 Three Leaskdale First World War soldiers

On 3 October 1911, Montgomery as Mrs Ewan Macdonald was inducted as the minister's new wife and honoured with a reception dinner at St Paul's Presbyterian Church. Dressed in her wedding gown, she stood at the front of the sanctuary, while Ewan, who had lived in the community for two years, introduced her to his Leaskdale and Zephyr congregations. Margaret Leask Mustard, then seven years old, was in "awe" of Montgomery's fame and recalls that the community was "honoured in having this already famous person as a resident."[3] Three of the families she met that evening – the Shiers, the Brookses, and the Lapps – would never have expected to be mentioned in her books. Catherine and James Shier's farm was located a few acres away from the Leaskdale church.[4] They had three children in 1911: Mabel was nineteen; Morley, sixteen, was a student at Uxbridge High School; and Harvey was nine. The Brooks family was in Ewan's Zephyr congregation. A hard-working, twenty-five-year-old farmer, Robert lived with his mother, Catherine, and thirty-year-old sister, Janet, when he met the minister's new wife. George Lapp was a farmer and the past reeve/mayor of the township; his wife, Effie Wright, was from Uxbridge.

24	P. Montgomery	J. Stevenson	J. Stevenson	E. Oldham	J. Tiffin	M. Quigley	
23	R.H. Graham	F. Law	J. Gray	F. Thompson	J. Quigley	L. Collins	
22	Mrs. Mooney / J. Barker	J. Cook	G. Leask + sons	J. Jones	Jas. Shier	John Shier	E. Hart
21	Non-resident	J. Kennedy	Mrs. Leask	G. Leask + sons	J. Colwell		J. Marquis
20	G. Blanchard	Mrs. Leask	Mrs. Leask	G. Leask + sons	LEASKDALE Wm. Oxtoby	J. Barry	Mustard
19	John Thompson	Thomas Thompson	F.J. Shier		J. Blanchard		
18	L. Vanderburgh / J. Vanderburgh / D. Walker		J.M. Shier	J. Blanchard	W. Hossack / A. Hossack		Ruddy
17	J. Acton, trustee		J. Vanderburgh	Blanchard	W.T. Lyons / E. Shier		J. Ruddy
16	W. Blanchard / F. Murphy		P. Murphy / G. Blanchard	Wm. Kennedy	D. Kennedy	A. Mustard	T. Merrick
15	Walter Barton		John Madill		Glebe of Presbyterian Church		G. Phair
14	John Card	John Barton	J. Sinclair	Wm. Kennedy	John Madill		F. King
13	Geo. Vernon		D. Ross	C. Ross	Robt. Kennedy		
12	I. Blanchard	Phillip Lapp	A. Mustard	J. Gibson	C. Whitney / Mrs. Bond		E. Acton
11	J. Hackner	Mrs. Galloway	D. Lapp	W. Ferguson	John Weldon	E. Acton	
10	H. Mustard	T. Gibson	P. Lapp	Hy. Madill	John Weldon		
9	W. Usher	A. Mustard	Wm. Ferguson		Geo. Abrahams		Acton

2.2 Leaskdale allotment map

Their oldest son, Ford, was nineteen; Goldwin was almost eighteen and in his last year of school in Uxbridge; Dorothy was thirteen and little Harvey three.

The sons would have known the Macdonalds for only a few years, but their families and relations became friends, especially the younger siblings (Harvey Shier and Dorothy and Harvey Lapp) because they grew up during the fourteen years that Montgomery created and directed the Young People's Association. Ewan provided the Presbyterians with two important assets: a mature minister who was a long-term resident and, as an added and significant bonus, a wife whose energy and talent would touch every aspect of the local life. The church youth adored her and appreciated her love of learning and guidance in debates, plays, and recitations.[5] Many of these young people became loyal friends and remained in contact with her as adults, giving her the opportunity to stay current with their evolving life stories and life in the Leaskdale community. Margaret Mustard, for example, visited Montgomery up until a week before the author died in 1942. As Elizabeth Waterston points out in the previous chapter, Shier and Lapp were adolescents in the Young People's Association when Montgomery arrived in 1911, and afterwards, they were poised to move on into adulthood; she did not know the young men well, but she shared in their lives and stories through their siblings and parents.

Morley Roy Shier knew "Mrs Mac" for about two years before he left to attend the University of Toronto's teacher-preparation program. Robert Forrest (Bob) Brooks was in Ewan's congregation for about six years before he enlisted. Goldwin Dimma (Goldie) Lapp was at home for only a year before leaving for Toronto to work and study pharmacy. They joined different military units at different times between 1915 and 1917.[6] These three young men represent the sacrifices that small communities all over Canada invested in the world conflict. Just as their stories are the very real stories of communities throughout Canada, *Rainbow Valley* and *Rilla of Ingleside* are their fictional counterparts. Montgomery planned, wrote, and revised *Rainbow Valley* during the final years of the war, from 1917 to 1918; it is, appropriately, the story of the children in Anne and Gilbert's Prince Edward Island village of Glen St Mary who reach maturity in the last years of innocence before they are pulled into war. Montgomery penned the dedication to the pilot Morley Shier and the two soldiers Bob Brooks and Goldie Lapp, when she finished the *Rainbow Valley* manuscript in late December 1918, three months after the death of the last casualty, Flight Lieutenant Shier.

Several Shier family members were Montgomery's friends, including Morley's cousin, Mary Shier McLeod. Mary often took part in community and church programs but left Leaskdale in 1913 to work at the *Mail and Empire* in Toronto. Readers of Montgomery's journals will recall Morley's uncle, Dr Walter Columbus Shier, who was a physician in Leaskdale and Uxbridge. Dr Shier attended the Macdonald family and was the first doctor to treat Ewan's depression. Another uncle was Rob Shier who lived in Zephyr; his third wife was Lillis Harrison (Lily Reid), Montgomery's household helper from 1912 to 1915 and a trusted friend throughout Montgomery's life.

Morley was a teacher, first at Corson's Siding, northeast of Leaskdale, and then at Earl Grey School in Toronto. Shortly after Montgomery began work on *Rainbow Valley*, Morley started pilot training. Planes could be seen in the air from Toronto to Georgian Bay in 1917. A local Uxbridge historian, Allan McGillivray, observes, "Something that brought the war feeling to Scott [Township] was the sight of planes travelling overhead ... In August of 1917, the paper noted that four planes had been seen over Zephyr."[7] Montgomery creates just such a "war feeling" for even a village as far removed from the action as Glen St Mary when, in *Rilla of Ingleside*, the Blythes and Susan Barker watch a plane, "like a great bird poised against the western sky," and imagine "Shirley away up there in the clouds, flying over to the Island from Kingsport."[8] Morley joined the Royal Flying Corps (RFC) in November 1917. Later that month, Montgomery wrote to her life-long correspondent, Ephraim Weber, "A friend of mine in the Flying Corps told me that when he first went up he felt neither elated nor frightened – only *desperately lonely and homesick* – as if he were adrift in space – like a lost star," sentiments that Montgomery gave almost verbatim to Shirley Blythe after his first flight in the flying corps.[9] The corps pilots were housed at the University of Toronto and trained at Armour Heights Field in North Toronto. During Morley's training, fatality records were improved greatly; however, there were sometimes more than two dozen crashes each day, and the airfields were littered with plane debris. Michael Skeet cites examples of "pilots learn[ing] to fly by the seat of their pants: resting hands and feet lightly on the controls while the instructor flew the plane" and of "a typical day (21 October 1917), [when] C.H. Andrews recorded 17 crashes at his training squadron." Although 129 RFC Canadian cadets died in training, fatalities of British cadets numbered in the thousands.[10] Susan's fear of Shirley's "machine crashing down – the life crushed out of his body"[11] is well warranted.

Morley went to England in May 1918, after basic flight training, to learn combat and reconnaissance skills at the British advanced flying schools.[12] He was assigned to the 256th Royal Air Force Squadron, formed in June 1918 at Seahouses, Northumberland, a busy fishing port not far from the Farne Islands and the border with Scotland (where the Macdonalds stayed during their honeymoon). The squadron did coastal surveillance for German submarines and flew two-seater, Canadian-built de Havilland DH-6 planes, with a range of about four hours of flight. One of the many nicknames for the DH-6 was "the Flying Coffin."[13] Shier became an active RFC pilot in July 1918 at the age of twenty-three. About one-quarter of the RFC squadron crews were Canadian.[14] Most RFC combat pilots survived an average of about three weeks once they began their combat flights. Although reconnaissance pilots were not exposed to enemy fire as often as combat pilots, the risk to them was still significant; they were not armed but could carry bombs, and parachutes were not allowed because they were too heavy.[15] Planes took off from a field just inland from Seahouses to patrol the misty coast for German U-boats. Pilots located and chased U-boats, forcing them to stay below the surface of the sea where they could not communicate, lay mines, or observe and attack ships. In this way, Britain kept control of the North Sea in the last year of the war.[16]

After two months of flying, Flight Lieutenant Shier and his plane went down in the fog in the North Sea on 6 September 1918, about twenty miles from shore. When he died, Montgomery was enjoying a long visit from her Aunt Annie Campbell. In the first week of September 1918, they viewed *Hearts of the World*, a First World War film set in France and made at the request of the British government to spur the United States out of neutrality. Montgomery saw the film, which she deemed "a wonderful thing," because her half-brother Carl, who had taken part in the battle of Courcelette featured in the movie, had told her stories whose landmarks she wanted to identify. Another attraction was a story that Annie's daughter, Frede Campbell, had relayed of attending the film in Montreal and becoming "so excited by the realism of the thing" that she yelled out a warning to the actress on the screen.[17] Montgomery was upbeat and happy after a summer trip to the Island and optimistic about the end of the war. She did not hear of Morley's death until a month later, three days before Germany and Austria agreed to peace in October 1918. He was one of the last local men to die before the war was over. Second Lieutenant Morley Shier's name is on the Hollybrook Memorial in Southampton, England, erected by the Imperial War Graves Commission with the names of those lost at sea. About one-third of the officers and men on the memorial are from Canada. Members of the Shier family placed a marker in the cemetery in Leaskdale and a plaque in the church to honour him at home.

Another member of Ewan's congregation to make the "supreme sacrifice" to protect "the happy valleys" of his home was Bob Brooks, several years older than most local enlistees and, unlike Goldwin and Morley, part of the battalion comprised of young men who lived near the Macdonalds. The battalion was formed in September 1915 by Sam Sharpe, an Uxbridge lawyer and member of the House of Commons; Sharpe's wife, Mabel, was Montgomery's friend through their membership in the Uxbridge Hypatia Club, a women's discussion group about books and authors. The 116th Battalion was part of the 3rd Division of the Canadian Corps and took part in all the major battles in France and Belgium, earning honours wherever it fought.

Private Bob Brooks took a leave from training in Uxbridge in March 1916 to go home to Zephyr and sell his machinery, horses, and livestock. His mother had passed away by then, and his sister, Janet, was displeased that he was closing down the prosperous farm. But Bob was unmarried with no dependents and felt that he was needed more in the fields of Flanders than the fields of Zephyr.[18] Later he arranged for Janet and her husband, Jake Meyers (the couple had been married by Ewan in 1914), to take over the farm. The recruits from Zephyr, Leaskdale, and Uxbridge, whom Sam Sharpe had trained so well, did what was required. For over two-and-a-half years, they moved in endless marches from one battle to another, carried bombs, set communication wire under fire, cut barbed wire, and built trenches and roadways. They lived in constant cold and wet, suffered gas attacks, and fought the enemy in acres of knee-deep mud and shell-torn burial grounds at Vimy Ridge, the Méricourt trench, Ypres at the Passchendaele Ridge, and Amiens.[19] Private Brooks received a field promotion to sergeant during the last half of 1917. After Passchendaele, Colonel Sharpe could find no relief from the exhaustion and the images of waste and carnage he had experienced, and he killed himself after he was sent back to Ontario in May 1918. He was loved and respected by his men, setting a courageous example for his troops with his own actions in No Man's Land and keeping the battalion together so neighbours could serve side by side, when many other units were split up as reinforcements.[20]

Near the end of the war, the 116th Battalion prepared for the Hundred Days Offensive that broke the German resistance. On 8 August 1918, at 4:28 a.m., the 116th attacked in a heavy dark mist in the Luce Valley, fighting the retreating enemy for three hours. Sergeant Brooks died sometime early that morning, five weeks before his thirty-second birthday. Lieutenant-Colonel George Randolph Pearkes wrote, "He led his platoon to their objective and well past it, but was killed early in the morning of August 8 in the third battle of the Somme while helping a wounded comrade to safety. He was a good soldier, keen, and showed marked ability in the leadership of men. His loss to his company cannot be overestimated."[21] As Jerry Meredith writes in *Rilla of Ingleside* of Walter's earning a D.C Medal for the same brave act, "In any war but this ... it would have meant a V.C."[22] Brooks was buried almost where he fell, with 143 others at Hourges Orchard Cemetery, Domart-sur-La-Luce, Somme, France, a cemetery that was created after the battle. His family received the news of his death in late August, and a memorial service was held in the Presbyterian Church in Zephyr on 1 September 1918.

Montgomery remained friends with Bob's sister, Janet Meyers. Janet and her little daughter, Olive, were with the Macdonalds at the time of the car accident that would plague the next decade of their life with legal proceedings and fears of garnisheed wages. Ewan was driving everyone to the Meyers' farm for tea after church when his car crashed into that of Zephyr resident Marshall Pickering. Janet testified on Ewan's behalf in the lawsuit that Pickering launched and kept them informed of happenings and conversations in Zephyr about the accident. In 1925, their friendship cooled when Janet appeared to leave the Presbyterian congregation and considered moving to the newly formed Union Church.

A poem by A.B. Lundy, "Men of the One-Sixteen," written for the 116th Battalion and published in the *Port Perry Star*, recalls Walter's premonition about war in *Rainbow Valley*: "For they heard the bugle's call, Sounding All! All! All! / While the throbbing of the drum / Answered Come! Come! Come!"[23] Montgomery mirrors the cadence and sense of urgency of this poem by giving it a voice through Walter, still residing in a happy valley. The young Walter envisions the call to war as "the Pied Piper [who] will come over the hill up there and down Rainbow Valley, piping merrily and sweetly. And I will follow him – follow him down to the shore – down to the sea – away from you all. I don't think I'll want to go – Jem will want to go."[24]

Goldwin Lapp was one of the boys from Leaskdale who, like Jem, first followed the call and enlisted when war was declared in August 1914. Goldwin is at the heart of a network of stories enmeshed with events that had especially painful personal associations for Montgomery. He signed his enlistment papers on 4 January 1915, joining one of the first authorized fighting units, the 20th (Central Ontario) Canadian Battalion, Canadian Expeditionary Force, which had been mobilized in Toronto. After months of training, Goldwin left for England on the ss *Megantic*, the same ship that the Macdonalds had taken on their honeymoon trip. Goldwin's first letter home on 23 May 1915 has been preserved and records the journey overseas. He told his mother about the daily routine, what life boat drills were like, his fear of torpedoes, and the *Megantic*'s escort ships, the British torpedo destroyers the *Legion* and the *Lucifer*.

Like most Canadians, the Macdonalds were immersed in the tension of a life focused on a far-away brutal conflict. Ewan was the chairman of the Scott Township Patriotic Committee and president of the War Resources Committee, responsible for recruiting soldiers. Montgomery hosted Red Cross activities in the manse and recited "In Flanders Fields" at recruitment meetings. Many of the young soldiers visited or shared meals with the Macdonalds before leaving for England. In church, the families cried while Ewan said prayers for the soldiers at the front and the new recruits still at home.

Since August 1914, Montgomery had deeply absorbed emotions of shock, grief, and anguish. She gave birth to a stillborn son within weeks of the beginning of the war, and the agony of that loss was overlaid with the grim daily war news. By the time Goldwin was boarding the *Megantic*, she was pregnant again. Throughout this period, her journals reveal that she was consumed with the sacrifice and suffering of mothers and children. She cried herself to sleep over stories of crimes against children in Belgium; she was ashamed at her relief that her own little boy was too young to be "sacrificed"; she, like Walter Blythe, was nauseated by the reports of fatalities of babies on the *Lusitania*. Her third son was born in October 1915. As a mother, she was deeply affected by the war news and could empathize completely with women like Effie Lapp, whose son was already on the battlefield and whose letters were undoubtedly shared with Montgomery by the worried parents.

By November of 1915, the women of Leaskdale had organized their own Red Cross Society; Montgomery was its president, Effie its treasurer. She admired Effie's work ethic and ability to organize and lead. Montgomery suffered from her position as the minister's wife because it constrained her from sharing the intensity of her feelings about the war with women in the parish. Likewise, other members of the congregation seem to have suppressed their own thoughts in her presence. As a result, she felt that many of her neighbours were not as affected by the war as she was, except for those whose sons had enlisted. But there were times when she and Effie worked alone together, and thus they developed a mutual respect and loyalty outside the group.[25]

Meanwhile, Goldwin was receiving special training for operations in the area of Lens, France, where the battalion was holding lines, patrolling, and raiding. He was a lance-corporal, second in command in a platoon, in charge of a section of about fifteen men. His nieces remember that "he could have been used as a spy as he looked like a German and spoke some German!"[26] Because of his training as a pharmacist, he may have had duties as a medic. On 5 January 1917, the soldiers began constructing "dummy" German trenches in Bully Grenay to practise for a large offensive. The drills continued for eleven days in cold, wet, grey weather. It was windy and snowy on the morning of 17 January as the troops moved into position at 4:30 a.m. in Calonne, waiting for the code word "Lloyd George" to start the attack at 7:45 a.m. Battalions charged the Germans on an 850-yard front, destroying dugouts near the railway, blowing up ammunition dumps, and taking prisoners. Goldwin was wounded in the action and transferred through a snowstorm to the 6th Casualty Clearing Station. He died the next day, 18 January 1917, at age twenty-three years, ten months, and was buried nearby at Barlin Communal Cemetery, Pas de Calais.

News travelled quickly to grieving parents during the war years as technologies like the telegraph and telephone outraced letters and dispatches. Goldwin's father received a cable about his son's death on 22 January and telephoned the family's friends. The Macdonalds went to see the Lapps immediately. Because Effie and George were special friends, Montgomery was deeply grieved. Margaret Mustard remembered that "the Macdonalds proved their friendship by claiming each sorrow as their own."[27] Montgomery helped prepare the sanctuary for the memorial service two weeks later. The church was filled with broken-hearted families on Sunday evening, 11 February, in spite of extremely cold weather. As Waterston writes in the previous chapter, Montgomery's "sombre response" to this young man's death in her journal on 22 January reflects the effects of this loss on the small community: "It seems to me that the very soul of the universe must ache with anguish."[28]

Effie died within two years of the end of the war, on 4 August 1920. Like most mothers, she seemed never to have recovered from her son's death. At her funeral, Montgomery probably heard a family story being repeated among the Leaskdale neighbours: one winter morning, the Lapps' dog could be heard howling and howling, a bad omen, Effie told her granddaughters.[29] It was the day they received the notice about Goldie's death. At the same time that stories about Effie were being remembered, Montgomery was working on the last half of *Rilla of Ingleside* and writing perhaps one of the most poignant scenes in any of her books, a scene about another grieving dog, the Blythe's Dog Monday foretelling the death of Anne and Gilbert's son Walter in France: "Whose dirge was he howling – to whose spirit was he sending that anguished greeting and farewell?"[30]

Montgomery shared the loyalty of little Dog Monday on 21 November 1921 when she spoke at Jarvis Collegiate in Toronto. *Rilla of Ingleside* had been published a few months earlier, in August, and she chose to introduce the students to her new work. In a loud, clear voice she read the chapter about Dog Monday's refusal to leave the railway station where he had been waiting since his master, Jem, left for service overseas. When she came to the part where Dog Monday recognized the tired soldier getting off the train, she tried to describe the joyful reunion between Jem and his dog, but something happened. Her voice broke, and she could not speak. There was complete silence. It seemed like forever until she spoke again. Everyone in the audience had goose bumps, and it was something that no one in the auditorium ever forgot.[31]

This very rare public display of emotion is tied to one of Montgomery's deepest personal losses. When she spoke at this school, she was thinking of her dearest friend, Frede, to whom she dedicated this new book. Frede, a victim of the postwar flu pandemic, died two weeks after Montgomery finished writing *Rainbow Valley*. Before her speech to the students, she had shared lunch with one of Frede's colleagues, and they had talked about their mutual friend, a pivotal incident in Montgomery's journal, discussed in greater detail by Lesley Clement in chapter 13.[32] Frede's absence was painfully fresh as she read about Dog Monday's happy reunion, something she would never experience for herself.

In the dedication of *Rilla of Ingleside*, Montgomery honours the memory of her cousin and best friend. She had already dedicated *The Story Girl* to Frede because of their nine-year friendship during their Prince Edward Island years. *Rilla*'s dedication commemorates their years together in Ontario. Frede had known Ewan since 1904 when they both boarded in Stanley Bridge, six miles from Cavendish, where Montgomery lived. Frede may even have facilitated the courtship between the two; when Montgomery faltered in 1910 during her long engagement, Frede encouraged her cousin to follow through with the marriage that would bring her to Ontario. With Montgomery's financial support, Frede left her teaching position on the Island to attend Macdonald College in Montreal. After graduation, she was employed there as superintendent of Women's Institutes for Quebec. Although her residence was not in Ontario, Leaskdale became a home to her almost as soon as the Macdonalds moved into the manse. She stayed with them for Christmas in 1911 and afterward for many weeks between terms and assignments. Frede became acquainted with Ewan's congregations alongside her cousin. She lived with the Macdonald fam-

2.3 Montgomery, Frede, Ewan, and Chester in the Leaskdale dining room

ily for five months in 1912 when their first son, Chester, was born and thus felt a special bond with him. This lengthy stay established her place as a member of the Macdonald family. She eased into the Leaskdale community because she was a long-time, trusted friend to both the minister and his wife. When Ewan made frequent congregational visits or attended out-of-town conferences, Montgomery was not lonely. Because the two cousins complemented one another, Leaskdale manse became the home that Montgomery always hoped to have. Her newfound contentment was due, in large part, to Frede's presence. When she was there, the Leaskdale neighbours heard the sounds of music and laughter from the manse. Everyone in the village knew her and was fond of her.[33] The tiny room at the top of the stairs was Frede's room; the Macdonalds' home was her home too.

Montgomery always viewed Frede and herself as allies against adversity as both worked to find personal happiness and professional fulfilment. They leaned on one another when their lives felt hard. While Ewan always seemed to be much older than he was, Frede preserved

2.4 Frede's room, Leaskdale manse

Montgomery's youth. Together they reached back in time through shared memories. They both recognized how the Montgomery and Macneill personalities intersected, not always harmoniously, in themselves; they admired each other's wit, intellect, work ethic, and sacrifice. In the war years, the strands of their lives were bound even more tightly because Frede was the only person to whom Montgomery could express her deeply experienced feelings about the terrible news she faced each day; Ewan would not talk about it. As several chapters discuss, particularly chapters 4 (Laura Robinson) and 13 (Lesley

Clement), they knew that their complete loyalty to and trust in each other meant they could be their true selves and confess feelings they could never express anywhere else.

When Frede's mother, Annie Campbell, returned to Prince Edward Island in October 1918 after her visit to Leaskdale, her son, George, became ill with influenza, and so did Montgomery. She recovered; George did not. His four-year-old son, Georgie, died too. Frede went home to help her family, with Montgomery joining her a few days later. They were together at the Campbell farm in Park Corner when the Armistice was signed on 11 November 1918. Montgomery returned to Ontario to finish *Rainbow Valley*, and Frede stayed on the Island through Christmas.

On 20 January, in Boston wrapping up her lawsuit against publisher L.C. Page, Montgomery received a wire from Frede indicating she was ill. The next night, Tuesday, she received an urgent phone call from Frede's colleague telling her to come to Montreal at once. Arriving on Thursday morning, not knowing if Frede was still alive, she went to her hospital room. Frede was conscious and had the strength to laugh. When the end was near, Montgomery asked Frede to remember an old promise they had made each other – that if one of them died, the other would come back to the survivor, "to cross the gulf." As she held Frede's hand, they agreed that they would never say goodbye to each other, and they never did. Montgomery ordered red roses – Frede's favourite – for the casket and accompanied it to the crematory where she watched the doors close between her and her former life.

Frede's death shattered Montgomery as well as her husband. Ewan suffered a double loss: he lost a friend, someone who had enlivened his family; and he lost the wife who had a capacity for resiliency that only Frede could fully replenish. It made him more vulnerable to his own fears and weaknesses. In addition, Montgomery lost someone who cared about her oldest son, Chester. Would his life have taken a different shape with Frede's interest and guidance?

Elizabeth Epperly describes Montgomery's fiction with the word "magic" and her journals with "lament."[34] Those two words, "magic" and "lament," also reflect the dual purposes of Montgomery's emotional outpourings in her journal about the person who understood her best. In her magical reminiscences of Frede, Montgomery resurrects the perfect friend, a partner in an enchantment of laughter and restoration. Her commemorative journaling about Frede is an enduring lament of her loss. Aside from her journal, Montgomery reached out to find other ways to keep a tangible connection to Frede in the months following her death. Frede's husband was Lieutenant Nathaniel Cameron McFarlane (recorded as MacFarlane by Montgomery). Frede and Cam were married in Quebec on 16 May 1917, at the beginning of his six-day leave from the New Brunswick Kilties (the 236th O.S. Battalion, CEF, known as the "MacLean Highlanders," was stationed in his hometown, Fredericton). He also served with the Princess Patricia's Canadian Light Infantry before and after his assignment with the Kilties. A chemistry teacher at Macdonald College, he met Frede when they both were hired as a result of the Agricultural Instruction Act in 1913. Montgomery was stunned and hurt when Frede wrote to her about the surprise marriage a week later. The Macdonalds had always expected they would plan and host a wedding for Frede in the Leaskdale manse. Moreover, Montgomery feared that Frede and her husband might relocate far away from Leaskdale after the war. After Frede's death, Montgomery wished to know Cam better; she and Ewan had met him briefly in late October 1917, before he went overseas, but there was no real spark in the meeting. She summoned him to Leaskdale in April 1919 as soon as he left the service, anticipating that they would share their mutual grief with a circle of Frede's Leaskdale friends. But the visit was a disaster. Montgomery was appalled by his immature behaviour, especially because he seemed untouched by his loss. She took him to visit the Oxtoby sisters, to whom Frede had always shown a special kindness. He made tasteless, insulting jokes about his late wife and about the Oxtobys, which bewildered the elderly hosts and humiliated Montgomery. She put Cam McFarlane out of her life.[35]

Instead, she kept "the Good Fairy," a bronze statue, a wedding gift from friends at Macdonald College, which was one of Frede's favourite possessions. It became a prominent fixture in the Leaskdale manse and Montgomery's later homes in Norval and Toronto as an artifact to memorialize her lost friend. As photographs that Montgomery took reveal, she rearranged the tables, books, and plant stands along the walls

2.5 Cameron MacFarlane

in the parlour where she wrote her manuscripts to set up a focal point between the tall windows: Gog and Magog, her china dogs from England, sat on the floor beside a bookcase upon which she placed the Good Fairy. Above it on the wall was a wedding portrait of Frede holding a flower. Every day as Montgomery looked out toward the western light toward the spot that, in the previous chapter, Waterston calls

2.6 Good Fairy, Leaskdale manse

a "haven from a grown-up world,"[36] she would see the Good Fairy standing on the top of the world, the wind blowing in her hair, gazing up with her arms outstretched in an arc that lifted the author's eyes upward to Frede. She never required a reminder of her lost friend, but she did need something on which to fix her vision, something beautiful that belonged to Frede. Through the enshrined Good Fairy, her friend was always there with her at the manse in the quiet hours while she sought inspiration and crafted her stories. The Good Fairy was an image that insisted on hope and optimism, even when Montgomery had neither.

Montgomery's early years in Leaskdale were rich in joy and sorrow. Here she lived some of her happiest times as a wife and mother, even during the war. She had a healthy husband and an intact young and loving family; the support of her beloved companion, Frede; and a village that appreciated and admired her. She placed a reminder of these poignant times in the first pages of *Rainbow Valley* and *Rilla of Ingleside*. The war and grief would bind her forever to many kind families in Ontario. She would never forget the effects that the war had on her community, or her friends' sorrows at the loss of their grown children in the Great

War, or the wooded haunts of those children who inspired the environs of *Rainbow Valley*. When the time came for her to leave Leaskdale, she wrote about the view beyond the windows beside the Good Fairy: "The beautiful woods behind Mr Leask's, the leaf-hung corner of the side road, the lovely hill field beyond with the elms on its crest. I love these things and grieve to leave them."[37] But more than that, it was the memory-filled home that summoned her deepest grief.

Montgomery was uniquely bound to her first Ontario home because, for a time, it was occupied by a family in the wholeness of their lives. To paraphrase a poem about the Good Fairy, the windows were lit with a buoyant light of hope, and the companionship within its walls provided the whispering voice of courage; it echoed of love.[38] The Leaskdale manse was, and would be forever, the only house inhabited by her little boys, Chester and Stuart, untouched by their futures. It would be the only place shared with a cheerful husband who still had a dimpled smile and roguish eyes unclouded by fear, confusion, and doubt. It would be the only home infused with the brilliance of her vibrant companion, Frede, and the only haven filled with her own potential for happiness and the life story she might have lived.

3

"Being a Christian" and a Presbyterian in Leaskdale

MARGARET STEFFLER

In her journal entry of 21 October 1921, L.M. Montgomery recalls a traumatic childhood incident in which her grandmother forced her to pray to God for forgiveness for being "a bad girl," a task she remembers completing "sorely against my will, and with a soul filled with humiliation, impotent anger, and a queer sense of degradation as if something in me was outraged."[1] Elizabeth Waterston, noting Montgomery's contextualizing of the journal entry as occurring "just after she finished writing the ninth chapter of *Emily*,"[2] connects such childhood memories with the creation of the character of Emily, who, like Montgomery, experiences anger and shame as a result of humiliation imposed by older relatives and oppressive religion. The result of this particular incident in Montgomery's life was "a lasting sense of disgust with and hatred for prayer and religion," a rather curious admission to be made by a minister's wife in early twentieth-century rural Ontario. While conceding that it was not "real prayer – real religion" that she "loathed," but her grandmother's version, which consisted of "pattering formulas and going blindly through certain meaningless ceremonies," the retrospective journal writer is still easily moved to extreme feelings of loathing for a religious style that requires constant resistance and is so obviously part of her present as well as her past. She believes that she retained the humiliation and loathing of the forced childhood prayer, which "manifest[ed] itself in a *feeling* ... that 'religion' and all connected with it was something which – like sex – one had to have but was ashamed of for all that." She explains that in her "subconscious mind" this childhood incident, traumatic at the time but also deeply disturbing in retrospect, was primarily responsible for her "irrational detestation of 'being a Christian.'"[3]

Montgomery assumed that she was "like most people in being a helpless victim to impressions made in early years" but thought that she was perhaps "more helpless than some owing to the exceeding sharpness and depth of the impressions made on a somewhat unusually sensitive nature." Her "helplessness" was supported, however, by the way in which she nurtured the retention and intensification of such impressions through revisiting, rethinking, and rewriting them. In the 21 October 1921 entry, for example, she talks about how she dislikes "the *name* 'Jesus' itself" because she remembers it being "howled forth" by "unctuous evangelists and revivalists"; she also comments on her lifelong aversion to the term "Christian," which came from being asked, "Little girl, isn't it nice to be a Christian?" by "old Secord," a grotesque Bible pedlar.[4] These girlhood experiences, which occurred before Montgomery kept a diary or journal, are recorded for the first time in retrospect from the distance of adulthood and Leaskdale, years and miles removed from the original events and feelings. Once written in the journal, such experiences are often copied word for word, over and over, in letters to various correspondents, impressing themselves on the mind and memory as if they had been recorded, fact and emotion, at the time of the event itself. In chapter 8 of this volume, Emily Woster points out how the process of rewriting confronts a former voice, thereby encouraging the emergence of a new pattern of identity.[5] Indeed, such remembering and rewriting is as much about the present as the past. According to Sidonie Smith and Julia Watson, "Acts of remembering take place at particular sites and in particular circumstances," with "the life narrator depend[ing] on access to memory to narrate the past in such a way as to situate that experiential history within the present"; the result is that "we inevitably organize or form fragments of memory into complex constructions that become the changing stories of our lives."[6] Montgomery, for example, in a letter to Ephraim Weber on 15 October 1922, recounts this same incident of forced prayer and aversion to the name of Jesus and being called a Christian, transcribing the words directly from her journal of the previous year but claiming that the incident was triggered by a squabble she had just settled between Chester and Stuart,[7] whereas in the journal account, it is apparently a catechism question asked by Stuart that triggers the memory.

The event is deliberately contextualized and framed differently, drawing attention to the artificial construction of the recounting without undermining the power of the memory itself, which remains constant. This practice draws attention to Montgomery's need to write out and write over key religious experiences. What is interesting is that Weber receives exactly the same account as the one recorded in the journal – the personal correspondence does not differ from the journal entry written with the intention of eventual publication.

Another form of rewriting was also taking place in the early 1920s. Mary Rubio outlines the process and years in Leaskdale when Montgomery, now in her forties, was "copying her childhood diaries into the formal journal ledgers," creating a new character, "Maudie," in the process.[8] Maudie, as Rubio demonstrates, is a more persecuted and marginalized child than was the fairly content and privileged young Maud. This complete journal of the PEI years, as recopied by Montgomery "sometime between 1918 and 1922," is now available in two volumes as *The Complete Journals of L.M. Montgomery: The PEI Years, 1889–1900* (2012) and *1901–1911* (2013), "uncut," in "the format she herself devised."[9] These years of recopying the PEI journals serve as the period studied in this chapter, which considers both what is being copied and what is being lived. Rubio points out that Montgomery's "brooding up" and writing of *Emily of New Moon* took place during this time when "she was once again reconfiguring her childhood in her journals."[10]

This was also a time when Montgomery was anxious about the effects of religion on her own children. Concerned about the impact of Christianity, and specifically small-town Ontario Presbyterianism, on the growth of the child, she was, in October 1921, remembering her own childhood brushes with religion as faced by "Maudie," creating those of the fictional Emily, and worrying about the effects of religious education on six-year-old Stuart and nine-year-old Chester. The journal entry of 21 October begins with the reference to completing the ninth chapter of *Emily* and ends with an anecdote relating how Montgomery went against the Leaskdale Sunday school teachers, "crude, ignorant old women," and the "Leaskdale grundyites" by providing Stuart with a different and better answer to the catechism question of "Why did

God make all things?" Rather than simply repeating what she considered the egotistical answer of "for his own glory," Montgomery supplied "a very much higher conception of God's creation" with her answer that "God made all things for the love and pleasure of creating them – of doing good work – of bringing beauty into existence."[11]

Woster notes that Montgomery's initial Ontario journal entry, in its retrospective stance, marks the first "major shift in her journaling process."[12] Even before she moved to retrospective entries, Montgomery noted that "in writing all this down I have seemed to live it over again."[13] Retrospective writing would have increased this sensation, but it is in the recopying and rewriting of her already composed life that such reliving becomes most intense: "I find that when I am copying those old journals I feel as if I had gone back into the past and were living over again the events and emotions of which I write. It is very delightful and a little sad." In her writing and rewriting, Montgomery creates Maud, a journal persona, in order to maintain, when desired or needed, an important distance between herself as journal writer and herself as depicted on the journal page. The presence of a persona, for example, allows her to respond to the space between her current self in the sterile present and her former self in the sensuous past, which calls up feelings of difference and loss: "I have made myself wretchedly homesick by writing all this and visualizing the memories evoked. It has been so real to me that it has filled me with a bitter longing to be in those spots once more – to taste the inimitable flavor of the wild fruit, to lie amid the sun-warm grasses, to hear the robins whistling, to tiptoe through the lanes of greenery and fragrance in the summer mornings of those faraway years. When I wrench myself away from their idyllic memories to the bitter, carking reality of life at present I sicken at the contrast."[14] The narrative, although speaking of acute pain, is constructed with an appreciation for the artistic balance and contrast achieved in the startling gap between the plentiful past and the destitute present.

It seems that the revisiting of her childhood, adolescence, and young adulthood through the recopying of the PEI diaries facilitated in Montgomery a reliving of both what was recorded and not recorded in those pages, including earlier childhood moments preceding the years covered by the diary and intense impressions not included in the original account. These moments and depths appear in various forms in the current Leaskdale journal as her writing triggers memories. Despite the immediacy and power of the actual childhood events and narratives, these accounts are obviously written out of the life of Mrs Ewan Macdonald, the minister's wife in Leaskdale, as much as they are written out of the Cavendish childhood and adolescence of Maudie. It is the startling intersection of these two lives that results in the extreme passion of the 21 October 1921 journal entry and other entries during this period. The intersections facilitate the transference and blurring of emotions between child and adult, nowhere more apparent than in the strong responses to Christianity and the Presbyterian Church. Sidonie Smith proposes that for the autobiographer "the doubling of the 'self' into a narrating 'I' and a narrated 'I' and, further, the fracturing of the narrated 'I' into multiple speaking postures" results in "several, sometimes competing stories about or versions of herself as her subjectivity is displaced by one or more multiple textual representations."[15] Montgomery's fractured representations during this time include Maudie, the child; Maud, bereft cousin and friend of Frede; L.M. Montgomery, celebrity author and creator of Emily; and Mrs Ewan Macdonald, mother of two sons and minister's wife to her husband and his congregations. A common thread connecting these disparate identities is the complex impact of religion as both supportive and destructive in past and present narratives, which are retrieved and constructed as continuous and complementary rather than competitive.

The importance of the creation of the character of Emily at this time, even beyond Montgomery's admission of its autobiographical tendencies,[16] is found in the theory of Sandra M. Gilbert and Susan Gubar, who argue that "life is enactment, art the outward manifestation of the scenes performed on an inner stage, and thus an author and her characters are one: they are, as we have said, one 'supposed person,' or rather a series of such persons."[17] Montgomery's concentration as an adult on the child identities of Maudie, Emily, Chester, and Stuart is similar in some ways to Gilbert and Gubar's account of Emily Dickinson "consciously enacting the part of a child – both by deliberately prolonging her own childhood and by inventing a new, alternative childhood for herself." Gilbert and Gubar's interpretation of Dickinson's poem "She rose to His Requirement" provides a relevant commentary on Montgomery's conflicting identities, particularly those of girl and wife: "The irony of the woman/wife's situation as it is described here is that in 'rising' to the rigorous 'Requirement' of a husband she has ... been cast out of the holy, Wordsworthian sea of imagination where she had dwelt as a girl." The husband/master's diminishment of creative works as "Playthings"[18] displays an attitude not far removed from Montgomery's assessment of Ewan's view of her fiction.[19]

There is then an intertextuality present in the fall of 1921, and more generally in the years 1918 to 1922, that involves the writing of the current journal in Leaskdale, the recopying of the diaries of the PEI years, and the composition of the first *Emily* novel – all written out of the Leaskdale manse, the official home of the local Presbyterian minister, with its complicated obligations to the congregation of St Paul's Presbyterian Church and the rural Ontario communities of Leaskdale and Zephyr. Within that manse, Ewan suffered from what was called at that time "religious melancholia," revealed to Montgomery when she pushed him for an explanation: "He said he was possessed by a horrible dread that he was *eternally lost* – that there was no hope for him in the next life. This dread haunted him night and day and he could not banish it."[20] I argue that the "physical repulsion to Ewan,"[21] as experienced and expressed by the journal persona Maud in response to this "malady," is a complex culmination of Montgomery's own contradictory and long-standing loyalty and aversion to institutionalized Christianity and Presbyterianism – which is as much about Montgomery as it is about Ewan. The complex feelings, highly controlled and not yet articulated in the girlhood entries of the PEI diaries being recopied into the journal format, are carefully formulated in the fiction but take full form and weight in the Leaskdale journal. The extreme diction used to describe Ewan's mental illness and Maud's reaction to it is the same diction used to describe retrospective childhood "feelings" about a detestable religion that was neither holy nor healthy. Such diction is not generally used in the early journals but is applied to these childhood experiences and feelings in retrospect. Montgomery's disgust for Ewan's condition encompasses a more general disgust for Christianity, which she was not free to acknowledge to herself or others as a child in Cavendish or as Mrs Ewan Macdonald of the Leaskdale manse. In chapter 13 of this volume, Lesley Clement describes the separate life that Montgomery carved out for herself in Toronto during the Leaskdale years,[22] and it was perhaps only in the city that she experienced relief from these recurring feelings of disgust and repression.

On one level, Montgomery is viewing the devastating effect on her husband of a particular brand of Scottish Presbyterianism, which depends on a belief in the doctrine of Predestination, thus corroborating her sense of religion's oppressive impact at its most extreme. In his short study of Montgomery's religious thought, Gavin White explains that Ewan would have heard "Predestination actually taught in the sermons of his youth, as had many of the settlers in Prince Edward Island," whereas Montgomery, on the north shore of the island, "was certainly made aware of Predestination, but probably was not taught it; in fact, she probably heard sermons rejecting it."[23] Ewan would not have been taught Predestination when he attended Glasgow's theology school, but Rubio outlines the pervasive persistence of the belief well after its exclusion from official doctrine.[24] Montgomery was convinced that Ewan did not believe in Predestination in a rational way but was a victim of its power when he fell ill and was unable to think rationally. This explanation is similar to her own belief that her detestation of being a Christian was a result of her subconscious rather than conscious mind. Montgomery's observations of Ewan's attacks of "religious melancholia," however, make it difficult to determine if a rational belief in Predestination caused the illness or if an irrational belief in the doctrine emerged as a symptom of the illness. Montgomery provides the diagnosis that makes the most sense to her and with which she can live most easily – the one that removes responsibility, choice, and will from Ewan.

Despite her intellectual attempts to explain and understand Ewan's condition, Montgomery actually partakes of the repugnance and self-loathing felt by Ewan – or that she attributes to him. Repelled by certain brands of religion since early childhood, she is intimately familiar with feelings of loathing directed toward the institution of religion but does not apply the loathing to herself until 1919 when she is weighed down by her cousin Frede's death and Ewan's illness.[25] Ewan calls forth Montgomery's disgust for what religion has done to him, but he also becomes a catalyst for her sense of what it has done to her to a lesser degree and what it could potentially do to her sons, considering the pervasive presence of the Presbyterian Church in their lives. Disturbingly, Ewan embodies for her all that is perversely dark and destructive in the institution of Christianity and more specifically in Presbyterian theology and doctrine. She concentrates her abhorrence on Ewan as both a representative and victim of the type of religion practised by her grandmother and imposed on her in childhood. Its shadow continues to haunt her as she uses her Leaskdale journal for the familiar process of "writing it out," "it" in this case being the shame for having religion, comparable in Montgomery's opinion to the shame for having sex.[26] Smith argues that "the autobiographer acknowledges, sometimes explicitly, more often implicitly, an uneasiness with her own body and with the sexual desire associated with it."[27] Montgomery is more explicit than implicit but is consciously working within what Irene Gammel identifies as a "remarkable awareness of both the risks and the empowerment involved in disclosing intimate subject matter."[28]

The fiction written by Montgomery during this period wrestles with the complexities of professing Christianity and Presbyterianism. *Rainbow Valley* (1919), in its exploration of the life of a minister, a manse family, and a judgmental community, serves as a preparatory text for *Emily of New Moon* (1923), which explores internal beliefs, including alternate forms of faith and spirituality. In *Magic Island*, Waterston describes *Rainbow Valley* as a novel concerned with "the institutions" as opposed to "theological beliefs" of religion and observes that it reflects the "tensions" of the "old-time Presbyterian community in which Montgomery grew up" and "her tussle with her own beliefs in the years when she was growing, perforce, into the role of minister's wife."[29] In her contribution to this volume, Waterston outlines the ways in which Montgomery's concerns about Ewan, Chester, and Stuart are transferred from the writing arena of the Leaskdale manse to the fictional manse of John Meredith.[30] *Rainbow Valley*, through its depiction of Meredith, deals with the many challenges faced by Ewan as a distracted minister in a small town and even touches on his adversary – Predestination. Treating beliefs in Predestination and damnation humorously through Harrison Miller, who "growls at everybody because he thinks he is fore-ordained to eternal punishment,"[31] and through the lightness of children's attempts to grasp heavy and irrelevant concepts, this novel touches on the darkness that is beginning to envelop Montgomery's life by exposing Predestination to views that render it powerless and turning the narrative's attention to other matters. Concentrating on topics less harsh than those of Predestination and damnation – the problems of a minister who does not connect with his congregation, a manse in disarray, and a community ever ready to find fault – Montgomery has selected areas over which she has some control in her own life. For example, she is able to compensate for Ewan's distance from those he serves, keep the manse in order by attacking it with regular cleaning campaigns, and defend her family and home from the watchful eye of Leaskdale. She is the minister's wife who is missing in the Meredith manse and thus writes herself into importance and service through demonstrating the negative impact of the absence in the fictional home and family. She heals and fixes the Merediths in a way that she could never heal and fix the Macdonalds. She cannot permanently cover for Ewan or completely protect her children from the invasive gazes and judgments that penetrate the walls of the Leaskdale manse. Neither can she protect the community of Leaskdale from the war, but as Mary Beth Cavert's chapter demonstrates, she can publicly honour and mourn Leaskdale's losses through the literary dedication.[32]

The PEI diaries she recopies in Leaskdale are filled with entries devoted to religion, but it is a much more socially enjoyable religion than that being lived by Montgomery in Ontario. Many of the references to religion, Christianity, and Presbyterianism in *The Complete Journals* focus on drives to and from church services and prayer meetings. Often the young Maud provides more detail about the drive than the service: "In the evening went over to the Baptist church at New Glasgow. It was a delicious evening for driving and I enjoyed that part of it quite well." When describing services, she often refers to views out the window, such as the one afforded by the family pew, which "look[ed] out over the slope of the long western hill and the blue pond down to the curving rim of the sandhills and the sweep of the blue gulf," or she refers to views of the congregation: "As usual I tucked myself away in the corner of Aunt Mary's pew where I could take a sly squint every now and then at Mary and Ida out of the tail of my eye." Services seem to provide more entertainment than worship, such as that provided unknowingly by "poor Mrs Albert Laird who came sailing down the aisle and plumped herself down in front of us with a sewing needle and a yard of white thread hanging from the crown of her bonnet down over her back. Every time she twitched her head – and she is noted for her twitches – the needle would fly."[33] The actual church is more of a theatre than a sanctuary.

Very aware of the different denominations of Christianity and sharply judgmental of the quality of sermons, Maud keeps track of her attendance at various churches, particularly when she covers a variety of brands in a single day. In Bideford on 5 August 1894, for example, she records that she attended the Methodist Church in the morning and the "Presbyterian service in Tyne Valley in the afternoon," where she "heard Rev. William MacLeod preach – or rather jump and rant and howl." She then "drove up to Lot 11 in the evening and heard him again." One month later, on 2 September, Maud writes that "we went to the English church in the morning and after dinner drove to the Presbyterian church at Lot 14." Such double-denomination Sundays become a motif in the journal, reaching a climax in Belmont on 22 March 1897: "Yesterday I experimented with three denominations. In the morning I went up to the Baptist church to hear Mr Robinson of S'Side. Then I went down with Mr Simpson and after dinner we all piled into a pung and drove up to Central to hear Mr Sutherland of Zion church preach. After tea we wound up our religious orgy by going to the Methodist church." The use of the term "orgy," like the earlier comparison of religion to sex, accentuates the forbidden indulgence in activity not sanctioned or approved. It seems to be both the amount of religion and the unorthodox mixture of denominations that render the day's activities orgiastic in Maud's view. In 1893, after having attended in Charlottetown a morning Anglican service at St Paul's and an evening "Roman Catholic in all but name" service at St

Peter's, Maud declares her loyalty to the Presbyterian Church, proclaiming "I felt devoutly thankful that I was a Presbyterian. If I went to that church a year I'd have nervous prostration – that is, if they always go through all the kididoes they went through to-night."[34] It is a loyalty arrived at through a negative elimination of alternatives and only achieved after experiencing strong feelings that the "Catholic church was the only right one" and repeated "fear[s] that the Baptists, and they only, were right."[35]

The potential darkness of the belief in Calvinist Predestination is treated quite lightly in the PEI journals. In an 1891 entry written in Prince Albert, Laura Pritchard, John Mustard, and Maud discuss Predestination, with Mustard arguing for it, Maud arguing against it, and Laura left in the middle. Maud comfortably and confidently concludes that "a million Mustards could never make me believe that God ordains any of his creatures to eternal torture for 'his own good will and pleasure.'"[36] Nineteen years later, in 1910, Montgomery writes a long paragraph in her journal in which she emphatically declares that the doctrines of the shorter catechism, which during her childhood taught "things that are no longer believed – and never should have been believed" – specifically "the doctrines of 'election' and 'predestination'" – "slipped over our minds like pebbles over ice, making little impressions."[37] Her entry of 7 October 1897, however, suggests otherwise. She writes of herself as a child "terribly frightened of hell," who regularly "fell under conviction of sin." The ease with which she claims to have dismissed the impact of such teachings in these early years, when they "drop[ped] away like an outgrown husk,"[38] questionable even at the time, becomes even more difficult once she moves from Prince Edward Island to Ontario, into her marriage with Ewan and into the Leaskdale community where the impressions of those pebbles reveal themselves as having made deeper and more permanent marks than previously acknowledged.

The dark undercurrent pertaining to religion in the PEI journals emerges not in the dreaded doctrine of Predestination but in non-Presbyterian theology and practices, with baptism by immersion, evangelism, and revival meetings receiving the sharpest criticism. Revival meetings are tolerated because, for Maud, "anything is welcome to vary the deadly monotony of life here [in Belmont]." Even her distrust of evangelical speakers and the pressure to "come out" are overcome to a certain extent by her conscientious decision to avoid having a negative impact on the faith of her friend, Mary Campbell. Maud signs the prayer card when it comes around so that Mary will feel free to do so without being intimidated by Maud's potential judgment and "sarcastic tongue." This action prompts Maud to admit that "there are some things I find it very hard to believe." Drawn emotionally to demonstrative displays of religious faith, she finds herself intellectually and spiritually wary: "The farewell service was held tonight in the Big Brick and 2700 people were present. The meeting was certainly very thrilling. But *feeling* and *belief* are such very different things – at least, after we begin *really* to think."[39]

The most serious criticism is reserved for baptism by immersion, but it is not so much the practice itself as the way in which it is presented that irks the young Maud. Mr Baker in Belmont "came out with a narrow, bigoted preachment on immersion," reports Maud, who had been playing the organ for his meetings and felt insulted that he would preach on immersion in her presence. When he acknowledged her Presbyterian presence with a "deprecating smile" and the comment that "of course I suppose you are all Baptists here. If you are not, you ought to be," she "gave no answering smile" but "looked as dour as my Scottish-Presbyterian great-grandfather himself could have done." With respect to the prospect of marrying Edwin Simpson and having to undergo "re-baptism by immersion," Maud uses the strong diction that reappears years later in the Leaskdale journal: "But to marry a Baptist minister would necessarily involve my re-baptism by immersion – a thing utterly repugnant to my feelings and traditions."[40] The yoking of feelings and traditions is telling here; the "repugnancy" is Maud's "feeling" transferred to the "tradition." For a Presbyterian, baptism by immersion may have been irrelevant and indefensible but not necessarily repugnant; this is a word and emotion that Maud claims and owns as the years progress, using it to describe both present and past experiences.

In the PEI journals, Maud presents her inclination and desire to substitute nature for religion as unorthodox and revolutionary. Calling herself "a coward" who "must drift on with the current of conventionality," she nevertheless writes out her yearning to spend Sundays in the forest "alone with nature and my own soul" but speculates rather dramatically that the "local spinsters would die of horror," crediting herself with more attention and importance than she would probably receive. In a more subdued framing of institutional religion by nature, she describes a "delicious" drive home from prayer-meeting "through the woods, so dark and rustling and mysterious" and refers to a ramble before the meeting "through the fields, starry with clover and buttercups, climbing old mossy fences, brushing through spruce copses, and startling blue-birds from their nests" without providing any information at all about the prayer-meeting itself. The emphasis on drives and rambles rather than on actual religious events, already noted earlier in this chapter, becomes a motif in the PEI journals to the point that an expected and familiar pattern is set: spiritual needs are met on the way to and from the formal services and meetings that are designed to serve such needs, but fail to deliver. This innocuous replacement of institutional religion with the worship of God as a creator is not as unorthodox or shocking as Montgomery makes it out to be. Her early reading of Emerson exposed her to Transcendentalism,[41] which she easily incorporated into her beliefs and which was not unknown in the Prince Edward Island of her childhood, having been "brought to the Maritime Provinces by settlers from New England."[42] Drawing attention to this rather tame (even at the time) religious transgression distracts both Montgomery and the journal reader from the shadow of much stronger and darker emotions that *do* threaten her religious faith and already exist in a muted form in the Cavendish years. These shadows emerge and expand in her religious struggles in Leaskdale as she performs her demanding roles as minister's wife, famous writer, and concerned mother.

Montgomery continued to explore other belief systems beyond Transcendentalism, including versions of spiritualism, theosophy, universalism, and the occult in attempts to find a faith more suited to her temperament than Presbyterianism. As Sylvia DuVernet accurately points out in *Minding the Spirit: Theosophical Thoughts Concerning L.M. Montgomery*, Montgomery's letters to her pen pals George MacMillan and Ephraim Weber contain extensive discussions of a "theosophical thinker."[43] The extent to which the well-read and informed Montgomery was aware of and searching among current trends of alternative religions is apparent in her journal entry of 29 March 1919 in which she reveals her desire to be convinced by Dr Albert Durrant Watson's *The Twentieth Plane: A Psychic Revelation* (1918), "the book which has made such a sensation in Toronto," and her subsequent disappointment in its "absolute poppycock."[44]

Rubio explains that in her fiction Montgomery "took emotions she knew and attributed them to a spectrum of imaginary characters," while "in her journals, she appears to have reversed the process, taking her emotions and attaching them – sometimes arbitrarily – to suitable real-life characters." Rubio's comment is made in reference to the description of the affair with Herman Leard of which Montgomery writes so passionately and which Rubio speculates could be partially due to displacement, her marriage with Ewan being extremely troubled "in 1920, when she recopied the Herman story into her entry of October 7, 1897."[45] While Ewan may be temporarily displaced by Herman Leard of the recopied journal, his continued presence remains necessary for other uses, namely as a receptacle for Montgomery's own fears and repugnance of sexuality and of certain Christian and Presbyterian dogmas. What Ewan has become – a religious melancholic – she could also be. The extreme reaction and language she uses are understandable as a defence against her own inclination to spiritual darkness, not dissimilar to Ewan's, which becomes more difficult for her to ward off with each passing year in Leaskdale.

Montgomery is surprisingly well versed in the symptoms of religious melancholia. Upon her realization of the nature of Ewan's disease, she responds through the journal persona of Maud with intense emotion and extreme diction, claiming that "unutterable horror seemed literally to engulf me," that he had "every symptom given in the encyclopedia on that type of insanity," and that "it was one of the things I had always had the most deeply rooted horror of." Her persona's insistence that the belief that "you were doomed to hell fire for all eternity" was a "hideous old mediaeval superstition which Ewan normally believed in no more than I did"[46] does not seem entirely convincing. Rubio, for example, believes that Predestination was "firmly lodged in Ewan's mind" and "provided him with the explanatory concept to understand precisely why he felt so miserable and depressed." She also points out that Ewan felt he had committed the "unpardonable sin" by doubting that he was one of the "Elect," thereby doubting God's power. In Rubio's words, "Ewan was caught up in circular reasoning within a complicated theology,"[47] a much more accurate assessment than Maud's rather simplistic explanation that he was not at all affected by thoughts of Predestination when he was in his "right mind." White points out that eventually Montgomery does resort to the doctrine of Predestination, despite her stated abhorrence. The most startling examples quoted by White occur in 1925 when Montgomery says, "It will all be according to predestination" and "Well, well, I really believe that everything is foreordained."[48] Although these could be dismissed as isolated and vulnerable moments, Montgomery's predisposition to such thoughts provides a plausible explanation for her violent reactions to Ewan's episodes, apparent in her persona's uncontrolled emotions at the time of their occurrence and reflected in the extreme diction used in the journal accounts. Her response to Ewan's depression forms it into a creature of her own making.

An example of excessive emotion and diction occurs in an entry on 31 August 1919. After finding Ewan "in his arm chair gazing gloomily before him" and making him "confess that he is again haunted by conviction of eternal damnation," Maud cries "wretchedly" in her room, saying that this "unnatural" "thing" fills her with "horror and repulsion" and turns her "against Ewan for the time, as if he were possessed by or transformed into a demoniacal creature of evil – something I must get away from as I would rush from a snake."[49] Montgomery's comparison of religion with sex in the passage describing her grandmother's forced prayer also seems relevant here in the reference to the snake. The repulsion felt towards religion strongly suggests sexual repulsion even as it evokes desire and temptation. Interestingly, a visit from Captain Edwin Smith in 1922 inspires Montgomery's comment that "Captain Smith is one of the few people I have met with whom I can discuss with absolute frankness, any and every subject, even the delicate ones of sex."[50] Edwin Smith, like Herman Leard, seems to provide an intimacy that is lacking in her relationship with Ewan.[51]

Just as Montgomery identifies a single event – the prayer forced by her grandmother – as the cause of her aversion to being a Christian, so she isolates and blames a specific sermon on hell, preached to Ewan as a child, as being "responsible for his delusion." In both cases, she approaches the problem by assigning responsibility to an external and oppressive force working through a specific, identifiable agent in order to impose suffering. During a period of reprieve when Ewan feels better, she makes the telling comment – "I feel as if I had been lifted out of hell"[52] – when it is more literally Ewan, in his temporary release from delusions of damnation, who should feel the effects of being lifted out of hell. Despite the distance that Montgomery establishes and maintains between herself and Ewan, there are similarities that suggest a closer alignment than she perhaps sees or admits. For example, when feeling that she will "be involved in lawsuits all my life – it is all dark and it will never be dawn," she says that she tries "to reason it away, but reason has no effect on it, any more than on Ewan's attacks of melancholy."[53]

Montgomery also makes comparisons between her sons and herself, but consciously, deliberately, and specifically with "Maudie" of the PEI journals, who in turn shares much with the fictional character of the novel she was creating at this time. She orchestrates and encourages these intersections involving Maudie, Chester and Stuart, and Emily. In her Leaskdale journal, she openly seeks similarities with her sons and draws comparisons between her own childhood and theirs. The attention is often on Christianity and Presbyterianism, as seen in the content of three "odd little things" spoken by Chester in November 1919. Similar to comments made by Montgomery's fictional characters, Chester's odd speeches have a serious element. In this case, he says he "kneeled down on the ground and asked God to make it warmer but when I got out of the gate it was just as cold as ever"; he explains that he could now eat celery because "God put the power into me"; and he tells Stuart that "a man and a woman go to a minister and he *preaches a sermon to them* and then they're married." Recording

Chester's comments, Montgomery turns the attention to herself, wondering if she "made many queer speeches when [she] was a tot."[54] The question provides the segue into a recounting of two such examples from her childhood, vivid and detailed because they were actually recorded and remembered. The question is also about all those moments that were not recorded or remembered and are thus lost.

Despite her desire for parallels, Montgomery cannot prevent herself from being drawn to contrasts and sees in the childhood of her sons a measurement of all she has lost. On 6 March 1922, she writes that Stuart enthusiastically tells her that "this is a happy life! I hope it will last always." She says "the contrast between my mood and his struck me rather bitterly," and she concedes that "neither he nor anyone else can wholly escape unhappiness in life." She writes that she tries "at least to give him a happy childhood" but then asks, "Is it any use trying to accomplish *anything* in this world! Are we not only puppets in the hands of destiny?"[55] Perhaps the outmoded doctrine of Predestination has had more of an impact on Montgomery, a committed if unorthodox Presbyterian, than she imagines or is willing to see.

Her recopying of the PEI diaries, along with her copying of other old journals, accentuates contrasts between the old and the new; the happiness of the two years after Chester's birth, for example, contrasts with the misery following the war, the deaths of Frede and baby Hugh, and the onset of Ewan's "malady." Montgomery takes that contrast between past and present and applies it to a more compact past and present: "As I wrote over that old journal I realized how unlike his old self [Ewan] is, even in the days when his trouble grows lighter. It is only in contrast with his dark days that he seems well."[56] The same could be said of Montgomery herself in her final years at Riverside Drive in Toronto. As she speaks of Ewan, she offers insight into herself, or perhaps premonitions. Her belief in Predestination is treated lightly in 1930 when she concedes that "one must just fall back on predestination," which at times "is a most comforting doctrine" and in 1933 when she calmly recognizes that "there are no 'ifs' in predestination – in which I have come to believe absolutely. We walk our appointed ways."[57] These statements are light only in contrast to later ones, such as the 1935 comment that "I seem to *live with fear*" and the final entry of 1937: "This has been a fitting close to a year of hell."[58] The fear and hell recall the sensations of damnation derived from a belief in Predestination that were prominent in Ewan from 1918 to 1922. These sensations continued to affect Montgomery directly and indirectly into the 1930s.

In her journal entry of 13 December 1920, Montgomery provides yet another contrast – between her religious feelings as a child and her spirituality as a woman in her forties, claiming, "In childhood I had very deep religious instincts but I do not seem to possess them now. I am not in the least spiritual – that is, in the ordinary meaning of that word."[59] The word "instincts" suggests innate feelings, while the "ordinary meaning" of the word "spiritual" is left to the reader to ponder. It is curious that she switches from "religious" to "spiritual," as "religious" suggests institutionalized Christianity, whereas "spiritual" has more of an air of transcendentalism to it. This account denying a spiritual temperament in general, written in Leaskdale, differs significantly from an earlier journal entry written in Cavendish in 1897. In that earlier entry, Montgomery explains that she is not "'religiously inclined,' as the phrase goes, but I have always possessed a deep *curiosity* about 'things spiritual and eternal.' I want to *find out* – to *know*."[60] The later reluctance and uncertainty about identifying as "spiritual" suggest a confusion comparable to Ewan's attraction and repulsion to a belief in damnation. There is a flirting with and withdrawal from what in both cases is perceived as dangerous but also powerfully attractive.

The Montgomery who waits for Frede to visit her from the dead and who sees the divine in nature certainly seems to be "spiritual" – more spiritually open than religiously observant. And in *Emily of New Moon*, being written when the 1920 statement denying spirituality was made, Montgomery explores the spiritual, in the sense of "of or relating to the human spirit or soul,"[61] as she has never explored it before. Emily's "flash" is the lifting of the soul and spirit beyond the material world. Kathleen Miller argues that Emily's journey "culminates in a spirituality that reinterprets traditional Christianity and values the power and energy found in feminized landscape, women's imagination, and female artistry." Miller also argues that "Montgomery succeeds in allowing Emily to abandon the patriarchal Christian religion, although she herself could not."[62] Although the patriarchy *was* objectionable to Montgomery, the church itself was not; in the end, she could not dismiss it, primarily because it stood as a type of home, making abandonment unthinkable, even in Leaskdale where it was the source of so much misery.

The autobiographical elements invested in the character of Emily were those of Maudie, the persona of the PEI journals, but were also those of L.M. Montgomery of Leaskdale, who was recopying and rewriting the Maudie of former years while creating Emily. Simultaneously, by necessity, the autobiographical elements were also those of Mrs Ewan Macdonald, the minister's wife. Montgomery's loyalty to the Presbyterian Church when the issue of Church Union was being bitterly fought from 1923 to 1925 is reminiscent of Maud's childhood preference for the comfort and familiarity of Presbyterianism above other denominations. The adult Montgomery resents the "feeling of 'homelessness'" that the forced union brings with it: "I feel that I have no longer a church. My Presbyterian Church has gone – I owe and feel neither love nor allegiance to its hybrid, nameless successor without atmosphere, tradition or personality." In the summer of 1924, she writes that the "feeling in Ontario is very intense. No matter what happens our Presbyterian church can never be what it was. We have to choose between staying in a broken, crippled church – which would be my choice were I free to choose – or going into a hybrid nameless 'United Church.'"[63]

Montgomery was never fully at home in Ontario, and the Presbyterian Church, even trailing its abhorrent doctrines of the elect and Predestination, spoke strongly of home – the home of Prince Edward Island, of Cavendish, of the Macneill and Montgomery families, and even of the ancestral home of Scotland. In chapter 9, Natalie Forest writes of how the view from Ontario, specifically from the Leaskdale manse, rendered the Cavendish home more uncanny and gothic with each return visit.[64] Montgomery's feeling of homelessness was as much about a lost time, approach, and emotion as a lost place, the gothic taking over as she carried back the uncanny of her Leaskdale life and landscape to her original home. In July 1899, she was forced to mourn actual changes and modernization when she writes of her sadness over the tearing down of the old church in Cavendish: "But the old church is gone now, with all its memories and associations. They will put up a modern one which will be merely a combination of wood and plaster and will not be mellowed and hallowed by the memories that permeated and beautified that unbeautiful old church. Churches, like all else, have to be ripened and seasoned before the most perfect beauty becomes theirs."[65]

Montgomery is repelled by what the Presbyterian Church and its doctrine brought to her and her family in Leaskdale. Never one to leave behind the past, memories, or tradition lightly or easily, however, she balanced this abhorrence by contrasting it with the stability and history of the institution and its provision of a home away from home. Her disgust for what she saw in Ewan was a fear of the emergence of what she felt within herself. Rather than an adversary, Ewan was a terrifying mirror, capable of inspiring loathing because of what he reflected. Even this fear and repugnance, however, is balanced by a loyalty to Christianity and the Presbyterian Church as one of many "creeds and religions, dead and alive" that Montgomery is "always poking and probing into" to find "what vital spark of immortal truth might be buried among all the verbiage of theologies and systems."[66] A master of contrasts and balances, Montgomery both denied and embraced the Christianity and Presbyterianism of her childhood, which followed her so closely, so passionately, and so painfully to her home in Leaskdale, Ontario, providing the deepest suffering but also providing complex memories of her PEI home that were written out over and over again in a life that depended on the creation of paradoxical connections and contrasts. In her ongoing search for home, Montgomery of Leaskdale, like Emily of New Moon, was compelled to "write it out."[67]

The Changing World of Women: Mother, Daughter, Friend

4

"A Gift for Friendship": Revolutionary Friendship in Anne of the Island *and* The Blue Castle

LAURA M. ROBINSON

L.M. Montgomery's fifteen-year sojourn in Leaskdale is framed by two novels – *Anne of the Island* (1915) and *The Blue Castle* (1926) – that showcase a houseful of women. In *Anne of the Island*, Anne rents a house with three other young women and a female housekeeper. Patty's Place becomes emblematic of what Eve Kornfeld and Susan Jackson call a "feminine utopia."[1] The house belongs to a woman, Miss Patty, highlighting the female ownership and empowerment that is the focus of the novel. The girls are mutually supportive, caring, and playful with one another, thus enabling each other's success in their university education. However, in the eleven years between the publication of *Anne of the Island* and *The Blue Castle*, enough had changed in Montgomery's life and in Canadian society to alter her representation of girls' and women's relationships with one another. Rather than offering playfulness and support, the women with whom *The Blue Castle*'s Valancy Stirling lives, her mother and Cousin Stickles, are demeaning, emotionally cold, and judgmental. In part because of Canadian society's shifting attitudes after the First World War, Montgomery's 1926 novel depicts women's same-sex relationships as problematic and troublesome. For Valancy, salvation is found only through marriage; she laments her social isolation – "I haven't even a gift for friendship" – and the narrator points out that Valancy "has never so much as had a girlfriend."[2] Ultimately, the troublesome relationships between women not only reveal the negative impact of these societal changes but also expose the complicity of the reader in desiring the conventional romantic ending. Montgomery shows her readers that they themselves impose unrealistic expectations on the young heroines.

Critics exploring Montgomery's representation of same-sex friendships and women's communities have often read them as idealized. Notably, in referring to the world of *Anne of Green Gables* as a "feminine utopia," Kornfeld and Jackson write, "Men appear only when they can perform a useful function, and only after it is clear that the women can manage perfectly well on their own."[3] Temma Berg suggests that Montgomery herself was conflicted about female friendships, but in *Anne of Green Gables*, she "successfully repressed" her misgivings to depict the enduring love between Anne and Diana.[4] Marah Gubar persuasively argues that Montgomery's *Anne* series postpones the inevitable heterosexual marriage in order to "make room for passionate relationships between women that prove far more romantic than traditional marriages."[5] While I agree wholeheartedly with Gubar, she reads the novels in the order of Anne's life rather than in the order in which they were written. As I will argue, Montgomery's attitudes towards women's friendships changed over the course of her life. Early on, she depicts friendship "as more satisfying to her than love," in Denyse Yeast's words; however, her later works construct much more troubled connections between women. Yeast touches on this shift when she contends that "with [her best friend] Frede's death [in 1919] Montgomery's writing changed significantly." Arguing that Montgomery's writing becomes more subversive, Yeast demonstrates that Montgomery's works become "more openly rebellious" because she expresses her growing anger at the losses and challenges she faced in her life.[6] In the next chapter, Caroline Jones discusses a similar subversive change in Montgomery's depiction of motherhood as her boys grew and developed.

In order to understand why Montgomery's representation of female same-sex bonds might have shifted between 1915 and 1926, it is important to ground her novels in their historical context. I have discussed elsewhere how Montgomery's attitudes towards female friendship and sexuality changed alongside shifting gender roles in postwar Canada.[7] Exploring Montgomery's journal entries that recount her experiences with a female schoolteacher, Isabel Anderson, who obsessively sought her attention in the late 1920s and 1930s, I argue that Montgomery deploys the figure of Isabel in order to heterosexualize herself in the face of a society newly fearful of lesbianism; yet, she does so in such a way as to maintain the centrality of her love for women. Montgomery labelled Isabel a lesbian and expressed a marked horror over Isabel's desire for her. I argue that Isabel's gushing attentions are a product of an earlier age – the romantic friendships of the Victoria era – that are no longer acceptable in the Canada of the 1930s. While I focus here primarily on the depictions of friendship and lesbianism in Montgomery's journals, my hope is that the argument lays the groundwork to explore the changing representation of female friendship in Montgomery's fiction. From her arrival in Leaskdale in 1911 to her departure in 1926, Montgomery's time there shows dramatically the pre-war and postwar possibilities for women's relationships with one another, as Jones also highlights in the next chapter through her examination of changing mother-daughter relationships.

Many historians and literary scholars have explored representations of women's relationships in the eighteenth, nineteenth, and twentieth centuries. Most well known, Lillian Faderman traces the history of female friendship in *Surpassing the Love of Men*, pointing out that a fashion for romantic friendship emerged in the eighteenth century and, unlike the early twenty-first century, was rarely regarded as erotic: women friends "embraced and kissed and walked hand in hand, and some even held each other all night in sleep. But unless they were transvestites or considered 'unwomanly' in some male's conception, there was little chance that their relationship would be considered lesbian."[8] This pattern of intense hyperbolic love between women reached its zenith during the nineteenth century when, as Carroll Smith-Rosenberg argues about Victorian America, families encouraged friendships between women in order to discourage "heterosexual leanings" in younger women unready for marriage.[9] Women in romantic friendships declared passionate love for each other, as Montgomery demonstrates in *Anne of the Island* by explaining how Philippa "adores" Anne: "I love you madly, and I'm miserable if I don't see you every day. You're different from any girl I ever knew before."[10] Faderman writes, "What the nineteenth century saw as normal ... [the twentieth] century saw as perverse."[11]

Importantly, Faderman links the increasing suspicion of women's same-sex love with the agitation for women's rights in the first three decades of the twentieth century, explaining that those "who had vested interests in the old order were happy to believe the medical views of lesbians as neurotic and confused and to believe that women who wanted independence usually were lesbians."[12] Faderman suggests that the spectre of the lesbian operated to frighten women back into traditional marriages and roles and ultimately affected women's attitudes towards friendship. She points to the widespread theories of the sexologists as playing a large role in shifting the discourse. These medical professionals, such as Richard von Krafft-Ebing and Havelock Ellis, first determined that women who would not fulfil traditional gender roles were "inverts" and thus ill. This belief placed women's passionate love for each other under the microscope, determining that such love indicated so-called abnormal desires. Ellis writes: "Among female inverts, there is usually some approximation to the masculine attitude and temperament."[13]

A lesser-known sexologist, André Tridon, also expresses the connection between sexologists' understanding of homosexuality and gender roles: "Homosexualism cannot be understood unless we associate it with a denial of life and all its duties." He offers a description of a lesbian that can be read as an inverse prescription for what a girl ought to be: "The homosexual girl prefers boys' games, does not care for sewing or other feminine occupations, is boyish in her disposition, her motions, often in her appearance ... She shows embarrassment in the presence of other girls. She often falls madly in love with a female teacher or some older woman."[14] In *Odd Girls and Twilight Lovers*, Faderman argues that the theories of the sexologists "finally came to be to discourage feminism and maintain traditional sex roles by connecting the women's movement to sexual abnormality." The cost of attempting to frighten women back into traditional roles was female romantic friendship: "These factors taken together – the concern over the ramifications of women's increasing independence; the sexologists' theories which came along at a most convenient time to bolster arguments that a women's desire for independence meant that she was not really a woman; and the poetry and fiction of the French aesthetes which provided anxiety-provoking images of the sexual possibilities of the love between women – guaranteed that romantic friendship, which had been encouraged by society in the past, would now be seen in a different, and most antisocial, light."[15]

Importantly, Montgomery not only had an awareness of the sexologists but also indicates in her journals of 1 March 1930, when she recounts her early communications with Isabel, that she has read their work: "The subject of 'sex perverts' has been aired sufficiently of late in certain malodorous works of fiction. I had learned of it in the cleaner medium of medical volumes. There was something in it that nauseated me to my very soul center but I did not think of it as anything that would ever touch my life in any way." On 2 July 1932, she writes that she has been reading the work of Tridon, whom she mistakenly identifies as "Thedon."[16] While we cannot know for certain if she was aware of these theories in the mid-1920s, the ideas of the sexologists and the discourse of perversion were obviously not new to her in early 1930.

As Faderman provocatively suggests, in the nineteenth century, people tended to overlook the "revolutionary potential of romantic friendship."[17] Similarly highlighting the rebellious possibilities in female friendships, Sharon Marcus writes about twentieth-century England: "Same-sex friendships would come to be defined as antithetical to the family and the married couple."[18] Cameron Duder sees the same pattern occurring in Canada after the turn of the century: "Perhaps not as rapidly colonized by the ideas of the sexologists and Sigmund Freud, Canada was nevertheless party to an increasing obsession with studying, classifying, and controlling sexuality in its many 'natural' and 'unnatural' forms. Heterosexual as well as lesbian and bisexual women were subject to the trends that Faderman describes. Expressions of romantic love between women, which previously could have been uttered without condemnation, were, by the 1920s, being viewed with suspicion."[19] As Faderman does, Duder connects the fear of women's same-sex friendships in Canada with the increase of education for women, of single women, and of women with viable jobs. As well, after years of protests and organized campaigns by suffragettes, Canada extended the vote to all women in 1918, before the United States (1920) and United Kingdom (1928).

Historian Veronica Strong-Boag suggests that the face of Canada rapidly and radically altered for its populace: "Whether it was because of the war, the flapper, or the Great Depression, Canadians only knew that domestic relationships had changed, and too often seemingly for the worse."[20] By the 1920s and 1930s, Strong-Boag reveals, Canadian women faced more overt pressure to marry and marry younger. Sheila L. Cavanagh's article, "The Heterosexualization of the Ontario Woman Teacher in the Postwar Period," demonstrates that the marriage bar prohibiting married women from teaching was quickly overturned as society became increasingly concerned with female homosexuality. She explains that "prior to the postwar period, it was possible for economically independent women to opt out of heterosexual and marital relationships with men."[21] Both these historians underscore the degree to which the threat of women's independence became linked to a fear of homosexuality.

Here it is worth noting that the geographical setting of each novel also reflects a difference in attitude towards women. According to Strong-Boag, PEI and Nova Scotia, the settings of *Anne of the Island*, maintained more opportunity for women to become economically independent, whereas in Ontario, where *The Blue Castle* takes place, women married earlier and did not go out to work in the same numbers. Montgomery no doubt encountered a more conservative attitude towards women's roles when she moved from PEI to Leaskdale, a conservatism bred not only of the historical moment but the geographical locale.

In 1915, then, *Anne of the Island*'s focus on passionate same-sex friendships, women's pursuit of higher education, and the postponement of marriage would not necessarily be problematic or threatening. However, by the time *The Blue Castle* was published in 1926, the world had changed dramatically. For example, unlike Anne and Diana in *Anne of Green Gables* (1908) losing track of time together in Lover's Lane, Valancy in *The Blue Castle* meanders down Lover's Lane by herself: "It was hard to go there at any time and not find some canoodling couple – or young girls in pairs, arms intertwined, earnestly talking over their secrets. Valancy didn't know which made her feel more self-conscious and uncomfortable."[22] The kind of friendship that Anne and Diana shared is now discomfiting.

Moreover, in her personal life, Montgomery experienced similar discouraging changes, a theme that recurs throughout the chapters of this book. First, and perhaps most importantly, she had moved to Ontario in 1911 to be a minister's wife; maintaining a high level of propriety in her life, and her fiction, was of paramount importance. As passionate female friendship gradually becomes suspect in the 1920s, her fiction alters its depiction of it accordingly. On 1 February 1925, she comments on Dr McMechan's *Headwaters of Canadian Literature*, in which he writes that her fiction shows the influence of her marrying a minister. She finds this laughable: "My 'marrying a minister' had absolutely no influence in any way upon my writings."[23] Despite her protestations, that a contemporary of hers identifies this influence suggests that it is quite likely, as Margaret Steffler similarly suggests in the previous chapter.

Highlighting Montgomery's difficulties in *Magic Island*, Elizabeth Waterston explains Montgomery's "litany of troubles" when she sat down to write *The Blue Castle* in 1924.[24] As other chapters discuss in different contexts, Montgomery had lost her best friend, Frede Campbell, in 1919 in the influenza epidemic; she mourned this death deeply for the rest of her life. In 1924, her husband was mentally ill, the duties of a minister's wife were overwhelming her, she had an ongoing lawsuit against her former publisher, she had money worries, and her son Chester was proving unmanageable, to name just a few problems. (The next chapter explores more completely the roller coaster of emotion surrounding Montgomery's experience of motherhood.)

By 1926, then, there was a societal backlash against women which, in addition to her own mounting troubles, clearly affected the content of Montgomery's fiction. In writing about *The Blue Castle*, Elizabeth Epperly notes a reversal in the courtship plot from the early *Anne* books: "Valancy recognizes the chivalry-in-disguise in a moment[,] unlike Anne Shirley, who cannot see Gilbert as anything but a school friend."[25] Indeed, *The Blue Castle* can be read as a mirror opposite of *Anne of the*

Island. In *Anne of the Island*, Anne leaves home for university where she lives with three other co-eds and a widow housekeeper in a supportive and lively environment. In *The Blue Castle*, Valancy is stuck at home with her impossible mother and Cousin Stickles. While both novels centre on courtship and marriage, Anne, declaring that she wants to be a "nice, old maid,"[26] rejects five marriage proposals, whereas Valancy, thinking she is going to die of heart disease, proposes to Barney Snaith. While *Anne of the Island* highlights Anne and her roommates' hard work and ambition alongside their full daily lives, *The Blue Castle* demonstrates the utter emptiness of a spinster's life. The narrator writes about "lonely, undesired, ill-favoured" Valancy: "The moment when a woman realizes that she has nothing to live for – neither love, duty, purpose nor hope – holds for her the bitterness of death."[27] On the surface, then, the backlash against women plays out in Montgomery's novel about a lonely spinster who needs to find a man in order to have any happiness.

While marriage seems to be the only ambition for women in *The Blue Castle*, Montgomery's earlier novel instead highlights women's educational and literary ambitions. The novel does not sugar-coat the difficulties the girls face in pursuing their dreams, however. Anne tells Gilbert of six women's responses to her going away to university: "They let me see they thought I was crazy going to Redmond and trying to take a BA, and ever since I've been wondering if I am. Mrs Peter Sloane sighed and said she hoped my strength would hold out till I got through ... Mrs Eben Wright said it must cost an awful lot to put in four years at Redmond ... Mrs Jasper Bell said she hoped I wouldn't let college spoil me, as it did some people ... Mrs Elisha Wright said she understood that Redmond girls ... were 'dreadful dressy and stuck-up.'" Gilbert protests, "You are the first Avonlea girl who has ever gone to college; and you know that all pioneers are considered to be afflicted with moonstruck madness." Philippa's math professor "detested coeds, and had bitterly opposed their admission to Redmond." Aunt Jamesina, the girls' housekeeper, reveals how Canadian society's attitudes have altered from one generation to the next: "When I was a girl it wasn't considered lady-like to know anything about Mathematics," she muses, wondering if times have changed for the better. She adds, "I am not decrying the higher education of women. My daughter is an MA. She can cook, too. But I taught her to cook *before* I let a college professor teach her Mathematics."[28] Montgomery's novel first exposes and then overturns the assumption that university education ruins women.

Moreover, Anne's ambitions are not restricted to education. She wants to be a writer. First, she encounters troubled success with her short story "Averil's Atonement," which won the Rollings Reliable Baking Powder contest after Diana revised it slightly. While Anne is dismayed by the product placement in her story and with the filthy lucre attached to the prize, the novel continues to focus on her literary ambitions. When she later publishes a short story in a legitimate magazine and the editor requests more work from her, "literary ambitions budded and sprouted in her brain."[29] In her four years at Redmond, she completes a BA and becomes a successful writer with promise. Not so for Valancy. The only ambition she has is tied up in her Blue Castle in Spain, a reference to her constant daydreams of riches and lovers which enable her to tolerate desperate daily conditions in her ugly home with her ugly room and her unloving relatives. The novel is silent, at best, on higher education for women. The only writer in it is John Foster, the nature writer whom Valancy reads and quotes obsessively. In the world of *The Blue Castle*, women are no longer capable of studying or writing. While Valancy is still reading, and rebelliously reading against her mother's will, she does not express larger ambitions. The heroine of *Rilla of Ingleside* similarly does not share in her mother's former ambitions: Rilla simply wants to have fun and attract a particular young man. Even Montgomery's most biographical and ambitious heroine, Emily of the *New Moon* trilogy, refuses an opportunity to go to New York with a woman as mentor to develop her writing further. Instead, she remains alone in Prince Edward Island until Teddy returns to her. Montgomery's fiction begins to shut down the possibilities for her young female protagonists.

Through the preponderance of happily unmarried women in one novel and the near absence of them in the other, Montgomery's two novels demonstrate a shift in the representation of women's same-sex relationships and underscore how these friendships can lead to women's potential independence. In *Anne of the Island*, women help other women, economically as well as emotionally. Not only do the Redmond co-eds rent a house together as a means of cutting expenses, but back in Avonlea, Anne's adoptive mother, Marilla, is living with widowed Rachel Lynde, also as a practical way to make ends meet. Anne's first boarding house in Kingsport is run by spinster twins. The house that she and her roommates rent belongs to an old spinster, Patty Spofford, who lives with her unmarried elderly niece, Maria. Tellingly, Miss Patty lowers the rent of the house for the students because she wants them to have it, demonstrating a woman's economic support for other women. When Anne explains that the girls cannot afford the listed price, the older woman asks her what they can afford. In response to Anne's figure, Miss Patty nods, "That will do. As I told you it is not strictly necessary that we should let it at all." Most notably, Anne comes into money when the wealthy and unwed Josephine Barry dies and leaves her $1,000. According to the Bank of Canada inflation calculator, that would be the equivalent of approximately $20,000 CAD in 2015. Anne's inheritance is strangely never referred to again, but Marilla's adoptive son, Davy, asks whether Anne needs to marry now that she has money, clearly exposing one of the primary reasons women did so. He explains his question: "When Dorcas Sloane got married last summer she said if she'd had enough money to live on she'd never have been bothered with a man, but even a widower with eight children was better'n living with a sister-in-law."[30] While Anne and her roommates are not in similar desperate straits, Montgomery's novel still draws attention to the fact that not all women are so lucky.

The Blue Castle no longer depicts unmarried life as a joyous, supportive condition. Valancy is single, as Anne is, but this state is regarded by her clan, and herself, as certain failure. The novel begins with Valancy's waking up on her birthday morning to the realization that she is "twenty-nine and unsought by any man." The narrator writes, "Deerwood and the Stirlings had long since relegated Valancy to hopeless old maidenhood." Unlike the books in the *Anne* series, *The Blue Castle* is not populated with unmarried women; Valancy is one of the few and feels the stigma. Widows abound, but they are regarded as superior to unwed women. The narrator explains Valancy's feeling about Cousin Stickles, who, simply because she "had once been desirable in some man's eyes" and been married, has the "right to look down on" Valancy.[31] Olive, Valancy's younger and more attractive cousin, is single but obviously marriage material in the clan's eyes because of her conventional good looks. The only other unmarried women are associated with illness. One is the Miss Sterling, spelled with an "e," who is the aged spinster dying of heart disease. Valancy, the Miss Stirling, spelled with an "i," gets the diagnosis letter intended for the other woman. Cissy Gay is another single female; however, Cissy became pregnant out of wedlock and refused to marry her lover when she realized he no longer loved her. The baby died at a year old. She is now shunned by the community of Deerwood and slowly dying. The narrative seemingly punishes Cissy for her refusal to marry.

On the surface, at least, *The Blue Castle* appears to reinforce the backlash against women's economic and social independence. The only way out of oppressive circumstances is to marry or face the scorn of the community. Female friendship seems to be out of the question. Valancy's relationship with her mother and Cousin Stickles is troubled. Both older women attempt to control every aspect of the younger woman's life, as Gabriella Åhmansson points out: "One of Montgomery's major aims in *The Blue Castle* is to expose, mainly through satire, the repressive society in which she herself had grown up ... in particular the double standards and the 'stigmatizing and controlling' of female sexuality that goes with it."[32] Valancy feels that her mother does not love her and is disappointed that she was not a boy.[33] Moreover, unlike Anne, Valancy is lamentably friendless.

However, Montgomery's narrative counters the backlash by its very exposure of Valancy's utter lack of choice. Her life changes only through random mistakes, such as her receiving the misdiagnosis that she will die shortly. Moreover, Montgomery's novel shows that Valancy's life changes *because* of other single women. Her misdiagnosis is passed to her instead of another spinster, Miss Sterling; the shared single-woman stigma is what causes Valancy to rise up against her controlling family. And, remarkably, her rebellion entails her leaving home to live with the ailing Cissy. When Valancy enters Cissy's house to look after her, the scene between the two women is touching. Cissy is thrilled to have a friend: "It – would just be like – heaven – to have some one here

– like you." The narrator writes, "Valancy held Cissy close. She was suddenly happy. Here was some one who needed her – some one she could help. She was no longer a superfluity."[34]

Not only does Valancy find emotional satisfaction in caring for Cissy but she also finds economic freedom. With her pay, she can purchase whatever clothes she likes, for example, rather than those chosen by her family. In some ways, similar to Anne at Redmond, Valancy manages to look after herself perfectly well before she proposes to Barney. However, she asks Barney to marry her because Cissy has died, and she has no other option but to return to the bosom of the clan. Since she believes she will die shortly, she explains her predicament to him, and he consents to marriage. Once again, however, this scenario highlights Valancy's utter helplessness. "I can't go back to Deerwood," she explains to Barney, "you know what my life was like there."[35] While she admits to loving him, she also confesses that living on his island is part of the reason she wants to marry him. She needs to escape her family. Montgomery's novel points out how few options uneducated women have in this kind of society. In doing so, her fiction offers up a muted protest against the shift in attitude towards women's increasing independence that she observed in both small villages such as Leaskdale and larger urban centres such as Toronto.

Montgomery's *The Blue Castle* presents a greater challenge to its readers than is first readily apparent, however. While *Anne of the Island* shows an Anne hesitant to succumb to marriage in the face of finishing her degree and her intense female friendships, *The Blue Castle* creates a Valancy desperate for marriage because of her economic dependence and loneliness. This may be the acceptable narrative trajectory in 1926, yet Montgomery's novel disturbs its own ending by making it completely unbelievable. Valancy discovers, of course, that her own husband, Barney Snaith, is not only Bernard Redfern, the son of a wealthy tonic and pill manufacturer, but also John Foster, the nature writer. Valancy's hopeless world is overturned by random good fortune. When she tries nobly to disengage from the marriage into which she feels she has entered unfairly – after all, she has never been on the brink of death, it turns out – she discovers that Barney loves her, is her favourite writer, and is wealthy. Because of Barney's wealth, her family finally embraces the couple with pride. Valancy gets it all: love, wealth, intellectual stimulation, familial approbation.

It is worth noting here, as Holly Pike also argues later in this volume, that this novel challenges the received wisdom of the medical profession, the very institution that introduced and promulgated the theories about perversion, sexology, and suspicious female friendships. The rector with a doctorate in divinity, the aptly named Dr Stalling, mistakes Valancy for a boy in her childhood; while Dr Stalling is not a medical doctor, the novel still calls this learned man into question. Valancy does not want to go to the family doctor, Dr Marsh, when she worries about her health later on. Indeed, she imagines that, if Dr Marsh were eventually consulted, she would be sent to specialists who would ultimately be powerless to help her. Instead, she departs from family tradition by visiting Dr Trent, whose massive mistake in diagnosing her is the impetus for the action of the novel. When she explains all that has happened to her clan at the end of the novel, they rejoin, "That's what comes of going to strange doctors."[36] Add to this mixture of mistaken medics Dr Redfern and his embarrassing yet highly popular tonics, and this novel ridicules not just doctors but the people who desperately want to believe what doctors tell them.

Similarly, readers want to believe the fairy-tale ending of *The Blue Castle*, and yet this climax calls itself into question. Valancy is about to set off on a European vacation: "She knew perfectly well that no spot or palace or home in the world could ever possess the sorcery of her Blue Castle," ostensibly referring to Barney's, and now her, island home. However, from the opening pages onwards, the Blue Castle has had another, more dominant meaning: Valancy's elaborate fantasies. Surely, the reprobate Barney Snaith is a surprising candidate for Prince Charming. When he appears early on in the novel, "It was very evident that he hadn't shaved for days, and his hands and arms, bare to the shoulders, were black with grease." The clan thinks he is "a jailbird" and, exposing their racism, "half Indian." Barney himself says to Valancy when she proposes, "You don't know anything about me. I may be a – murderer," and she later jokes that he has dead wives in his locked room, which she calls Bluebeard's Chamber. Valancy's family believes that he is the deadbeat father of Cissy's baby, but Valancy knows this to be untrue. The words to justify her faith again call attention to Barney's potential for violence: "A man with such a smile and lips might have murdered or stolen but he could not have betrayed." The figure of Barney Snaith/John Foster/Bernard Redfern resonates with the possibility of evil-doing and deception. That this novel transforms the reprobate into a prince indicates that the book itself is a Blue Castle fantasy, hence the title. Most old maids would more likely wind up like the other Miss Sterling, a "lonely old soul," who dies alone in her sleep.[37] Montgomery's novel places the reader in the position of the Stirling clan who might judge spinsterhood harshly and who greedily embrace the turn of events that transforms the unlikely Barney into a prince. The ironic excess of the ending keeps it clearly in the realm of an impossible Blue Castle fantasy.

Moreover, the end of the novel silences Valancy's voice and restores traditional marriage and family ties, showing what must be given up for the happiest of happy endings. Montgomery's later novel thus points a finger at readers who crave the heterosexual romance. In the final pages of *Anne of the Island*, Anne accepts Gilbert after spending three novels evading him. While the narrator explains that, after Gilbert proposes, "Still Anne could not speak," the last words of the novel are hers.[38] This novel maintains a clear focus on Anne's voice and empowerment. On the other hand, in *The Blue Castle* after Valancy's last words, when she asks Barney never to remind her that she proposed to him, two more chapters follow in which she is mute. The penultimate chapter is, intriguingly, an extract from a letter written by a single woman, Valancy's cousin Olive, who is furious with Valancy's good fortune. Again, the novel highlights the unbelievable nature of this tale and indicts the readers (and Valancy's family members) who want to believe that Valancy's misery can be overturned so easily. Olive writes bitterly about Valancy's newfound status as the golden child in the family: "And they can't see that Valancy is just laughing at them all in her sleeve."[39] *The Blue Castle* certainly seems to be poking fun at the reader who is well satisfied that Valancy has found her prince. Montgomery's later novel can offer only a quiet protest to the conditions that have altered women's lives from 1915 to 1926, but her message's ironic twists suggest it is up to readers to rebel.

5

The New Mother at Home: Montgomery's Literary Explorations of Motherhood

CAROLINE E. JONES

When L.M. Montgomery moved to Leaskdale as the Mrs Rev. Ewan Macdonald, she encountered a series of new challenges and roles she would be required to fulfil. Although she was a new wife and a new manse mistress, she already had experience in keeping house and assuming leadership roles within the church, but this was her first opportunity to create her own home. Montgomery delighted in putting the manse to rights and creating her own spaces for living, entertaining, and writing. In Ontario she had, she hoped, the opportunity to make a home according to her own needs and tastes, free from the scrutiny of family, friends, and overly familiar neighbours. She also had the task of setting up a suitable home for the minister, blending propriety, elegance, and hominess. Montgomery devotes almost eight pages of her published, edited journal to the making of her home, including eight photographs.[1] No one from Cavendish or Park Corner came to help her settle in, but these sporadic entries, recorded in a notebook even when she was not keeping up with her journal, reflect a time of comradeship and intimacy with her husband unprecedented in her discussions of Ewan to date.

These early Leaskdale entries reflect a sense of isolation from the people of her new community; in the first entry, as she brings her journal up to date, Montgomery reflects, "there is no one here whom I could admit into my inner circle. To all I try to be courteous, tactful and considerate, and most of them I like superficially. But the gates of my soul are barred against them. They do not have the key."[2] Thus, the physical landscape of Montgomery's life became increasingly important – creating a congenial and cosy home, finding lovely spaces for walking and thinking – and her work would have to function as her support system until she could build friendships.

The majority of Montgomery's time in Leaskdale, however, centred on her role as mother. Making a home for her husband and establishing a manse household undoubtedly gave her great pleasure, but in producing sons, she was able to meet the more fundamental expectations of her world: it allowed her to enter the privileged sisterhood of mothers and to fulfil her wifely and womanly duties, important concerns both personally and socially. Significantly for her writing, becoming a mother also gave her the opportunity to reflect upon the institution of motherhood from a panoply of perspectives: to consider her own mother (and surrogate mother and stepmother) as mother and to experience – and construct – the memory of her mother in an entirely new way, and also to reflect upon – and construct – herself as mother in varying phases of her own and her sons' lives. Sara Ruddick suggests that "three interests ... govern maternal practice" – "preservation, growth, and acceptability of the child" – and Montgomery's mothering practices reflect each of these at different points in her sons' lives. As she mothers her sons, so too does she construct her own identity as mother, alternately succumbing to "the temptations of fearfulness and excessive control" characteristic of the preservation interest of mothers of infants and young children, embracing change as "innovation takes precedence over permanence" as her sons develop agency and independence, and struggling with the inherent contradictions between her own desires for her sons, society's expectations for them, and their own choices. Notably, Montgomery struggles with all three interests at varying points in her life as mother, and each of these interests manifests in her fiction as well.[3]

In her fiction, Montgomery returns repeatedly to motifs and subtexts of motherhood, but her depictions of mothers in their various incarnations and relationships, are, like her depictions of fathers, vague, shadowy, and idealized. Rita Bode suggests that "the absent mother, essentially unknowable, keeps reasserting herself and forms the source of a lingering tension for Montgomery,"[4] an idea borne out by the fact that mothers, when present in her novels, tend to inhabit the extremes of either perfection or cruelty. Since her mother,

Clara Woolner Macneill, died when her daughter was only twenty-one months old, Montgomery had little memory and no experience of a relationship with her own mother.⁵ Her maternal surrogate relationships, with her mother's mother, Lucy Woolner Macneill, who raised her, and her stepmother, Mary Ann McRae, whom she met at the age of fifteen when she spent a year with her father in Saskatchewan, were notable failures at intimacy and trust. Perhaps because most of Montgomery's novels are deliberately child-centric, or perhaps because of a failure (or excess) of imagination, she never produced a realistic, loving, firm mother-child relationship in her work. Although her depictions of motherhood shift once she experiences motherhood herself, the relationships between mothers and their children, particularly their daughters, still rarely approach verisimilitude.

Montgomery gave birth to her first son, Chester, in 1912, when she was thirty-seven years old and had already published four novels and a great many short stories. As she grew into motherhood, as her support systems shifted, and as her relationships with her sons evolved and changed, Montgomery's intimate understandings of motherhood quietly emerged in her novels, offering subversive interpretations of the mother figure. With her boys maturing and beginning to differentiate in what she perceived were unacceptable ways, Montgomery effaced, idealized, and infantilized her fictional mothers. I explore below these complex engagements with literary motherhood over the course of her actual motherhood, focusing on two of the early *Anne* novels, *Anne of the Island* (1915) and *Anne's House of Dreams* (1917); *The Blue Castle* (1926); the two *Pat* novels, *Pat of Silver Bush* (1933) and *Mistress Pat* (1935); and *Jane of Lantern Hill* (1937).

In the *Anne* novels, I focus not so much on mother-child relationships as on mother-mothered relationships: the relationship of Anne to her own mother and Anne's understanding of her new role as mother. Both of Anne's intensive contemplations of motherhood, which inform the narrative mother, occur at significant moments in Montgomery's own life as mother. Her conflicting experiences of motherhood especially inform *Anne of the Island* and *Anne's House of Dreams*, which explore motherhood from a duality of perspectives. The former centres on a daughter coming to know her own mother for the first time, written by a woman relatively young in her own experience of motherhood; it is a nostalgic speculation from a daughter missing her mother in a way she had not been able to articulate earlier. Yet that novel is also shadowed by the author's dreaded loss of a child. *Anne's House of Dreams*, in contrast, explores the joys and tragedies of new motherhood: the birth and same-day death of a first child and the later, healthy, birth of a second child. Each of these writing exercises allowed Montgomery to process her feelings about motherhood, to develop her own lens for reading her life, and to reclaim the tragic losses of first her mother, and then her stillborn son, through her art.

Cecily Devereux suggests that Anne's ambition, despite Queen's and Redmond, where she earned her BA, and despite teaching and writing, has always "tended" toward the domestic, and that, for her, "the highest 'womanly' ambition is realized in motherhood."[6] In *Anne of Green Gables*, Montgomery indeed establishes Anne's need, above all, to belong to someone;[7] it makes sense that, as a grown woman, Anne would ultimately want – *in addition* to education, career, and avocation – a family that belongs to *her*, an opportunity to *be* the mother and create the family she lost. Montgomery lost her chance at a loving, nurturing family with her mother's death and her father's subsequent move from Prince Edward Island. In fact, we see in Montgomery's actual life an attempt when she was only fifteen to recreate a loving family with her father and stepmother. In her 22 April 1890 entry, she confides, "Do you know, journal mine, I may take a trip out west to see father this summer ... I feel so excited about it ... to see darling father again!" On 8 August, the eve of her departure, she anticipates her relationship with her father's second wife: "Shall I like [Prince Albert]? And my stepmother? I do not know. She seems nice from her letters and I mean to love her if I can, just as if she were really my mother."[8]

Unfortunately, three days into her stay in Prince Albert, Montgomery records an antipathy in her stepmother resulting, she believes, from a jealousy of her father's affection: "It is lovely to be with father again ... His eyes just *shine* with love when he looks at me. I never saw anyone look at me with such eyes before. But, to speak plainly I am afraid I am *not* going to like his wife. I came here prepared to love her warmly and look upon her as a real mother, but I fear it will prove impossible."[9] In this second mention of her desire for a "real mother," Montgomery, even as a fairly mature teenager, demonstrates a desire for family intimacy. In her work, children of widowed parents betray a touching faith that their parents will do well in their selection of replacement parents; her own disappointment in her father's choice resonates in this trope. Paul Irving, for instance, expresses confidence that his father has chosen "a nice little second mother" for him – not, notably, a "step"-mother.[10]

When her own motherhood becomes a real possibility, Montgomery notes in her journal: "Early in November I began to suspect that what I had intensely longed for was to be mine and now I know it. I am to be a mother. I cannot realize it. It seems to me so incredible – so wonderful – so utterly impossible as happening to *me*! But I am glad – so glad. It has always seemed to me that a childless marriage is a tragedy – especially in a marriage such as mine." Her journal through the winter and spring of 1912 records the happy preparation and anticipation expected of an eager new mother, but as she enters her last weeks of pregnancy, her tone becomes more anxious. She meditates on the existential aspects of birth, life, and death, weighing the equally terrifying possibilities that she might die and leave her own child motherless or that her child might die, prompting her to reflect, "If I were to live but lose my baby I think the disappointment would almost kill me," a tragic anticipation of a loss that awaits her.[11] Chester's birth in July 1912 opened an idyllic period in Montgomery's life. She was a new mother, basking in the glory of her son and enjoying the company of her cousin and dear friend, Frede, who shared her delight in "baby Punch." In fact, Montgomery's journal entries for at least five months after Chester's birth are filled with rhapsodic descriptions of the baby and the fun she and Frede have doting on him. In many ways, his birth cements her position as manse mistress within the Leaskdale and Zephyr communities and makes the transition from the Island to Ontario more manageable: she is no longer Maud Montgomery, orphan or spinster; she is Mrs Rev. Macdonald, mother.

Her first journal entry after Chester's birth is a paean to motherhood and mother love. Its intense, occasionally religious language prompts Margaret Steffler to suggest that Montgomery's "exaggerated and pas-

5.1 Mother and child: Chester and Montgomery

sionate performance [of motherhood] calls into question the narrow and tame emotions allocated by society to the institutionalized and public role of motherhood as sweet and nurturing."[12] This journal entry is full of passages like "Love – such love! I never dreamed there could be such love. It seems blent and twined with the inmost fibres of my being

– as if it could not be wrenched away without wrenching soul and body apart also and the love of motherhood, exquisite as it is, is full of anguish, too. I see and realize deeps of pain I never realized before. Motherhood is a revelation from God."[13] Steffler reads such entries as an "inflated and exaggerated maternal performance." Perhaps, as Steffler suggests, this "performance" is "an indictment of the public and patriarchal institution" of motherhood;[14] perhaps it reflects the deep relief of a woman who had wondered whether she would ever be a mother, fearing that her marriage would remain empty not just of passion or deep romantic love but also of the gift of children. Or perhaps it is the reflection of a woman for whom writing and words are *more* natural than motherhood – in consecrating the experience of motherhood with the act of writing, she marries her two great gifts.

In her 10 October 1912 journal entry, Montgomery reflects upon Aunt Mary Lawson's death, wishing her aunt had been able to see Chester, and then muses on other friends and family members who will never know him. Most prominent in the list is her own mother: "In certain lights my baby's eyes and brows are strangely like my mother's ... My mother! How near I feel to her now in my own motherhood. I know how she must have loved me. I know what her agony must have been in the long weeks of her illness when she was facing the bitter knowledge that she must leave me. My dear, beautiful young mother whose sun went down while it was yet day!"[15] The fullness of that kinship stayed with Montgomery; we see that over a year later, in *Anne of the Island*, she offers Anne that painful pleasure of motherhood borrowed from the mother herself, Bertha Shirley, whose experience of motherhood, like Clara Macneill Montgomery's, was fleeting. As she began writing her third *Anne* novel, Montgomery little realized how the lines between bereft daughter and bereft mother would blur and dissolve. Embarking upon the story of Anne's coming of age, Montgomery could not have anticipated the ways in which her own life and loss would inform – and perhaps delay – Anne's coming into womanhood.

Montgomery began blocking out "Anne of Redmond" on 1 September 1913 and realized that she was pregnant for the second time in November 1913. This time she hoped for a daughter. She began the actual writing of "Anne of Redmond" in April 1914 and lost baby

Hugh in August. On 20 November of that year, she writes, "I finished 'Anne of Redmond' to-day. And I am very glad. Never did I write a book under greater stress. All last winter and spring I was physically wretched and all this fall I have been wracked with worry over the war and tortured with grief over the loss of my baby."[16] In *Anne of the Island*, in which Anne is neither married nor a mother, Montgomery successfully incorporates both the joy of Chester's birth and the anguish of losing Hugh through Anne as daughter. Anne herself is still a girl, unready to receive or return Gilbert's romantic love; after rejecting his proposal of marriage, she instead seeks the love of her parents at the place of her birth. When Anne returns to the little yellow house where she was born, her idyllic image of it is fulfilled to the letter – with the exception of the honeysuckle over the windows – allowing Anne to live a bit longer as a girl, while showing her the incipient joys of womanhood. In this scene of homecoming, Montgomery allows Anne to inhabit the sacred space where she was born, not simply as herself, a daughter, but also as her own mother: "Here her mother had dreamed the exquisite, happy dreams of anticipated motherhood; here that red sunrise light had fallen over them both in the sacred hour of birth; here her mother had died."[17] The sweetness of birth is mingled with the grief of death, just as it was in Montgomery's own heart.

Devereux maintains that "the foundation for the construction of Anne's 'house of dreams' is quietly but unmistakably established in the first three novels ... even *Anne of Green Gables* ... serves ... to entrench her story within the maternalism that comes to dominate the series."[18] While Devereux references not the novel but the concept of the house of dreams, she acknowledges that within that house resides what many of Montgomery's initial – and subsequent – readers required for "happily ever after." The *House of Dreams* novel provides Anne with the husband that readers expected and, perhaps more significantly, the home that eleven-year-old Anne Shirley so deeply craved. The addition of children to that perfect home seemed, at least to my adolescent self, an afterthought. As an adult, however, I read quite clearly the abundant foreshadowing of Anne's own motherhood: Anne's "thrill" at Diana's cuddling of small Anne Cordelia, Montgomery's pointed references to Miss Cornelia's preparation for unwanted "eighth babies," and Anne's own unarticulated "poignantly-sweet dreams."[19] Yet, as William Thompson notes in the next chapter, the loss of Montgomery's stillborn second son deeply informs the story of Anne's motherhood experience.[20] Before she could write Anne as mother, even as bereaved mother (and Montgomery knew she could not simply leave Anne with the loss of baby Joy), she needed to process Hugh's death in her writing and to work through her grief. With Stuart's birth in October 1915, having given voice to her grief in her art, she was able to take up her life with new hope. She even offered homage to the daughter she had hoped for by giving Anne a first-born girl.

When Montgomery records Stuart's birth in her 23 October 1915 journal entry, she references the contrast between the "gay time" after Chester's birth and the "horrible time last year after dear little Hugh's coming – and going," adding, "for the first time the ache has gone out of my heart. And yet this baby does not, as someone said, 'fill little Hugh's place.' None can ever do that. He will always have his own place ... Wee Stuart is doubly precious for his life was purchased by 'little Hugh's' death. But he has his own place; he does not fill that where a little cold waxen form is shrined." Montgomery began writing *Anne's House of Dreams* in June 1916, almost two years after Hugh's death. She records "getting the material for it in shape all winter and spring," starting within months of Stuart's birth. The manuscript was finished on 5 October 1916, just shy of Stuart's first birthday. Of *Anne's House of Dreams* she says, "I never wrote a book in so short a time and amid so much strain of mind and body. Yet I rather enjoyed writing it and I think it isn't too bad a piece of work."[21] In finally writing Anne as "mother," Montgomery embodies Ruddick's interest of "preservation" without the hazard of "excessive control"[22] and simultaneously allows herself freedom from her own pervasive grief over Hugh's death.

In contrast to the images of motherhood Montgomery created in the *Anne* books, the primary mother in *The Blue Castle* is simply absurd: mean, petty, and tyrannical. Montgomery first mentions the novel in a 10 April 1924 journal entry, but it is not referenced again until seven months later, on 27 November, when she says she is "finding much pleasure" in it.[23] At this point in her life, her primary source of stress appears to be Ewan's psychological problems; her boys continue to be a source of confidence, even as Chester approaches the cusp of adolescence. Because motherhood is still a comfort, and because she has settled into her Leaskdale life, able to see kindly the humour in the wide variety of motherly experiences around her, Montgomery can use an overdrawn mother as a source of comedy and an initially repressive mother-daughter relationship as a source of liberation for her protagonist.

Valancy Stirling is Montgomery's only protagonist whom readers never see as child or girl – she is a young woman, waking on the morning of her twenty-ninth birthday, when her story opens. Her relationship with her mother is outwardly respectful but inwardly contentious. Valancy requires a situation in which she believes she has nothing left to lose before she can confront and defy her mother, thus finding agency and empowerment – or so we hope. She is a spinster with nary a beau in sight. She is cowed not just by her mother but by a host of uncles, aunts, and cousins. She has allowed herself to become the butt of their jokes, subjected herself to their unkind remarks, and settled herself into the role of the family's old maid. It is not until Valancy (mistakenly) believes she is dying that she finds the strength of mind to resist her family and challenge the limits they have set for her. Valancy decides, "I've been trying to please other people all my life and failed ... After this I shall please myself. I shall never pretend anything again ... What a luxury it will be to tell the truth!"[24]

While Valancy has never felt "mothered" – her mother is critical and unloving, concerned more that her daughter (like all of Montgomery's heroines) does not meet her expectations or conform to the norms of her community – she does not seem to miss that aspect of her life. Rather, she seeks, like Anne Shirley, the role of mother and caretaker. And, as she does in the *Anne* series, Montgomery interweaves and overlaps the various "mother" roles. Valancy's surrogate child is Cecilia Gay, a childhood friend, and daughter of the town drunk and reprobate. Cissy herself was a mother for a brief shining year: she bore a child out of wedlock and chose not to marry the baby's father, thus estranging herself from the "proper" elements of her society. The child died after a year of life, a typical punishment for the sinning mother of late nineteenth- and early twentieth-century novels, visited on the innocent child. So, as Laura Robinson discusses in the previous chapter, nothing is left for the wilfully unmarried Cissy, "shunned by the community of Deerwood,"[25] but to die, which she does, slowly and painfully, of consumption. Valancy empowers herself and develops a sense of subjectivity by choosing to nurse Cissy in the last months of her life. She learns the truth of Cissy's story in those last few months, that the child's father had offered to marry her but Cissy refused: "I couldn't [marry him] when he didn't love me anymore. Somehow ... it seemed a worse thing to do than – the other."[26] Cissy has long understood and lived by the truth that Valancy has just learned: that personal integrity has more value and worth than meeting the expectations of her society.

Montgomery's relative equanimity during this period of her life allowed her to critique the smallness and pettiness of Valancy's world, and the more mature intended audience for this novel allowed her to step beyond the expectations of societal norms to do that. Valancy admits to herself that she does not love her imminently respectable mother: "What's worse, I don't even like her." In contrast, Cissy's year of forbidden motherhood is a precious memory: "My baby was so sweet ... When he died, oh, Valancy, I thought I must die too – I didn't see how anyone could endure such anguish and live."[27] Valancy understands the mother-love Cissy feels for her lost son and offers Cissy the motherly understanding and love that both girls have lacked throughout their lives. As Robinson points out, "Valancy's life changes *because* of other single women," especially Cissy.[28] The socially outcast young women nourish each other in ways that conventional families – and mothers – cannot. Each embodies an ability to mother regardless of society's expectations, thus avoiding Ruddick's concern that in shaping a child acceptable to the mother's "social group," the mother inevitably "betrays [her] own interest in the growth of [her] children."[29] Of course, this feminist model is ultimately subverted by the deaths first of Cissy's son and then of Cissy herself. The desperation that allows Valancy to disregard societal norms and please herself frees her to follow her heart, to look for her "blue castle" rather than just imagining and longing for it impotently. That freedom leads her into traditional romantic love (in the previous chapter, Robinson effectively asserts the inevitability of such an outcome), but the stronger discovery may be Valancy's own inner mother, willing and able to love, nurture, and accept herself unconditionally.

The Macdonalds have been living in Norval for five years when Montgomery begins *Pat of Silver Bush* in late 1931. Here she has been enjoying more fulfilling personal relationships than she initially found in Leaskdale. She seems, largely, to take pleasure in Chester and Stuart. As Chester finishes at St Andrew's, a boarding school in Aurora eighty kilometres from Norval, she worries over his grades and choice of university program but appreciates his company when they are together. She describes a day when Chester, then aged nineteen, shows her the film he took with the family's movie camera: "It is just capital. I was so amused and tickled that for a time I forgot all my woes." Stuart, at age sixteen, is still at home, although he will be at St Andrew's the next year, and is doing well in both academics and gymnastics and offering no cause for expressing anxiety in her journal.[30] Montgomery's main worries seem financial, primarily as a result of the worldwide economic depression. She is also in the midst of a perplexing and generally frustrating relationship with Isabel Anderson, which has been explored elsewhere by Laura Robinson and Mary Beth Cavert.[31]

As Montgomery begins to write in earnest, she wonders how she can continue when she is "worried and nervous and insomniac," citing in particular her anxieties about finding time to write and about the "world and market news," which "continues bad." The fourth volume of the *Selected Journals* offers few mentions of the writing process of *Pat of Silver Bush*, and what references there are focus on the stress of writing and lack of time to devote to the novel. However, in the final days of writing the *Pat* book, Montgomery makes a trip to the Island, enjoying a "whole month of happiness – what a treasure!" She spends time at Park Corner, the basis for Silver Bush, which no doubt inspired her as she finished this "simple story of a child's unfolding." Upon its publication in 1933, Montgomery writes, "Somehow, I love *Pat* as I have not loved any book since *New Moon*."[32] Her ultimate success with the novel reflects a relatively uncomplicated sense of her own motherhood. Her sons experience the rebellions and difficulties expected of teenage boys, but, undoubtedly, Montgomery reconciles those difficulties with her awareness of her sons' "unfolding" into young men.

In contrast, *Mistress Pat*, published only two years later, demonstrates Montgomery's increased and intensified maternal anxiety as Chester and Stuart, both out of the house, more actively resist her attempts to manage their lives. They are more able to explore their own impulses, likes, dislikes, and desires, seeing girls outside of their mother's supervision and pursuing extracurricular interests of which their parents were undoubtedly unaware. The earlier novel, the tale of the child's development, relies very little on Pat's need for or relationship with her mother. It is a very interior novel, focalized through Pat and her primary relationship, her home, Silver Bush. Unlike Green Gables or New Moon before it, Silver Bush obsessively dominates Pat's emotional attachments; Mary Gardiner, Pat's mother, plays a secondary role in the narrative. However, unlike Anne before Green Gables and Emily after her father's death, Pat is mothered, regardless of her mother's health or physical presence. She has Judy Plum, the family's faithful retainer, to tell her stories, comfort her grief, and offer her "liddle bites" to assuage discontent. In contrast to Montgomery herself, who regresses to Ruddick's interest of preservation and becomes fearful and obsessed with the control she has lost, the mother figure in the *Pat* books is idealized through both absence and presence. Of course, as Pat becomes a young woman and assumes the role of "the Chatelaine" of Silver Bush,[33] the role of her mother, ostensibly the mistress of Silver Bush, must be addressed.

Mary Gardiner is one of Montgomery's idealized mothers: she is absent from the daily life of Silver Bush, mostly because her ill health keeps her removed from the busy and active world of Judy's kitchen. As she becomes stronger, toward the end of the second *Pat* novel, she travels, absenting herself from the home completely. However, Mrs Gardiner offers an emotional presence for Pat; for example, although she is silent until after the rift between Rae and Pat is healed, she knows that Rae feels Pat has stolen her lover.[34] Readers see Mrs Gardiner on special occasions, in which she is generally quiet and good humoured, but have no sense of her except as a feature necessary to keep Silver

Bush as unchanged as possible. Judy Plum is, similarly, the idealized surrogate mother: loving, indulgent, and affectionate. Both of Pat's "mothers" accept and love her unconditionally. They fret over her choices of men (as Montgomery did over her sons' choices of women), and they worry that no man will ever be able to supplant Silver Bush in Pat's affections. It is easy to see Montgomery as daughter in Pat, especially with her intense love of place and nature. In both *Pat* books, Montgomery rewrites her own youth with the maternal support she lacked as she idealizes Pat's relationships with her mother figures. But we must also read these relationships through the lens of Montgomery as mother, and thus reflective of her sense of maternal inadequacy: she offers Pat the unconditional acceptance and freedom of autonomy that she, as mother, could not give her sons. No real woman could hope to live up to the bar of motherhood set by either Mary Gardiner or Judy Plum: in idealizing these mother figures in the *Silver Bush* books, Montgomery effectively, if unconsciously, exempts herself from even attempting to meet those standards.

When Montgomery is beginning to think about "Pat II," Chester brings home a bride, Luella Reid, who is already pregnant with the Macdonalds' first grandchild. Both Montgomery and Ewan Macdonald have difficulty accepting this turn of events, particularly because of Ewan's position as the community's Presbyterian minister but also because this scenario is one that Montgomery, at least, had long dreaded given Chester's early sexual precocity. Through the beginning of 1934, her journal entries reflect her struggle to reframe her own dreams about and desires for Chester's marriage and family.[35] The second mention of "Pat II," on 31 March 1934, is the first in a long series of entries expressing difficulty in focusing on her work. Initially she attributes this difficulty to her own ill health, aggravated by her anxiety and disappointment over Chester's behaviour. But in May 1934, Ewan relapses into melancholia,[36] and her entries on "Pat II" from that point on are bleak, the few positive mentions of work expressing surprise at her ability to focus or the quality of the work. For instance, on 21 May 1934, she records, "I wrote the 'Christmas' chapter of *Pat II* today and lost myself for a few blessed hours in 'Silver Bush'"; on 30 July 1934, "I read over what I have got written of *Pat II* today and find it better than I expected. It has been so hard to get it written." However, as she moves through the sequel, Ewan's precarious health, the lost loyalty of the Norval congregation, and one of Stuart's girlfriends all claim her attention and generate more anxiety and distress. Entries about the book's progress are more typically the following: on 12 June 1934, after a bad day with Ewan, she reports, "I tried to write some of *Pat II* but found it almost impossible," or, on 17 July 1934, "I worked at *Pat II* this evening but felt very bad. What a dreary, makeshift sort of life this is!" However, as she nears the book's end, she allows herself some praise. On 28 November 1934, she notes, "Wrote a *Pat* chapter – 'Judy's' death – and did it rather well," and two days later (on her sixtieth birthday), she finishes: "I got the last chapter of *Pat II* done. Such a relief! I thought so many times this fall I should never get it done. I never wrote a book in such agony of mind before." Finishing the book was indeed a relief: three days later she mentions that she has revised all day after "a lovely natural sleep of nine hours – nothing like it since last April." The typescript is complete and ready for the publisher in January 1935.[37]

Montgomery made a remarkably similar observation about her state of mind in 1914 after the birth and death of baby Hugh; the similar circumstances, twenty-one years later, of a mother living with the consequences of a son's perceived failure and a wife facing her husband's mental illness and imminent job loss, result in a book with a very different tone and outlook than *Pat of Silver Bush*. *Mistress Pat* is a novel of loss: Pat's loss of Judy to death, of Mary to her own past, and most significantly, of Silver Bush, first to May Binnie and then, perhaps more mercifully, to fire. Jingle's arrival and rescue of Pat are negligible and have only six pages in which to redeem six unhappy years. The book may end "happily," but it is not a happy book.

Both Mary Rubio's and Elizabeth Waterston's 2008 biographical works on Montgomery – *The Gift of Wings* and *Magic Island*, respectively – reveal a woman only glimpsed in her body of fiction: a woman often seized by depression, insecurity, anger, and resentment, entirely human qualities but qualities we tend not to associate with Montgomery's optimistic and hopeful heroines. Yet, in much of Montgomery's later work, and particularly in *Jane of Lantern Hill*, human nature is revealed as flawed, tainted by bitterness and resentment. Mothers, particularly, come across very poorly: weak, ineffectual, or just plain mean. There are redemptive characters – Jane herself is one – but Montgomery's anger and pain are neither hidden nor masked in this novel, nor are they presented as extremes or anomalies; they simply *are*. We might speculate, as Lesley Clement does later in this volume, that while Montgomery's public "personae must be consistently self-effacing and optimistic," her journals "reveal ... a deteriorating strength to fight on in an increasingly alien world."[38] In other words, Montgomery had not the mental or emotional resources with which to soften the bitterness of her first draft, as her life had become almost untenable. Similarly, in the next chapter, Thompson notes the juxtaposition of Montgomery's "private and public" spheres in her journals as she struggles with the loss of baby Hugh and the simultaneous and grim war news.[39] By the time she writes *Jane*, she cannot confine these juxtapositions to her journal; they seep inexorably into her fiction. Jane Stuart, like Anne before her, plays the role of mother but without any external role model. Montgomery constructs Jane, again like Anne, as an innately maternal figure, someone who does not need to learn how to mother; she simply knows. Jane seeks out others who, like herself, have no functional, nurturing mothers and offers herself as surrogate.

According to her journal, Montgomery worked on *Jane* from May 1936 to February 1937, a period during which she worried obsessively about the state of Chester's marriage (which she had only reluctantly accepted as a *fait accompli*), Stuart's actions and romantic entanglements, the death of her beloved cat, Lucky, and an unexplained event on 29 January 1937 of which she says only, "On that day all happiness departed from my life forever."[40] In Mrs Kennedy, Montgomery recognizes the tensions at work in her own mothering style, as she too closely involved herself in her sons' lives. Hence, the strained three-generational relationship and the bitterness and resentment, present primarily in the daughter-mother-grandmother triad of Jane and her mother, Robin Stuart, and Robin's mother, Victoria Kennedy, become central in the new novel.

Deborah Luepnitz suggests that, "in Lacan's view, the most important thing a mother can do is to be *not* in a state of 'primary maternal preoccupation' with her infant, but instead a subject in her own right, who does not look to the child to complete her. Who or what else she desires – husband, lover, or work – is not as important as the *fact* of her desiring something beyond the child."[41] This idea is echoed by Andrea O'Reilly in her work on empowered mothering. She suggests that "empowered mothers do not always put their children's needs before their own nor do they only look to motherhood to define and realize their identity. Rather, their selfhood is fulfilled and expressed in various ways: work, activism, friendships, relationships, hobbies, and motherhood."[42] Montgomery was a prototypical empowered mother, refusing to relinquish her entire self to her sons, although the last novel published in her lifetime demonstrates not just the motherly failures of both mother-characters in the book but also her own inability to move beyond the need to make her elder son "an adult acceptable to the next generation."[43] In *Jane of Lantern Hill*, both mothers, in different ways, violate the Lacanian precept and O'Reilly's criteria for empowered mothers. Mrs Kennedy lives almost entirely through her daughter. When Robin married against her wishes, Mrs Kennedy, rather than cut off her daughter financially or, less dramatically but more radically, support her decision, simply sets out to bring her back home. She manipulates Robin, planting seeds of doubt and distrust in the marriage, which, nurtured by Robin's own insecurity in her status and skills as Andrew's wife, eventually bears fruit, driving Robin back to her mother's house and her role as perfect and obedient daughter. Deceit seals the estrangement when Mrs Kennedy destroys Andrew Stuart's letter asking his wife to come back. Robin, with her full social calendar, cannot dote on Jane to the extent that either of them would like, but, notably, she relies on Jane's weakness to find her only moments of strength; Montgomery's narrator notes that "the only times [Robin] ever dared to contradict grandmother were in defence of Jane."[44]

Robin's relationship with Jane is much sweeter and more tender than her own with Mrs Kennedy. She focuses on Jane what little intimate attention that she can: endearments like "heart's delight" and "darling"; small and private moments of praise, sometimes in the face of her own mother's disapproval; and kisses at bedtime or before Robin goes out for the evening. Much of Jane and Robin's time together is covert, mornings in Robin's suite over her breakfast, with Jane's maternal nature manifesting in a longing to *do* things for her mother and already recognizing the impulse to protect her. Montgomery offers one such morning: "Jane slipped down the hall to mother's room ... She was not supposed to do this. It was understood at 60 Gay that mother must not be disturbed in the mornings. But mother, for a wonder, had not been out the night before, and Jane knew she would be awake ... They had a lovely time, laughing and talking beautiful nonsense, very quietly, so as not to be overheard. Not that either of them ever put this into words; but both *knew*." They are conspirators in preserving this time together, for it occurs so infrequently, and Mrs Kennedy's jealousy would prevent even these few moments if she knew they were happening. Jane wishes "it could be like this every morning," but she has learned to hold her tongue, for "she would not hurt mother for the world."[45]

Jane is made in the pattern of Valancy: a poorly mothered girl who is herself an innate nurturer. She mothers her orphan friend, Jody, and the stray cat she wants to keep. She wants to learn cooking and cleaning, the skills of making a home, despite the unsuitability of this pastime according to Grandmother Kennedy. After an idyllic trip to Prince Edward Island, where her father allows her to home-make to her heart's content, she emotionally mothers Robin, becoming shrewd in analyzing and interpreting her grandmother's and mother's relationships with each other.[46] Jane recognizes the fear that drives Grandmother Kennedy, coming to see that she desperately fears losing her daughter. Modern readers can see the parallel between Montgomery and her maternal villain: the author similarly feared the loss of her sons to people or occupations that she deemed unworthy of them and their talents. Rubio suggests that "Jane's grandmother bears uncanny similarities to the woman Maud could sometimes be: a mother who meddled in her children's romantic affairs, who tried to break up relationships she considered unsuitable, and who had fierce ambitions for her offspring."[47] Montgomery gives Jane strength beyond Robin's scope, strength that rivals and redeems the negative power of Grandmother Kennedy. In her penultimate paragraph, Montgomery sets Jane in direct opposition to her grandmother. Jane reflects, "Grandmother, stalking about 60

Gay, like a bitter old queen, her eyes bright with venom ... could never make trouble for them again. There would be no more misunderstanding. She, Jane, understood [both her parents] and could interpret them to each other."[48] Jane becomes the ultimate and final mother in her own story.

Montgomery's own experiences of motherhood were complex; she was at once daughter of absent, surrogate, and step- mothers, present mother of sons, bereaved mother, and disappointed mother. In her work, she was able to uneasily align these roles, first and most positively in Anne Shirley and later, more caustically, in the characters and stories of Valancy, Pat, and Jane. Her high expectations for her own experience of motherhood, and for the sons she raised as she had not been raised, set her up for intense disappointment when those sons chose their own paths for their lives. The idyllic and idealistic portrait of motherhood so potently portrayed in the earliest *Anne* novels is comedically reconstituted in *The Blue Castle* and poignantly but confusingly reshaped in the *Pat* novels. But those portrayals of mothers who mean well inexorably give way to the lost, angry, and bitter depictions of motherhood in *Jane of Lantern Hill*.

Montgomery's time in Ontario was marked by remarkable highs and lows, as Waterston suggests in chapter 1, a veritable rainbow valley of experience. She came as a bride to Leaskdale, and there learned to be a pastor's wife and became a mother; while there, she lost a child and several dear friends and lived painfully through the First World War. In Norval, she experienced the joy of new and renewed friendships, even as she struggled to let her boys become men and make their own (devastating, for her) choices. At Journey's End in Toronto, she wrote her final books and reflected on a life that she believed had failed. Perfectionism hobbled her own self-perception and compromised her relationships with her husband and her sons. Yet in her novels, she offers her protagonists a wide sense of family and empowers them with the ability to both find their own mother figures and shape themselves as mothers.

Shadows in Rainbow Valley: Loss and Grief

6

The Shadow on the House of Dreams: Montgomery's Re-Visioning of Anne

WILLIAM V. THOMPSON

After the move to Leaskdale, Ontario, in 1911, L.M. Montgomery's journals are characterized by the energy of a woman who is a working writer, a mother, and the wife of a minister. As has been explored in the previous chapters, central to these first years in Leaskdale is her ecstasy that comes with the birth and babyhood of Chester, her firstborn son. By the end of August 1914, however, Montgomery is grief-stricken over the stillbirth of Hugh, her second child, and she is in constant trepidation over the news after the outbreak of the First World War. These events, devastating in their impact on Montgomery's private and public selves, eventually lead to the re-visioning of the character of Anne Shirley. *Anne of the Island* appears in 1915, but the distress and anxiety of August 1914 filter down to become part of Montgomery's creative expression, marking a change in the fictional life of Anne. The books that most reflect this distress and anxiety are *Anne's House of Dreams* (1917) and *Rilla of Ingleside* (1921). Anne's joy in her House of Dreams is marred by the stillborn birth of her first child, while *Rilla of Ingleside* centres on the response of the community, the Island, and the country to the events of the Great War. Both of these texts incorporate a level of darkness and anxiety, tension and distress, not present in the earlier *Anne* books. The tenor of these later books reflects Montgomery's growing melancholia and anxiety, her efforts to cope with Ewan Macdonald's struggles with depression, the initiation of the lawsuit with L.C. Page, and the beginning of a growing dependence on pharmaceuticals. *Anne's House of Dreams* and *Rilla of Ingleside* are also the texts that best represent the intersection of Montgomery's private and public lives. While she tirelessly worked to maintain control of her fiction, both financially and creatively, the suffering she details in her journals from 1914 onwards, discussed in more detail elsewhere in this collection, shows a constant negotiation between her private and public selves, which in turn finds a literary expression in the life and experiences of one of her most beloved fictional characters.

More than any other, Anne Shirley has an iconic status among Montgomery's characters. In terms of a Canadian and an international readership, the adoration of Anne extends to Montgomery herself, and critics have commented extensively on the impulse that draws readers to both character and creator. Poushali Bhadury, for example, points to the "blurring of real and fictional worlds" in the creation of Prince Edward Island's Green Gables National Park as a site for literary tourism. She comments that "what was once a real-life space for the author's inspiration has been redesigned and re-presented as an 'authentic' copy of what is essentially the imaginary dwelling place of a fictitious character."[1] This fictional orphan from Bolingbroke, Nova Scotia, constitutes an industry for Prince Edward Island, which often foregrounds the fictional world of Anne at the expense of the author. Linda Rodenburg, in chapter 11 of this volume, offers a comparable connection between the Bala Museum and Montgomery's visit to the Muskoka region of Ontario in 1922, which inspired *The Blue Castle*. As Rodenburg argues, incorporating this region as part of Montgomery's internal landscape marks it as an expression of the importance of place for her and another site for the literary tourism surrounding the figure of Anne. Apart from tourism and the national park, Val Czerny comments that readers are drawn to discovering Anne's origins through the life of Montgomery, while suggesting that satisfying such an impulse has more possibilities in the character of Anne than it does in Montgomery's biography. She writes: "Thus, although we tend to seek after Montgomery's mind and inspiration in order to find Anne, we can more directly discover the wild element that Anne brings to the text by going straight to the 'window' of access that Montgomery pursued." This "window of access" is Anne's imaginative ability to look beyond the mundane, into what Czerny calls "the wild" or "lunacy": "Anne paradoxically matures without maturing, and so she inspires her readers – regardless of age – to look forward through those figurative 'windows.'"[2] Readings of Anne can and do exist apart from the author, but Montgomery's journals shed light on her creation of this iconic character in significant ways, revealing how Montgomery's experiences of grief, in particular those during her early years in Ontario, find their way into Anne's experiences.

Montgomery's journals are the constructed expression of a literary life. More specifically, and in the context of women's autobiography, the journals constitute the private diary of a writer, wife, and mother. According to Judy Nolte Lensink, female diarists "both tell their truth and create female design – a supersubtle design, similar to a quilt's, made up of incremental stitches that define a pattern."[3] Emily Woster, in chapter 8, observes that Montgomery is as much a diarist as she is a novelist. The nearly five decades of Montgomery's journals reveal the pattern of her life, but the "truth" of that pattern is not always clear. Further, while certain limitations exist in interpreting her fiction in the context of her journals, the direct crossover between Montgomery's journals and her fiction represents a further blurring of the lines between the real and the fictional. Montgomery was becoming aware by 1910 of the importance of the record she was constructing. In chapter 3, Margaret Steffler argues that Montgomery created an identity in relation to the various aspects of her life and that, moreover, the self-constructed nature of the journals gave rise to the divide between her private and public selves. This divide occurs early in her writing career; it constitutes a permeable separation between these private and public selves and remains one that she refines throughout the Ontario years. The journals situate Montgomery between these private and public expressions of self and further provide a detailed means of self-scrutiny. As Woster's chapter points out, later entries often correct, comment, or criticize entries from earlier years, while the progression of the journals details Montgomery's daily life and writing, further offering her a place to rant, vent, and process both her emotions and her experiences. Montgomery thinks of her journal as a friend and confidante as much as she does a place to voice her thoughts and feelings. She emphasizes this relationship at the end of her third volume, 11 March 1916: "How I love my old journal and what a part of my life it has become. It satisfies some need in my nature. It seems like a personal confidant, in whom I can repose absolute trust."[4] Such a comment reinforces the separation between the journals as an account of Montgomery's life and Montgomery as the author of that life, emphasizing the journal as a record from which she felt free to draw.

The direct crossover between her journals and her other writings shows the developing public Montgomery while detailing the private Maud. The divide between these public and private spheres enables her to move between one and the other throughout her journals, shifting between private reflection and public commentary. From this fluidity emerges her awareness of the need for the creation of something more appropriate for public consumption. In chapter 13, Lesley Clement argues that Montgomery's proximity to Toronto in the years after the move to Ontario results in her becoming "a product of the cultural industry in which she participated," suggesting the reciprocal nature of her relationship with that industry and her increasing status as a celebrity author.[5] An example of the consumable Montgomery comes with the publication of *The Alpine Path*, her autobiography published serially in *Everywoman's World* in 1917. The book demonstrates Montgomery's borrowing from her own journals in order to construct a public version of herself as precocious child and budding author. *The Alpine Path* represents a careful construction of Montgomery's early life, ending with the anticipation of her return from the honeymoon trip to Britain and the pending move to Ontario. The move to Leaskdale is for her "a new consecration,"[6] but the conclusion of her autobiography prior to the actual return and move to Ontario, not to mention the use of her travel journals to flesh out the end of the book, is notable. *The Alpine Path* specifically establishes Montgomery as an author in relation to the early years in Cavendish, years that remain separate from her pending life in Ontario as a minister's wife and soon-to-be mother.

Montgomery creates her account of the Cavendish years through the lens of her life in Ontario during the war years and her journal from 1910. Because *The Alpine Path* is Montgomery's official record of the Cavendish years, it becomes necessary to position the book in relation to her growing awareness of herself as a public figure – as both author and minister's wife. Its publication also coincides with her early motherhood and follows the stillbirth of Hugh and the beginning of the Great

War in 1914, factors that contribute to a re-visioning of her early life as separate from her later grief and anxiety while living in Leaskdale.

Notable in *The Alpine Path* is the manner in which Montgomery casts herself as the romantic, precocious child, constructing the autobiography from the details of her journal. She writes: "So ran the current of my life in childhood, very quiet and simple, you perceive. Nothing at all exciting about it, nothing that savours of a 'career' ... But life never held for me a dull moment. I had, in my vivid imagination, a passport to the geography of Fairyland."[7] This passage casts Montgomery's childhood into a particular light, unselfconscious and coloured by imaginative bliss, using the address to the reader as a means of furthering the bond between reader and writer. Moreover, it provides a connection to the character of Anne by recalling Anne's raptures over the nearness of fairyland in the first book of the series. In describing Idlewild, Anne tells Marilla, "We have the fairy glass there, too. The fairy glass is as lovely as a dream ... It's all full of rainbows – just little young rainbows that haven't grown big yet – and Diana's mother told her it was broken off a hanging lamp they once had. But it's nicer to imagine the fairies lost it one night when they had a ball."[8] Anne's comment operates as the fictionalized, child's version of Montgomery's description of having a passport to fairyland in *The Alpine Path*. The older Anne of *Anne's House of Dreams*, the twenty-five-year-old Anne who sits in the garret talking to Diana on the verge of marriage, reflects too on her childhood. She is less rapturous than her younger self but equally determined as the Montgomery of *The Alpine Path* to preserve the sanctity of her childhood home: "But somehow I feel as if I didn't want Avonlea spoiled by what Mr. Harrison, when he wants to be witty, calls 'modern inconveniences.' I should like to have it kept always just as it was in the dear old years."[9] In writing the autobiography for *Everywoman's World*, Montgomery imports passages directly from her journals, but those passages are recast in such a way as to reflect a particular childhood – the constructed childhood of a woman who is intent on creating for herself a public image that excludes the grief of motherhood and the harrowing years of the Great War.

A long journal entry dated Friday, 7 January 1910, forms the basis for Montgomery's description of her Cavendish childhood in *The Alpine*

Path. Even in 1910, she is aware of writing for a public arena, which she presents as the justification for recording some of her early memories: "I wonder if it would do any good to write out all of the recollections that have crowded into my thoughts today ... Besides, I am always being bothered by publishers and editors for 'information' regarding my childhood and 'career,' and it will be handy to have it all ready for them at the cost of copying out."[10] Such a comment indicates her clear sense of needing to begin the negotiation between her private and public selves. The understatement in the passage further reinforces her deliberateness. Having such an account "handy" speaks to an offhandedness that is belied by her extensive use of the journals.

Those passages that find their way into the autobiography are necessarily lacking in context and constitute a more consumable account of the writer's early life. For example, in *The Alpine Path*, Montgomery records her first experience of death as a child. Fittingly, it is the death of a pet, the nine-year-old Maud's beloved Pussy-Willow: "It was the first time I *realized* death, the first time, since I had become conscious of loving, that anything I loved had left me forever ... the curse of the race came upon me, 'death entered into my world' and I turned my back on the Eden of childhood."[11] The passage suitably paints a romantic portrait of the loss of childhood innocence, and, from the perspective of 1917, it couches that description in biblical metaphors that seem most appropriate to a woman writer and wife of a minister.

A later entry further illuminates that of 7 January 1910. Montgomery's assertion that she wants to record the events of her childhood for the later purpose of culling them for publication is true, but only partly so. She explains her despair that characterizes this entry in an entry from 25 February 1918, near the end of the war and several months after the publication of *Anne's House of Dreams*. Montgomery's nervous breakdown of 1910 is partly owing to what she refers to as a "kernel" she discovers in her breast: "There were a couple of weeks that winter [1910] in which I tasted all the bitterness of death – and a dreadful and lingering death. It induced a nervous breakdown to which I made reference in my journal at the time. But I did not explain the *cause* of it – I could not."[12] Convinced she has discovered the first evidence of breast cancer, Montgomery is driven to recall her Cavendish childhood in detail. Her inability to give voice to what she believes to be the unspeakable truth eventually results in her breakdown. The description of her Cavendish childhood in *The Alpine Path* is lacking in such a context, the account offering no hint of the anxiety and despair that motivated the recollection in the first place.

A poignant intersection between Montgomery's journals and her fiction comes with *Anne's House of Dreams*. She uses the stillbirth of her second child to inform Anne's grief over the death of her baby Joyce in the spring after she and Gilbert move into the House of Dreams. In order of publication of the *Anne* books, *Anne's House of Dreams* follows *Anne of the Island*, the third book in the series that ends with Anne and Gilbert walking home together in the recognition of their love for one another. *Anne's House of Dreams* opens with Anne and Gilbert's wedding and their subsequent move to Four Winds Harbour. The House of Dreams itself embodies Anne's marital bliss, but the change to Anne's character, coming as a result of Montgomery's growing anxiety during the war years, is most evident in her connection to the landscape, her friendship with Leslie Moore, and her impending motherhood.

Anne's connection to the natural world appears immediately upon her arrival on the Island at the beginning of the series. She begins to rename features of the landscape as she rides in the buggy with Matthew from Bright River to Green Gables; however, this romantic aspect of her character has another side. Anne's habit of romanticizing natural beauty works to separate her from the present moment, a tendency that Ashley Cowger calls her "distractibility." Cowger comments on manic-depressive episodes throughout early books in the series, suggesting that a "hypomanic well-being but a pervading tone of melancholy underscores the books as chapter by chapter Anne learns that the real world is not the fairy tale land she so desperately wants it to be." More important, *Anne's House of Dreams* is, according to Cowger, "bursting with images of suicide, death, and depression."[13] The mania that Cowger describes in the earlier books underscores Anne's grief and depression in *Anne's House of Dreams*, in addition to characterizing the relationship she develops with Leslie. This relationship becomes bound up with Anne's depression and anxiety. While her friendship with Leslie is not reflective of Montgomery's wartime journals in the same way as is Anne's grief over the death of Joyce, it becomes redolent of the emotional turmoil so characteristic of the journals during this time.

In *Anne's House of Dreams*, the most marked change in Anne's character is her social and domestic position as Mrs Blythe. No longer the figure of the maiden, she is wife and soon-to-be mother. While the figure of the matron and the old maid populate the *Anne* books from the beginning, as Caroline Jones develops in the previous chapter, the new mother or the expectant mother does not emerge fully until *Anne's House of Dreams*. Diana is a new mother at the beginning of the book, while Anne is soon to become the middle-class mother, the wife of a doctor who will have a permanent housekeeper to look after her by the time she is brought to bed with her first child. Anne enters into her new life at Glen St Mary in the expectation of maternal bliss, but she first finds distress and anxiety in the friendship with Leslie and then depression and grief after the death of Joyce.

Anne's expectations around motherhood are clear from the book's beginning, reflecting and recalling Montgomery's maternal feelings after the birth of Chester. Anne's response on the eve of her wedding to the sight of Diana holding Anne Cordelia speaks to the depth of these expectations. The sight "always sent through Anne's heart, filled with sweet, unuttered dreams and hopes, a thrill that was half pure pleasure and half a strange, ethereal pain."[14] Her sense of "ethereal pain" upon seeing the mother and child embodied in her childhood friend anticipates Anne's earthly pain upon Joyce's death. It elevates the figure of the mother and child to something semi-divine in nature, only matched by Kenneth Ford's sight of Rilla holding her war baby in the half-light of a summer's evening in *Rilla of Ingleside*, looking "exactly like the Madonna that hung over his mother's desk at home. He carried that picture of her in his heart to the horror of the battlefields of France."[15] This idealized vision of Rilla, according to Elizabeth Epperly, is "characteristic of the novel's romantic view of womanhood and sacrifice."[16]

Motherhood for Anne becomes further tied up with the uneasy friendship with Leslie. Anne's friendship with Leslie is not the bosom friendships of Anne's girlhood nor the supportive, idealized friendships of *Anne of the Island* that Laura Robinson describes in chapter 4, "'A Gift for Friendship'"; it is fraught with tension and anxiety, while Leslie's attachment to Anne is tied up with bitterness and resentment. Unlike Anne's, Leslie's life is defined by personal loss: her brother's death under the wheels of a hay wagon and her father's suicide, as well as her marriage to the simple Dick Moore, combine to create a spiteful jealousy of which Anne becomes the target.

Anne is at first shocked by Leslie's attitude, but Leslie is neither a girl nor an inhabitant of the lush and forgiving landscape of Avonlea, a landscape that Irene Gammel suggests provides a safe place for the young Anne and her companions to enjoy and explore their sensuality. Gammel encapsulates Anne's earlier friendships in her description of Montgomery's girls in relation to the landscape they inhabit: "Montgomery's girls are profoundly modern in that they do not wait for pleasures to materialize in heterosexual romance. Montgomery empowers her girls to be agents in their erotic universe, to indulge in sensualized pleasure without feelings of guilt; indeed, to cultivate and map their erotic imaginary."[17] In "'Sex Matters,'" Robinson furthers this point by commenting on the nature of same-sex friendships among girls, both in terms of the period and for Montgomery herself: "Montgomery represented herself as seeking out and deriving great sustenance from her female friendships. This emotional intensity, and the often flamboyant descriptions of the affections, both physical and emotional, emerged from a society that generally encouraged this style of female friendships."[18] While Robinson's description of Montgomery's attitude towards female friendships fits with Anne's relationship with Leslie, the tension that Anne experiences as a result of that relationship is markedly different from the girlhood friendships of the first three books in the series, as Robinson further details in chapter 4 of this volume.

Montgomery's girls may be, as Gammel suggests, "profoundly modern," but Leslie is a complex character, jealous and spiteful, with psychological depths informed by Montgomery's experience as a woman and a mother writing during the war. Unlike Anne, Leslie is a woman trapped by legal and social convention. She is torn between her desire for Anne's friendship and her desire for Anne's wealth of happiness in heterosexual love and pending maternity. For Leslie, this desire is "some hideous creature" locked away in a dark inner room. Leslie must overcome this "monster"[19] in order to love Anne in a manner more appropriate to the normative standards of female desire. The friendship with Leslie is further coloured by the landscape of Four Winds Harbour itself. Of Montgomery's depiction of the sea in *Anne's House of Dreams*, Epperly writes: "Abiding, yet ever-changeful, at times serene and at times savage, the sea suggests the quality of Four Winds life. The apparent power, beauty, mystery, melancholy, caprice, and joy of the harbour and gulf reflect as well as affect the moods and personalities of the novel's main characters."[20] Four Winds Harbour is a landscape both wild and lonely, haunted by the sea and the shadows of the past and entirely unlike the ordered and domesticated Avonlea of the earlier books.

Anne senses the tension with Leslie, but she fails to explain it fully to herself or anticipate its barbs: "She felt, with an instinct that was not to be combated by reason, that Leslie harboured a queer, indefinable resentment towards her." She further feels the thorn of Leslie's resentment when she confides "what she hoped the spring would bring to the little house of dreams."[21] While never stated openly, Anne's pregnancy, much to her bafflement, becomes the centrepiece of Leslie's bitterness. According to Elizabeth Waterston in *Magic Island*, "Leslie's horrible dilemma, more tragic than anything Montgomery had ever introduced into her stories up to this point, shows among other things the darkening vision inflicted by the war."[22] The tension that characterizes *Anne's House of Dreams* no doubt comes in part from Montgomery's experiences of wartime, but it also marks a change in Montgomery's depiction of female friendship. Leslie's dilemma is the duty that binds her to Dick Moore, while the tragedy of her life seems underscored by her beauty, something with which Anne is struck – romantically, of course – the first time she sees her. Leslie, on the other hand, is less struck by the sexual intimacy Anne's pregnancy implies than she is by Anne's impending motherhood. Her envy of Anne extends to her maternity but more so to her maternal bereavement: "And I'd envy her even if she had died! She was a mother for one beautiful day. I'd gladly give my life for *that*!"[23] Leslie's jealousy speaks to a sublimated desire to possess Anne, or at least Anne's life, which she is not able to relinquish until fully witnessing Anne's grief. The two women become in turn bound by grief and personal trauma, which has the effect of defusing Leslie's desire and in turn enabling them to become friends but in a manner that relies on Anne's loss.

As Waterston suggests, the darkness and anxiety present in the book reflect Montgomery's anxiety during wartime, but the death of Joyce represents the emergence of Montgomery's private grief into a public, if fictional, context. Apart from reforging the friendship between the two women, Anne's grief over her infant's death becomes the direct point of crossover with Montgomery's journals. In August 1914, Montgomery's consciousness of the divide between her private and public lives takes a different form. She is pregnant with her second child, and the war intrudes into her life, causing grief, sleeplessness, and anxiety. Montgomery writes of the outbreak of war in her journal on 5 August 1914, but as Mary Rubio suggests, "Maud could not have imagined how much the war would eventually affect her husband, her community, and her own life."[24] The war has an immediate effect on Montgomery's life, but specific events take longer to filter down into her fiction, finding an initial foothold in the darker depictions of character, such as that of Leslie in *Anne's House of Dreams*.

The private and the public spheres are interestingly juxtaposed in Montgomery's journals at this point, the anxiety over the outbreak of war sitting alongside her grief over the death of Hugh. On 30 August 1914, Montgomery writes in her journal: "Oh, it is not fair – it is not fair! Children are born and live where they are not wanted – where they will be neglected – where they will have no chance. I would have loved my baby so ... Yet I was not allowed to have him. And while I was lying helpless bad war news began to come, too."[25] This passage captures Montgomery's private grief, while she goes on to exhort herself to carry on with her work as a wife, mother, and writer. These words, minus the bad news from the war, have a different impact from the mouth of Anne. Anne is torn by grief and loss, and she speaks that grief to Marilla, who becomes the witness to something bordering on religious doubt: "'It doesn't seem *fair*,' said Anne rebelliously. 'Babies are born and live where they are not wanted – where they will be neglected – where they will have no chance. I would have loved my baby so – and cared for it so tenderly – and tried to give her every chance for good. And yet I wasn't allowed to keep her.'" Marilla's response that Joyce's death is "God's will"[26] in no way pacifies Anne's rebellion or her anger at being robbed of her maternity. The change in Anne's character is subtle but noteworthy. Knowing motherhood and the loss of a child on the same day galvanizes her in a particular way, enabling her to speak directly from her grief.

Montgomery extracts another passage from her journal to put into the voice of Anne, with one important difference. Anne's passionate speech to Marilla as to the purpose in Joyce's death comes directly from Montgomery's journal, 4 September 1914, but for Anne, God's will remains a question: "Why should she be born at all – why should any one be born at all – if she's better off dead? I *don't* believe it is better for a child to die at birth than to live its life out – and love and be loved – and enjoy and suffer – and do its work – and develop a character that would give it a personality in eternity. And how do you know it was God's will? Perhaps it was just a thwarting of His purpose by the Power of Evil. We can't be expected to be resigned to *that*."[27] Anne's question as to God's will, and whether to be resigned to the thwarting of that will, is Anne's, not Montgomery's. Anne does not blame God outright for the loss of her child, but her rebellion and passion speak to a defiant dismantling of the religious platitudes that Marilla raised her to believe. The words are Montgomery's, written in the private grief over the loss of Hugh. Spoken by Anne, the words have a different force.

Anne's words give a public, if fictional, voice to one of the many changes the war brings. Rubio points to this alteration in the foundational nature of faith for Montgomery and many of her contemporaries: "The old view of the world, ruled by an omnipotent God who took an active and benevolent interest in all human affairs, was for many nearly impossible to maintain. Decimating a generation of young men hardly seemed benevolent."[28] Lacking the context of the war, this attitude coming from Anne speaks of rebellion and anger, of a denial of the pat Christian values in which she has received instruction from the first time she prays in her room at Green Gables. Moreover, the challenge to Anne's faith goes some way towards reflecting Montgomery's own efforts to grapple with the realities of being a Christian wife and mother, as previously detailed by Margaret Steffler in chapter 3.

Given the poignancy of Anne's grief and the excruciating nature of her friendship with Leslie, Montgomery's description of the arrival of Jem by stork comes close to trivializing the emotional intensity of these earlier scenes. If nothing else, it undercuts the book's emotional intensity and sentimentalizes the dangers and difficulties of childbirth: "One morning ... a certain weary stork flew over the bar of Four Winds Harbour on his way from the Land of Evening Stars. Under his wing was tucked a sleepy, starry-eyed, little creature."[29] Notably, this passage comes from the narrator rather than Anne. While it is only possible to speculate as to why Montgomery places the birth of Jem in the context of a nursery tale, it nonetheless forms a jarring counterpoint to the description of Anne's first experience of childbirth earlier in the book.

The re-formation of Anne's character in *Anne's House of Dreams* from girl to woman carries over to *Rilla of Ingleside*. After the death of Joyce, and in spite of the birth of Jem, "there was something in the smile that had never been in Anne's smile before and would never be absent from it again."[30] Part of this change has to do with Anne's own acknowledgment that she and Leslie are no longer girls; they are women – women who have experienced pain and suffering. And it is Anne as a woman who appears in *Rilla of Ingleside*.

Setting aside here *The Blythes Are Quoted*, *Rilla of Ingleside* represents the final book in the chronology of the *Anne* books published during Montgomery's lifetime. *Anne of Windy Poplars* (1936) and *Anne of Ingleside* (1939) are inserted into the chronology of the series: *Anne of Windy Poplars* before *Anne's House of Dreams*, and *Anne of Ingleside* before *Rainbow Valley*. The Anne of *Rilla of Ingleside* emerges directly out of the Anne of *Anne's House of Dreams* and the Anne of *Rainbow Valley*. The Anne of *Rainbow Valley* has moved on from the House of Dreams; she is more removed from the main action of the book, and she has become mother and mistress of Ingleside. Bearing in mind the chronology of publication rather than the chronology of the series, the character of Anne in *Rilla of Ingleside* is no longer the Anne of the House of Dreams. She is Mrs Blythe, mother, or Mrs Dr Dear, and she is further in the background while Rilla becomes the focalizing character of the novel.

Unlike *Anne's House of Dreams*, *Rilla of Ingleside* was written after the Great War. According to Waterston, the texture of *Rilla* is also substantively different from the earlier books in the series: "*Rilla of Ingleside* substitutes directness in reporting events for the prettiness of descriptions of nature, and adds the humour of Susan Baker's sturdy resistance to melodrama or pathos."[31] While *Anne's House of Dreams* carries the anxiety of both wartime and Montgomery's personal grief, *Rilla of Ingleside* encompasses the anxiety of the community as the war progresses.

Mary Beth Cavert's earlier chapter in this volume poignantly describes the overwhelming part that the war played in Montgomery's life for four years. Her intense anxiety and sleeplessness often caused by news from the front speak to a growing pathology of depression and general anxiety disorder, but news from the war also figures into the day-to-day of domestic chores and child rearing. On 10 June 1916, Montgomery writes in her journal: "This war is slowly killing me. I am bleeding to death as France is being bled in the shambles of Verdun." Such a passage shows her manner of internalizing the news from the front. However, a later entry that summer demonstrates the way in which news from the war is simply part of her day as a mother and working writer: "I do my writing in the parlour now, as said parlour possesses the only door in the house which young Chester cannot open ... Wednesday and Thursday I was miserable with an attack of bowel trouble. Naturally, visitors took that day for appearing. The Russians have captured Tarnapol heights and the British and French have renewed their offensive."[32] This passage from 19 August 1916 encapsulates much of Montgomery's life: writing, motherhood, physical discomfort, duty to the community, and the Great War collide with and collapse into one another. While lacking the narrative presence of earlier books, Anne's character in *Rilla of Ingleside* represents a similar stoic determination to that of Montgomery herself.

The events of the war form the structure for *Rilla of Ingleside*. Montgomery's personal, familial, and communal anxiety inform that structure. In chapter 2, Cavert fleshes out Montgomery's place in the community and the grief and loss Leaskdale experienced as a result of the war. In *Rilla*, Anne's character is removed from the foreground of the action; nonetheless, she is the matron of Ingleside. She bears the responsibility of a household and a family; she has a position in the community as the wife of Dr Blythe; she is a middle-class wife and mother. Anne deals with Rilla, her daughter and a somewhat flightier version of herself at the same age, while later, just as she does in *Anne's House of Dreams*, she copes with the death of a child.

Anne is no less important in *Rilla*, in spite of being largely removed from the main action. Epperly suggests otherwise, stating that "this Anne, like the Anne of *Rainbow Valley*, is a mere place marker for her former self. The energy of the book is with the other characters, and Anne serves sometimes as a device within the narrative, an audience for Rilla's resolves or a recipient of Susan Baker's pungent remarks."[33] Anne, however, seems more than simply a place marker. Her maturity is that of a parent and mother, and she shares, both personally and communally, in the sufferings of the war. Her interactions with Rilla, for example, are those of mother and parent. Rilla recalls a younger Anne, but as Waterston suggests, Rilla "has no intellectual ambition, no desire to go to college like her sisters Nan and Diana. She doesn't write, except in a girlish journal. She certainly doesn't enjoy the kind of frank friendly exchanges that marked the development of Anne's love for Gilbert."[34] This difference in their characters is underscored through their exchange over Rilla's green velvet hat. Rilla writes in her diary that when "mother saw the hat and the tag she just *looked* at me. Mother is some expert at looking." The relationship between Anne and Rilla is clear: Rilla is the defiant, vain teenager, while Anne is the determined, rational parent. Anne comments on the price of such a hat during wartime but concludes, "If you think you did right, Rilla, I have no more to say. I leave it to your conscience."[35] Anne's methods here are notably modern. She is secure in her parenting style in a way that Rilla simply finds frustrating. Rilla has to learn about parenting as well while caring for Little Jims, but she takes the baby on as a project or a duty of wartime, continually consulting "Morgan" as to Little Jims's moods and ailments.

A more poignant example of the change in Anne's character from *Anne's House of Dreams* comes in the form of her nostalgia. She is much less the romantic than she was as a bride coming to Four Winds Harbour, partly because of the anxiety of the war and partly because of the weight of motherhood and responsibility. She sits gazing out upon a summer's evening, but she is less struck by the romance and poetry of the scene than she is with the memory of her children in the Rainbow Valley years: "I was just taking relief from intolerable realities in a dream, Gilbert – a dream that all our children were home again – and all small again – playing in Rainbow Valley. It is always so silent now – but I was imagining I heard clear voices and gay, childish sounds coming up as I used to."[36]

Motherhood and loss become intertwined for Anne as the novel progresses. However, Rilla and not Anne first receives the news of Walter's death at Courcelette, and, as Melanie Fishbane discusses at greater length in the next chapter, Rilla serves as witness to the family's loss, carrying on while Anne is in bed overcome by grief: "For weeks Mrs Blythe lay ill from grief and shock. Rilla found it was possible to go on with existence, since existence had still to be reckoned with ... For her mother's sake she had to put on calmness and endurance as a garment in the day; but night after night she lay in her bed, weeping the bitter rebellious tears of youth." Rilla carries on, and Anne recovers. As Rilla matures, she assumes the stalwartness and determination of her mother, but she never has to endure the private grief of loss that Anne suffers during the war. For Anne, the war is only part of that experience of grief. It spans her life as a mother, beginning with the anguish over Joyce's death and her subsequent rebellion against God. When Shirley comes to tell his parents that he wants to join the Flying Corps, Anne is struck by the prospect of losing another child: "She was thinking of little Joyce's grave in the old burying-ground over-harbour – little Joyce who would have been a woman now, had she lived – of the white cross in France and the splendid grey eyes of the little boy who had been taught his first lessons of duty and loyalty at her knee – of Jem in the terrible trenches – of Nan and Di and Rilla, waiting – waiting – waiting, while the golden years of youth passed by – and she wondered if she could bear any more."[37]

Critics agree that *Rilla of Ingleside* is about heroism – not the romantic heroism of Anne's fancies from the first three books in the series, but the heroism of determination, endurance, and steadfastness. Epperly poignantly states that Anne "serves as a reminder in the novel as a whole of the millions of quiet, nameless women who watched their sons and brothers and lovers and husbands and friends go to the front. And Montgomery makes it clear that for this she is heroic, for this and for running the Red Cross and carrying on her daily life."[38] Montgomery returns to the character of Anne more than a decade later in *Anne of Windy Poplars* and *Anne of Ingleside*. These later novels attempt to reposition a more romantic Anne in relation to the earlier books in the series, while *Anne of Ingleside* serves to anticipate, particularly in the figure of Walter, the grief and loss of *Rilla*. Nonetheless, both *House of Dreams* and *Rilla* incorporate a level of tension and anxiety distinct from any of the other books in the series, underscoring the profound effect of the war years evident through Montgomery's journals. The overlay between her private and public selves manifests both directly and indirectly in the character of Anne from these two books, reinforcing her position among the many strong female characters Montgomery represents throughout her fiction.

Over the course of *Anne's House of Dreams* and *Rilla of Ingleside*, Anne's character embodies the womanhood forged through grief that Montgomery came to know in married life and motherhood in Leaskdale. Anne's womanhood in *Rilla* is markedly different from the matronly, community-minded womanhood that appears early in the series. By the time of *Rilla*, Anne's womanhood is written in grief and pain against a much larger backdrop than that of the church socials and friendships of Avonlea. More than this, her experience of child-bearing and motherhood, of the domestic and of wartime, is informed by Montgomery's entrance into a new life in Ontario. Her marriage to Ewan, her domestic and parish responsibilities, and her growing fame as an author all contribute to the change in Anne's character. Montgomery's journal, the life record that she kept so carefully for nearly five decades, represents the point of connection in understanding this change to Anne's fictional life. The freckled, skinny Anne of the first book in the series is the Anne who is central to the industry that brings thousands of tourists to Prince Edward Island every year. She is the Anne of the National Park near Cavendish and of the Anne of Green Gables Store in Charlottetown. She is the Anne who attracts visitors to Ontario's Bala Museum, with its annual "Everything Anne Day" and "Cran-Anne Look-a-Like Contest." However, the older Anne acquires a presence that is unmatched by any of Montgomery's other characters, and she does this by receiving something of Montgomery herself through the journals that span the author's first ten years in Ontario.

7
"My Pen Shall Heal, Not Hurt": Writing as Therapy in Rilla of Ingleside *and* The Blythes Are Quoted

MELANIE J. FISHBANE

Literary scholars have long shown interest in how an author's personal loss, specifically a death, fuels his or her creative work. Harold K. Bush Jr, for instance, explores how the death of Mark Twain's daughter, Susy, characterizes the author's later work; Keverne Smith considers how the death of William Shakespeare's son, Hamnet, changes the way in which the playwright discusses and describes death and grieving in his plays; and Christian Riegel focuses on how the death of Margaret Laurence's mother when Laurence was young informs her fiction, arguing that Laurence's writing about grief and the grieving process is an attempt to bring back what has been lost.[1]

Writing has always been a form of meditation for me. At thirteen, I started a journal, and at various stages of my life, I have turned to writing non-fiction and poetry, and recently to finding my voice in young adult fiction, to seek understanding and heal wounds. Creative writing instructors and theorists have much to say on this. Anne Paris suggests that immersion in a creative endeavour can be good for one's psychological health.[2] Sheppard B. Kominars argues with his "Write for Life" workshops that the act of journal writing can heal the body, mind, and spirit. Richard Stamelman takes this one step further, stating, "Writing is an act of survivorship; it is what the survivor does in order to keep on going, to understand what has happened in his or her own life, and to give form, shape, and sound to the pain of losing."[3] Susan Zimmermann provides daily exercises to help people transform their grief and loss through writing and argues that the "act of writing brings a structure and order to the chaos of grief."[4] One of Natalie Goldberg's writing exercises challenges writers to think deeply about why they write and to see how writing permeates their lives.

"Writing is not therapy," she states, "though it may have a therapeutic effect." She continues: "Writing is deeper than therapy. You write *through* your pain, and even your suffering must be written out and let go of."[5]

For these personal and professional reasons, Montgomery's writing out of and through her grief has intrigued me. As an outlet that allowed her to retreat into her ideal world when the real one "bruised [her] spirit," writing brought Montgomery great pleasure and often relief. Whether it was in her journal or fiction, from an early age she used writing as a productive way to cope with what she had learned were inappropriate emotions. Writing provided a means to channel her darker moods and doubts about self and society. In a letter to G.B. MacMillan dated 3 December 1905, Montgomery tells him, "When I get very desperate I retreat into my realms of cloudland and hold delightful imaginary dialogues with the shadowy, congenial shapes I meet there. It is not so satisfying as the *reality* of such might be but it is far better than to let one's soul slip down to sodden levels for lack of the stimulation which comes from the flash and meeting of other intellects."[6] As Goldberg says, writing "is an opportunity to take the emotions we have felt many times and give them light, color and a story."[7] Through her creation and recreation of characters such as Anne, Rilla, and Walter, in *Rilla of Ingleside* and *The Blythes Are Quoted*, written two decades apart, Montgomery tapped into what writer Anne Lamott counsels in her craft book *Bird by Bird*: "You must risk placing real emotion at the center of your work. Write straight into the emotional center of things."[8] Perhaps recalling Emily Dickinson's "Dare you see a soul at the white heat," Robert Olin Butler echoes Goldberg's and Lamott's challenge to write from the emotional "white hot center": "You have to go down into that deepest, darkest, most rolling, white-hot place ... whatever scared the hell out of you down there – and there's plenty – you have to go in there; down into the deepest part of it, and you can't flinch, you can't walk away."[9] Montgomery intuitively understood how emotions and craft worked in tandem to inform one's art; she writes in her journal on 8 April 1898, recalling the occasion of her grandfather Macneill's death, which prompts memories of her mother's funeral, "I am going to write it out fully and completely, even if every word cuts me to the heart. I have always found that the writing out of a pain makes it at least bearable."[10] This idea later finds its way into *Emily of New Moon*, when Emily pours her pain over her father's death into letters to him: "When she had covered the backs of four letter-bills she could see to write no more. But she had emptied out her soul and it was once more free from evil passions."[11]

This relationship between pain and writing aligns with my interest in how a writer's personal history affects his or her craft. Did Montgomery's periods of depression affect her creative impulse? What does her creative process reveal about her psychological health? How did writing help her balance her hypersensitive, moody, and brooding nature with the discipline, self-control, and dignity her grandparents had expected of her and that were required of her as a Presbyterian minister's wife and mother of two boys after she moved to Ontario?

Riegel's research on Margaret Laurence is suggestive for the study of Montgomery. Riegel examines how "death and mourning [are] pervasive in Laurence's writing, [and how] her personal life was deeply informed by her first-hand experience of death." Laurence's posthumously published memoir often discusses the profound effect her mother's death had on her life and her writing. Riegel argues that, as part of working through the grieving process, mourners engage in attempts to bring back what has been lost, and for Laurence that meant writing fiction that explored autobiographical material. Riegel says that this is "work that needs doing, as in the psychological, social, and cultural processes of mourning themselves; and work that results from mourning, as in the creatively articulated texts that result from grief."[12] By giving her characters Morag and Hagar the opportunity to grieve, Laurence could also revisit her own complicated feelings about her mother's death and loss. Similarly, William Thompson and Caroline Jones in this volume examine this theme with reference to Montgomery. Thompson (chapter 6) shows a direct link between Anne's grief over the death of Joyce in *Anne's House of Dreams* and Montgomery's own mourning over the death of her stillborn son, which marks a shift in Anne's character that can be seen throughout the rest of the *Anne* series;

Jones (chapter 5) presents a compelling argument on how Montgomery processed her complex feelings around motherhood through Anne, Valancy, Pat, and Jane.

As seen throughout this collection, the publication of Montgomery's *Selected Journals* and now of her *Complete Journals* has allowed Montgomery studies to make connections between her life writing and fiction. Within this significant area of Montgomery research, my interest focuses on how personal losses inform her fiction to create grief narratives in which storytelling is tied to the attempt to make meaning out of profound sadness. While personal storytelling is an accepted method in grief counselling, my interest is not clinical but driven rather by my need as a writer to understand and illuminate another's writing out of psychological and emotional desolation. My interest rests also on the link between emotion and craft, on the techniques that transpose the personal experience into the creative work. The compulsion to create through suffering is particularly relevant when applied to the tumultuous years leading up to and through Montgomery's writing *Rilla of Ingleside* and *The Blythes Are Quoted*. This chapter thus explores how Montgomery uses her characters to question public and private forms of grieving and how the act of writing and reading or hearing words is part of her characters' mourning process.

Rilla of Ingleside centres on Anne and Gilbert Blythe's youngest teenage daughter, Rilla, during the First World War. Scholarly work on this novel focuses on the tragedies that characterized Montgomery's life before, during, and after this war as well as her obsession with the war and the interpretation of her views of women's roles during wartime. Montgomery's loss of her stillborn son, Hugh, on 13 August 1914, the impact of the war on her psyche, and the death of her best friend and cousin, Frede, of the Spanish influenza on 25 January 1919, set the stage for this wartime novel. A few months after Frede's death, on 24 August 1919, Montgomery writes in her journal, "This afternoon I was alone and bitterly lonely. I took a wild spasm of longing for Frede. It seemed to me that I *could not* go on living without her – and that it was no use to try."[13] *Rilla* was born out of this rubble of emotional turmoil, as Montgomery started writing it six weeks after Frede's death and would later dedicate it to her "true friend." As Mary Beth Cavert discusses in chapter 2, *Rilla* is the fictional response to these losses and to the deaths of three young soldiers from Leaskdale to whom Montgomery dedicated *Rainbow Valley*.

Scholars of women's history have given much attention to the importance of journal and memoir writing in the evolution of women's literature. In many cases, these personal writings gave women the means to articulate suppressed female perspectives. In *Grief in Wartime: Private Pain, Public Discourse*, Carol Acton suggests that during wartime, the diary emerged as a way for writers to control their experience through language and create a narrative in which they participated with the "self as a central character."[14] Acton examines the different private narratives of grief and the discourses that controlled the public expressions of that grief. While product advertisements from the period often glamourized weeping and mourning women, the diary allowed women to explore honest expressions of grief in private. As the development of a female literary tradition shows, journal and memoir writing constitutes a significant part of women's literature. During wartime, the diary provided a literary form for women in which they could voice their war experiences in a safe place – that is, outside of the mainstream public discourse with its strictures on acceptable emotional responses.

In *Rilla of Ingleside*, Montgomery varies her narrative methods to reflect different expressions of grief and mourning during the period. A third-person omnipresent narrator acts as the public voice, whereas Rilla's journal, which slowly develops and becomes the dominant point of view in a number of chapters, functions as a way to show private expressions or observations of grief as well as to give voice to those whose perspectives have been historically silenced.[15] As the diarist, Rilla is the observer, the record keeper, of grief. When Jem goes off to war, she writes, "I shall never forget Susan's face when Jem came home in his khaki. It worked and twisted as if she were going to cry, but all she said was, 'You look *almost* like a man in that, Jem.'" Susan's public teasing covers what Rilla (privately) detects as the family housekeeper's worry. Rilla also recounts Anne's emotional reaction when Susan mentions in passing that the mayflowers are blooming in Rainbow Valley: "Her face changed and she gave a queer little choked cry. Most of the time mother is so spunky and gay you would never guess what she feels inside; but now and then some little thing is too much for her and we see under the surface. 'Mayflowers!' she said. 'Jem brought me mayflowers last year!' and she got up and went out of the room."[16] While propriety demands that Anne should hide her feelings in public, Rilla's diary entry reveals her own and others' true emotional states.

Indeed, Montgomery shows the kinds of pressure women were under as twice in the novel the already vilified Irene Howard accuses Rilla of not behaving appropriately. In both circumstances, Rilla chooses to keep her emotions to herself and show a distant "businesslike" attitude to the world and continue her work with the Junior Red Cross. The first occurs when Walter leaves for the front and Irene tells Olive, "You would never suppose ... that Walter had left for the front only this morning. But some people really have no depth of feeling. I often wish *I* could take things as lightly as Rilla Blythe." The second occurs after Walter dies, when Irene claims that "every one is talking about" Rilla's calm demeanour and refusal to wear mourning garb, which she does out of respect for her mother's wishes.[17] Despite being an emotionally shallow gossip, Irene represents the larger society's attitudes towards the public's idea of appropriate grieving. Yet through Rilla's journal, we are aware that she and her family feel a profound loss over her brother's going to war and his subsequent death.

Rilla also observes and records the inner life of those beyond her immediate family. Gertrude Oliver returns to work immediately after hearing that her fiancé, Robert Grant, is missing and possibly dead, but Rilla's private narrative reveals Gertrude's anguish: "I heard Gertrude walking up and down her room most of the night ... And once I heard her give a dreadful sudden little cry as if she had been stabbed." And later, when Rilla tells Gertrude that her fiancé is still alive, the diary bears witness to Gertrude's collapse: "She said, 'Rob – is – living,' as if the words were torn out of her, and flung herself on her bed and cried and cried and cried ... All the tears that she hadn't shed all that week came then. She cried most of last night."[18] Here we see what was publicly expected of Gertrude in contrast to what Rilla's journal reveals about her friend's private grief. Through Rilla's journaling,

Montgomery gives Anne, Susan, and Gertrude a space to reveal their true grief, while highlighting the public pressure to mourn in private.

When Walter dies, however, Montgomery chooses the third-person perspective, giving her readers a compassionate distance from Rilla's pain. In response to the news that Walter has been killed in action at Courcelette, Rilla "crumpled up in a pitiful little heap of merciful unconsciousness" in her father's arms. "Nor did she waken to her pain for many hours." The profound emptiness that follows the loss of a loved one is keenly observed, as Anne lies "ill from grief and shock," and Rilla realizes that she must "go on with existence, since existence had still to be reckoned with." Yet, later when Rilla is in bed, she cries "the bitter rebellious tears of youth until at last tears were all wept out and the little patient ache that was to be in her heart until she died" takes a permanent hold."[19] This perspective indicates how devastating Walter's death is for Rilla; she cannot even write about it. She is hollow. Instead, she goes through her daily life as expected and then weeps until she is left with a dull emptiness. Through shifting perspectives and changes in narrative form, Montgomery provides insight into public and private notions of grief and pushes her characters to their emotional core.

Words also have the power to bring solace to a grieving heart. When Rilla receives the letter Walter wrote the evening before he died, she reads it in the same spot in Rainbow Valley where she sat with him at the beginning of the novel. The power of his words lifts her spirits: "Walter, of the glorious gift and the splendid ideals, *still lived*, with just the same gift and just the same ideals. *That* could not be destroyed – *these* could suffer no eclipse. The personality that had expressed itself in that last letter, written on the eve of Courcelette, could not be snuffed out by a German bullet. It must carry on, though the earthly link with things of earth were broken." Here, in the light, Rilla can find the strength to move beyond her grief for a moment and find solace. Similarly, after being worried that Kenneth might be drowned at sea, she receives his first love letter from the front and finds a moment of peace in his way of "expressing things in a few poignant, significant words which seemed to suggest far more than they uttered, and never grew stale or flat or foolish with ever so many scores of reading."[20] While the act of writing allows her to work through her emotions and show the conflicting ideologies between private and public forms of grieving, the act of reading can also be a balm for pain.

Montgomery further explores these themes in her final novel, *The Blythes Are Quoted*, in which writing and reading are an important part of the Blythe family's healing. As Benjamin Lefebvre outlines, it is impossible to know when Montgomery started writing this novel because the three typescripts that survive in the Guelph archives are undated.[21] Still, we can ascertain that Montgomery was writing *The Blythes* approximately twenty years after *Rilla of Ingleside* and after a number of years of personal struggle.

Both *Rilla of Ingleside* and *The Blythes Are Quoted* were written after or during times of war, but because *The Blythes* is so new to Montgomery scholarship, there is still much we do not know. Montgomery's journal stops in 1939 with only two more entries before her death in 1942. And while we have some clues in her correspondences with G.B. MacMillan and Ephraim Weber, much is clouded in Montgomery's emotional fog. Her last journal entry on the 23 March 1942 is of a woman deep in despair: "My mind is gone – everything in the world I lived for has gone – the world has gone mad. I shall be driven to end my life. Oh God, forgive me. Nobody dreams what my awful position is."[22] The final journal entries, her letters, and the note left by her bedside the day she died provide a complex story of the author's overall declining physical and mental health.[23]

As with Montgomery's time leading up to writing *Rilla of Ingleside*, a series of personal tragedies from 1937 onwards inspired the themes in *The Blythes Are Quoted*. The Second World War was looming, and the loss of life – both present and past – weighed heavily on her. The death on 18 January 1937 of a beloved cat, Lucky, who seemed to give her more companionship than the people in her life, deeply affected her. Her vigil by his deathbed speaks to her devotion to him, and even years later, she continued to miss him. Soon after Lucky's death, she found and recorded the "ten-year letters" that she and Frede had written in 1907 and 1917 and spoke of dreaming of Frede. Chester's graduation reminded her of not only how much Frede had loved him but also how much she continued to miss her friend: "the pain of her loss has grown bearable but it has never ceased – and never will."[24] As Kate Sutherland's discussion in chapter 12 on the Canadian Authors Association indicates, Montgomery was also suffering with the loss of her literary reputation. With Ewan's declining mental health and Chester's betrayals, her world was crumbling. In 23 February 1938 and 23 July 1939, she reports to MacMillan that she had severe sciatica pain and insomnia and had fallen, hurting her arm so badly that her ability to write was compromised, meaning that she did not have this emotional outlet on which she had depended so heavily throughout her life.[25]

It is difficult to know exactly the extent to which ill health affected Montgomery's creative process, but her journal entries clearly indicate that her usual strategies to channel adversity into creativity were failing her. In an entry dated 28 August 1937, she complains, "I have felt a little better today and was able to do a little spade work on my book. But I had no heart for it. All my old pleasure in my work is gone – I can't *lose myself* in it."[26] Writers experience creative cycles and often have "blocks," during which they are unable to find joy in their work and lose faith that they will ever find that spark again. That *The Blythes Are Quoted* did come to fruition shows that Montgomery found the creative will she needed to continue to write and that through craft she was still exploring the emotions of grief and loss.

The Blythes Are Quoted becomes a companion novel to *Rilla of Ingleside* because both have similar subjects, which echo many of the situations Montgomery was dealing with later in life. However, the idealism and hope that characterize the final pages of *Rilla* have disappeared. While words and writing are the elements that the Blythes use to work through their grief, there is little reprieve, reflecting Montgomery's despair at a world heading back to war, which may very well require the participation of her now-adult sons.

The Blythes Are Quoted features Anne and Gilbert and their family at Ingleside and is divided into sections of poetry, dialogue (or vignettes), and short stories. Part 1 is set before the First World War, and Part 2 begins after this war, concluding after the start of the Second World War. While there are changes in perspective within the short stories, Montgomery's experimentation with different styles has been of greatest interest to scholars. As Lefebvre notes, while Anne and Gilbert speak often in staged dialogue, they are rarely in the stories and instead are made "the objects of gossip."[27] Thus the poetry and prose illuminate how various family members behave in the privacy of their own home. Elizabeth Epperly explores why Montgomery grouped these pieces and why there is no easy closure for the Blythes.[28] These are compelling questions, particularly when we consider how Montgomery was trying to reframe her best-known characters into a post–World War I world – a world from which she felt alienated. After Frede's death, Montgomery writes how she is now living in two worlds, one before the war and one after: "I have lived one life in those seemingly far-off years before the war. Now there is another to be lived, in a totally new world where I think I shall never feel quite at home." When she starts writing *Rilla of Ingleside*, Montgomery specifically connects this idea to Anne, who "belongs to the green, untroubled pastures and still waters of the world before the war."[29]

The fragments of prose, poetry, and story are one way that Montgomery addressed this divide because then she had to stay within these broken spaces only for a short time. While many of these pieces were appropriated from previous works, especially the short stories, by reframing the poetry and dialogues within this context, Montgomery tells a different story, one that reflects the Blythes in a new light. In "Fancy's Fool," for example, Allardyce's perception of the Blythes, while a reflection of his own character and his annoyance that Anne has not responded to his flirtations, suggests how others see them. When Allardyce believes that his fiancée, Esme, will do whatever she is told, the narrator indicates that, even if Gilbert told him differently, Allardyce would not believe him because he "did not know Dr. Blythe or would not have had much opinion of his views if he had."[30] The Blythes may not be the main story, but Allardyce's petulance underlines his dismissal not only of Gilbert and the prominence in which the community holds him as a doctor and counsellor but also of the family's esteemed position generally.

Within each poem and dialogue, similar threads connect *Rilla of Ingleside* to *The Blythes Are Quoted*, such as Walter's poem "The Piper," which differentiates the call to arms in the First World War from that in the Second World War, showcasing how Montgomery's perspective has changed since the earlier novel, and with the expectation that her readers would know of Walter's fate. Montgomery, as narrator, indicates that readers have often asked her for the poem that Walter wrote in *Rilla* and explains that at that time "the poem had no real existence" but has been "written recently." Only with the threat of the Second World War looming does she find the "white hot center" she needed to write it. The narrator even says that the poem feels "more appropriate now than then."[31]

Like Rilla, who writes in her diary as a way to handle emotionally what is happening in the outside world, in *The Blythes Are Quoted*, Anne and Walter write poetry to channel their grief and anger, poetry that the family now turns to as a way to heal their suffering. As Susan muses, "As far as I can understand it, writing poetry is just putting into rhyme what everyone feels," thus giving Montgomery an opportunity through character to describe how important the act of writing is to the writer's emotional well-being. While there is a haunting tone in Anne's poetry in the first half of the novel, that tone turns morbid after Walter's death. In response to Anne's reciting her gothic poem "The Bride Dreams," Susan thinks that Anne never wrote so darkly before Walter's death. After Gilbert suggests that Anne's writing in "The Wind" is so strong because she is healing, Anne replies, "But the scar will always be there, Gilbert," confirming that, even though she is writing, the pain still lingers and the scar is a permanent reminder of the family's loss. When Anne finishes writing one of Walter's poems, "The Parting Soul," which he started before he "went away," the poem becomes her tribute to her son and brings mother and son together through words.[32] Anne is moved by her grief to write verse that might be darker than what she had written before because it speaks to her suffering, which may be eased but never completely vanquished.

Walter's natural inclination to use words to understand his world echoes that of his mother and younger sister. The poem "The Aftermath" was written on the battlefield, perhaps on the same night he wrote his letter to Rilla, and the tone is one of regret, combined with the boldness and bloodthirstiness of battle, the effectiveness of propaganda, and the belief that what the soldiers were doing meant something. It is the only poem that Anne reads that was written while Walter was at war. As opposed to Walter's "I Want," written before the war, which describes the virtues of country life, the darkness in "The Aftermath" addresses Walter's personal shift.[33] The soldier wishes to forget the person he killed, wishes to forget the blood of the battlefield, even wishes to forget his own cowardly nature, but he cannot, reminding the Blythes that Walter was once perceived as a coward and even thought of himself as one for not fighting.[34] Walter's poetry shapes the narrative and emotional arc of *The Blythes Are Quoted* and raises difficult questions concerning patriotism and self-sacrifice.

For the Blythes, hearing and reading poetry allow them to work through their grief and reconnect with the dead. While Walter destroyed most of his poems before leaving, he bequeathed a few to his mother. Now in the evenings, Anne reads Walter's and her own poetry partly to keep "his memory keenly alive in the hearts of his brothers and sisters and partly to please Susan, who now treasured every scrap of Walter's scribblings," signifying that words – whether written, read, or recited – carry the energy of the person who penned them and have the power to heal, even if simply during the experience of connection they provide. When Jem leans over and whispers to his wife that he wonders if reading Walter's poems is good for Anne, Faith says, "Yes, it is. It helps an old ache. Do you think if you hadn't come back from that German prison I wouldn't have cherished and reread every letter you ever wrote me?"[35] Her answer shows how important Jem's words were for her while he was missing and how, although not an absolute cure, words do help Anne.

As the poetry becomes multi-layered in meaning between the life before Walter's death and the grief that follows, the dialogue accompanying each poem contributes to the melancholy and sombre tone. In Part 1, Anne's poem "Sea Song" may be discussing the lure of the sea and was originally inspired by *Captain Jim's Lifebook*, but there is also the idea of a very different kind of call – the call to war. The lines "Sing to me / Of the terror and lure of the sea, / Of the beautiful creatures it clasped to death ... / Wondrous-eyed children, women fair" speak of this dangerous lure. As the conversation following the poem "Grief" indicates, the meaning of the poem shifts after Walter's death. The poem personalizes "Grief" as a faithful companion who accompanies the narrator wherever s/he goes, replacing "Joy," also capitalized as if it were a person, possibly again reminding readers of Anne's loss of baby Joyce:

> Music lost its tender grace
> When I looked on her grim face,
> Flowers no more were sweet for me,
> Sunshine lost its witchery,
> Laughter hid itself in fear
> Of that Presence dour and drear,
> Little dreams in pale dismay
> Made all haste to steal away.

In the poem's last line, although Grief leaves, there is still an ache, which works in tandem with the dialogue that follows. Anne discounts the last line, saying that she had written the poem when Matthew died but has since learned that "some griefs are more faithful," to which Una Meredith responds, "Ah, indeed yes."[36]

In this final work, Montgomery explores how writing and reading poetry can be a form of therapy. If, as Kominars argues, the act of journal writing is a form of therapy, it seems that Montgomery certainly understood the power that it had in her own life. *Rilla of Ingleside* and *The Blythes Are Quoted* were written after a number of years of intense emotional, physical, and psychological circumstances that shook Montgomery's foundation, forcing her to change her worldview. Written twenty years apart, these novels show a writer who knew that the only way to her story's truth was by writing through her own experience, however painful it might be. Anne's story ends not with a blissful dream but with more questions. Epperly writes, "Montgomery the artist triumphs in shaping this final book: there is no easy closure for Anne's story, and we care how and why this is so."[37] What is it about some losses – such as the death of Frede – that they can never be totally forgotten and the pain completely relieved? Why do writing and reading fail Montgomery in the end? These are questions that writers throughout this volume come back to and address from various angles.

Although healing is about coming to terms with loss, there is always something more to discover. Part of the joy of writing from the perspective of Dickinson's "soul at white heat" is the journey to Butler's "white-hot center" and the discovery of "the flash" (to use Emily Byrd Starr's term) found there. Montgomery's grief narratives are the creative manifestations of a writer who was compelled to channel her emotions into her fiction – even if that meant, as in *The Blythes Are Quoted*, a revisiting and revising of older texts, laden with memories. Both these novels speak to lost ideals, lost hope, and a family coping with loss, experiences of which Montgomery had intimate knowledge. Although she intuitively channelled her anxiety and pain through her characters, finding the heart of her fictional stories, this became more difficult towards the end of her life, which her later fiction reflects. Through writing fiction, Montgomery found a way back to her heart and to her own story, whatever form that story might take.

Interlude

L.M.M.

KATHERINE CAMERON

Take down Volume II, the last years when she was happy. The tiny woman in the pince-nez, the veiled black hat, black gloves, and a smartly tailored suit stares out at the reader. Her thoughts, too, were veiled: from her husband, her congregation, her readers, who expected only sunshine from their favourite writer. Only in her journals could she *let off steam*, as if she were a volcano about to erupt, words flowing from her pen like molten tears.

She wished for *an hour out of the past*, a time when she was happy but didn't know it. She wished to go back to Park Corner, when she was still young and hopeful: before her father died, her husband fell into madness, Frede died, and the world changed.

She wrote about that hour out of the past, turning back to a time when the world seemed safe, before motor cars, world wars, madness, death. She gave her readers marriage in the final chapter, the happy-ever-after ending.

She wrote about marriage failures, war, despair, madness, death. The anger we carry in our bones because life cheats us, steals what we hold most dear, gives us back our dreams with tarnished corners. The secrets we never reveal.

"L.M.M." appears in Kat Cameron's *Strange Labyrinth* (Fernie, BC: Oolichan Books, 2014).

A Sense of Place: Reading and Writing

8

Old Years and Old Books: Montgomery's Ontario Reading and Self-Fashioning

EMILY WOSTER

Between 1911 and 1942, L.M. Montgomery's journals allude to, discuss, quote, or generally reference books, literature, and reading more than three hundred times. These references clearly exhibit Montgomery's attachment to reading and allusion, but her continued reliance on literature as an autobiographical tool suggests that she is a life writer who is intensely concerned with literary expression and the evocative use of text-within-text. During these years in Ontario, Montgomery also expands and redefines her autobiographical output by recopying her early journals into uniform ledgers, constructing a more formal autobiography in *The Alpine Path* (1917), and then typing her ledger journals in preparation for their eventual publication.[1] Her assertion that the journals "should have a certain literary value" to her descendants and her "literary heirs"[2] – which the epilogue to this volume, Kate Macdonald Butler's "Dear Grandmother Maud on the Road to Heaven," addresses – and the care with which she copies and types them suggest that she is aware of the journals' significance to future readers. The sheer volume of her autobiographical efforts during this period is remarkable given her personal struggles and simultaneous literary production. Her Ontario years offer a particularly rich site for an analysis as her reading and life-writing projects shift and change with the transitions and accommodations prompted by life events. Her ability to balance professional writing and life writing while constantly making time to read and record her responses indicates that these textual occupations are not only linked but also foundational to her identity and the subsequent construction of her autobiographical self in the journals. Her records of reading in the Ontario journals provide a suggestive map of the ways in which her encounters with text are spun into self-creation. Separate from and enfolded in her journals, these encounters can be read as an autobiographical act, one facet of her complex, layered self-definition.

Montgomery's earlier journals also contain evidence of her reading self; her life writing in Prince Edward Island is filled with allusions to her reading habits. In Ontario, however, the entire body of her textual work undergoes significant changes, parallel to those in her life overall. Marriage, children, new professional and personal responsibilities, and a change in geography all left their mark in Montgomery's journal and on her reading life within it. The first entry in the *Selected Journals* after her move to Ontario is also the first significant "retrospective" journal entry, marking a major shift in her journaling process. On 28 January 1912, she ends a nine-month break in her journaling to describe the events surrounding the death of her Grandmother Macneill, her wedding and honeymoon, and her move to Leaskdale: "I was so busy I could not keep this journal up in any regular fashion ... But occasionally through the spring, when I had a little spare time, or when the pain demanded some outward expression, I wrote some stray entries in a notebook."[3] These "stray entries" occupy nearly thirty pages of the published journal and are illustrated with photographs of her trousseau and her honeymoon tour. These entries and photographs imply that her journal and her journaling have altered in direct response to her life's circumstances.

The frequent integration of allusions and literary references in this section, however, shows that some of her journal processes have not changed: she uses two of Byron's lines from *Don Juan* to describe her longing for Prince Edward Island, "that far shore / Beloved and deplored." The section on her honeymoon reinforces her attachment to the book world in its many entries on literary sites in Scotland and England. As the years pass, she continues to rely on allusion and references to her reading to record the successes and tragedies of her life, as well as the quotidian and the commonplace. Throughout the journals, she can, for example, with biting clarity, use literature to describe a visitor as "'Mrs Nickleby' in the flesh." When she finally writes of her cousin Frederica Campbell's death in 1919, she quotes *Macbeth*, using a particular line to help her explain and cope with this devastating experience: "*She died*. And I live to write it! Frede is *dead*. 'After life's fitful fever she sleeps well.' But *I* wake and must face the dreary years without her."[4] In order to describe these people and events fully, Montgomery relies on allusion and literary memory. Perhaps this is not surprising given that the culture of reading to which she belonged both sanctioned and permitted her to read widely and voraciously, and she was herself an author attentive to language and expression. However, as Kate Flint points out in *The Woman Reader, 1837–1914*, "records of reading after marriage are scarce in autobiographies" of this period, as the authors' duties presumably shifted to the running of a household, the raising of children, and other domestic responsibilities.[5]

If, as Flint claims, reading is "an assertion and organization of private space,"[6] then Montgomery took this organizing principle seriously enough to maintain her reading/allusive habits and preserve them in her journal, itself a theoretically private space for expression and reflection. The nature of this reading-writing relationship then exposes the text-based layers of Montgomery's identity and self-construction. Mary Kelley, studying women readers from 1500 to 1800, explains that many readers used reading to produce "pluralities of meanings" of and for themselves; readers then "relied on those meanings as they fashioned subjectivities as autonomous and communicative thinking women."[7] Reading is thus part of the autobiographical process, serving as inspiration for the journaling and reflection that define a diarist's life. Flint supports this notion of reading as a means of identity construction in that "autobiography ... involves self-fashioning through selectivity and arrangement" that is influenced by reading itself.[8] Although she does not mention specific titles in the entry, in December 1919, Montgomery neatly illustrates this principle: "But my givings-up never last very long. When I get rested and cheered up by a bit of a dip into some interesting book – or even by a dose of confession in this, my diary – I rise up again and resolve to endure to the end. This little outburst here has quite refreshed me."[9] On one hand, she is journaling and recording a typical expression of her current feelings; on the other, she is fusing the reflective work of journaling with the meaning-making of reading. Montgomery is a thoughtful reader-writer whose "organization of private space" is indicative of her relationship with text.

Her reading record, moreover, is remarkable not only for its thoroughness or for its powerful presence in her journals but also for the way in which both her Ontario reading and journaling are informed by her attentiveness to the future value of her self-constructions. When, in 1919, she writes that she has been copying her collection of "blank books" into uniform ledgers and illustrating them with photographs,[10] she implies that the journal has its own textual and personal importance. As Lynn Z. Bloom emphasizes, many life writers are attuned to questions of audience despite the supposed privacy of the journal space. Bloom maintains that "it is the audience hovering at the edge of the page that for the sophisticated diarist facilitates the work's ultimate focus, providing the impetus either for the initial writing or for transforming what might have been casual, fragmented jottings into a more carefully crafted, contextually coherent work."[11] When Montgomery edits her journals and considers that they "should have a certain literary value" for others, she indicates that a future audience will not only read them but value their contents.[12] As a result, this project requires her to reread all of her earlier autobiographical selves while simultaneously keeping up with her contemporary journaling and maintaining her current reading/writing regimens.

Subsequently, she uses her past journals as she does literary texts: as a reason for journaling, a way to describe her current feelings, and a way to reflect on her life and work. She admits that "when I am copying these old journals I feel as if I had gone back into the past and were living again the events and emotions of which I write. It is very delightful and a little sad."[13] This short reflection functions much the same way as her allusions to literature. Her old journals provide the impetus for the current entry just as any text she has read inspires her autobiographical writing. What defines her Ontario reading and self-fashioning is the intersection of her new and old reading, reading that calls for both literary and self-study. By analyzing the recursivity of Montgomery's reading-writing work in her journal, we can read this text as a site of dialogue as well as autobiographical narrative. Both reading and autobiography are largely concerned with communication and interaction (often with oneself); in combining the two acts, Montgomery reveals the textually preoccupied part of herself that is perhaps hidden in other parts of her journal. Her Ontario journaling/reading is thus shaped by her past and present writing/reading projects, compelling her to layer self and text. In chapter 3, Margaret Steffler observes a similar layering of reading/writing selves in Montgomery's Leaskdale journals and religious thought. Layering, and the need to "write out and write over"[14] her experiences, permeates and defines her journals. This reading-inspired layering goes through three distinct phases as Montgomery reads both books and herself in Ontario.

The first period of this autobiographical and literary work occurs between 1911 and 1918, before Montgomery began the task of rereading and copying her journals. In these early years in Leaskdale, she reminisces about Prince Edward Island, her childhood and adolescence, revelling in the nostalgia of rereading favourite texts. Reading an "old paper on 'Kipling's verse'" to the Guild in Leaskdale, a paper she first gave to the Cavendish Literary Society, makes her "homesick": "My soul ached when I lay awake in the darkness afterwards ... [thinking] over the old days."[15] Rereading Friedrich de la Motte Fouqué's *Undine* prompts a recollection of a childhood dream: in a curious blend of text and memory, Montgomery remembers dreaming "as vividly as if it were yesterday" about a tunnel through an "Enchanted Forest" with a hero barred from her path by a "hideous head and face." In December 1914, she rereads Mrs Felicia Hemans's poems, a "source of great pleasure" in her childhood. She admits that "I love them yet, partly for their own sake, partly because of the old associations connected with them." On one hand, this text is an artifact from Montgomery's former life and from her youth; on the other, it is a contemporary inspiration for her journaling and reminiscing. "I think Mrs Hemans has been hardly dealt with by our hurrying, feverish, get-rich-quick age," she writes. "Surely sweetness and charm of sentiment have their place in literature."[16] This comment is as much a statement about Montgomery's feelings for her old life as it is about her opinions of the changes in literary movements. She suggests that her childhood reading and her childhood home still preoccupy her present. The preoccupation is, in essence, channelled through her literary activities. Certainly, most readers experience a similar connection between past reading and present selves, but for Montgomery the power of these moments is particularly poignant given the significant changes in her life and her tendency to journal about them.

In August 1916, Montgomery purchased for her sons four volumes of the children's magazine *Wide Awake*, which she had read occasionally in her Cavendish days. She writes, "It is impossible to tell how much I have enjoyed re-reading them and what delight they gave me – a strange, eerie pleasure as of a journey back into the past. It was not only that their contents had still a literary relish even for my mature taste; but as I read I seemed to be back again in the surroundings of the days in which I read them first. I was back in the old home in Cavendish. Grandfather and grandmother, and Dave and Well were there ... I went again to the white washed school on the crest of the hill; the stars were in their right places in the heavens ... a world utterly passed away was my universe once more. I felt curiously homesick and strange, every time I shut the book and came back to this one."[17] The pages of *Wide Awake* serve as a conduit into her own past and to her past self, with the power to elicit homesickness and the feeling of having been somewhere else. Her journaling about this feeling serves as yet another layer of text over this already intertextual autobiographical moment. Later that year, she describes the way the First World War widens the gulf between her past (reading) self and the present: "I re-read Kipling's 'Kim' tonight ... And yet how strangely far away everything written before the war seems now. I felt as if I were perusing some classic as ancient as the Iliad."[18] The implication that there is "homesickness," distance or text-inspired time travel inherent in the act of rereading – an act that then leads to new journaling activities – exposes the layered nature of her first period of Ontario reading.

After marriage and the births of her children, Montgomery's reading seems to turn backwards, and thus so does her journaling. Patricia Meyer Spacks argues that, for many women writers, marriage serves as an "implied relative loss of self."[19] Flint expands this statement in differentiating the more formal, and traditionally male, autobiography from women's private diaries. This loss of self is then accentuated in "those autobiographies which present childhood and adolescence by way of an act of reminiscence, and which attempt to assert or create the permanence and significance of some of the most private and transitory moments which have gone into the formation of their subjects' sense of self."[20] Montgomery's nostalgic turn reveals that her early reading was so deeply influential as to inspire entries in her journal decades later. Significantly, it is reading that inspires this nostalgia. She is devoted to text as a means of remembering and recording experience.

In a chapter titled "Woman's Story and the Engenderings of Self-Representation," Sidonie Smith contends that "autobiography simultaneously involves a realization that the adventure is informed continually by shifting considerations of the present moment." A life writer may have to "rely on a trace of something from the past, a memory" that is itself a story. "As a result, autobiography becomes both the process and the product of assigning meaning to a series of experiences ... by means of emphasis, juxtaposition, omission."[21] Montgomery's use of published stories (whether novels, poetry, or otherwise) to emphasize, juxtapose, and even mask her life story gives multiple layers of auto-biographical/textual meaning to these recollective reading experiences. Much of her reading allows her to (re)live and write in a space of near-constant homesickness and longing, even while there is plenty of "new" reading and casual allusion in the journal. As Natalie Forest points out in the next chapter, Montgomery's fiction also undergoes a similarly gradual shift in focus as she engages with various manifestations of gothic and romantic aesthetics. Her records of that reading allow her to return to old places and times and, most remarkably, prolong the act of reading itself. In referencing works that she read years before, she strives to characterize herself and the changes she has undergone. Rereading the poems of Mrs Hemans in 1914, she admits "I love them yet," despite how she has changed. Kipling's *Kim*, which she "cared little for" when she first read it, she now finds "charming."[22] She uses these examples better to paint a picture of herself as an individual in her own journal. She is thus an individual who *used* to read, just as much as one who *re*reads. The journal as a space for her reading record allows her to prolong her reminiscing. When she rereads Bulwer-Lytton's *Zanoni* in 1924, she claims that "I seemed to open a magic door and step at once into a world of enchantment."[23] In her extended discussion of the book's effect on her childhood when she used to play at living out different parts of the book – another result of a bout of reading – Montgomery's past and present selves converge.

Between 1919 and 1930, her nostalgia eventually gives way to more direct self-confrontation and self-construction through reading. She still spends time rereading favourite texts and responding to them, but she more consciously documents her present rather than past through the textual occupations of the moment. By 1921, she has finished copying her old journals, effectively "catching up" with her autobiographical self, perhaps influencing her active presence in the journals themselves and the connection to reading and literature that they record. In an eerie parallel to the nostalgic rereading she did previously, she writes, "Last night I copied a lot of my old diary. It is like living over the past again and I always come back to the present with a little sense of unreality. Some of those old entries hurt me too." She goes on to record some details from the most recently copied entry, and she fills in the changes from that particular past moment to the one in which she writes. This time, her reading-inspired journaling is a reading of herself, her journal self, whom she faces just as she once faced the child-Montgomery. When she finishes recopying the Cavendish years of her journals, she reports that she has "come to 'modern history'" in her life: "I have lived over those old years in this writing them over – relived them more vividly and intensely than I have ever done in reading them. I am a little sorry that I have finished with them."[24] Earlier, it was novels and a children's magazine that brought her past rushing back; now it is a textual encounter with her previous (and previously constructed) self.

This middle period of Montgomery's Ontario reading and journaling is thus shaped by her rereading of her past autobiographical work. In *Mapping Our Selves: Canadian Women's Autobiography in English*, Helen Buss discusses what she calls "serial autobiography," suggesting that it "seems to be a useful mode by which women overcome limitations in their identity patterns and facilitate their self growth."[25] Buss refers to women who write more than one autobiography or who write multiple volumes of autobiographical work over time, but Montgomery's multiple revisions of her journals seem to denote the same impulse. She had already written *The Alpine Path*, and here she returns to "rewriting" her earlier journals. She is continually concerned with her autobiographical constructions, as she confronts and rewrites them frequently. This rewriting, predicated on both reading and writing her life, then influences other textual choices within it. If her earlier reading indicates her nostalgia for the pleasure of past reading, this middle period seems to be about confronting and (re)reading her journal voice, revealing a new "identity pattern" in the journal that is informed as much by literature and text as it is by her own past.

At the same time, many of her discussions of literature seem to take a more straightforward turn as she lets go of her intense nostalgia for Cavendish in favour of a more general literary wistfulness. She wonders about May Sinclair's *The Romantic* (1920), comparing it to older works: "It is hard to see just why anybody should have written it or wanted to write it – unless it is to show the difference – the unfathomable gulf – between the heroines of the Victorian age and the 'heroines' of today." About Walter Scott's *The Betrothed* (1825), she declares, "It is one of his poorest novels. But I was struck by his immeasurable superiority to the novel-writers of today – even those who are acclaimed as the strongest and most virile." And she compares another reread book to the novels of the present: "Today I wrote a poem, canned six jars of tomatoes, and re-read *Trilby*. One never hears *Trilby* mentioned now. It made the most tremendous sensation twenty years ago … Yet beside some of the heroines of today's novels *Trilby* was chaste as ice and pure as snow."[26] Rather than recalling all the previous selves that read these texts, Montgomery's new reading inspires her to discuss a larger picture of her literary tastes. In essence, these textual exercises depict a Montgomery who is no longer layering text in the same personal way as she did upon her arrival in Ontario; she is focusing more broadly on literature as a whole rather than on her specific memories of it.

This new autobiographical focus on her present connection with books and literature is also evident in her confession that books serve as important companions. While she makes such a declaration in regards to her childhood in Cavendish, where books were a "faithful old key to the gates of fairyland,"[27] books now serve as important tools for communication and intellectual companionship. In 1922 she writes, "Today my reading Tennyson's life filled me with a sort of envy of that intercourse with congenial souls that was always his – going and coming. That is so wholly lacking in my life. But if Ewan only keeps well I will be content – I will not complain of what is lacking. After all, books are wonderful companions."[28] Books have become companions that can serve as interlocutors in her journal and connect her to worlds and lives beyond Ontario in addition to serving as imaginative escape. While she cannot have the fulfilment that Tennyson's companions provided him, she can use the space of her journal to respond to his texts (themselves her companions), speak to his ideas, and, in essence, construct herself as a woman within a greater intellectual community than her circles in Leaskdale, Norval, and even Toronto provide. This constant communication with and through her reading has been preserved in other ways as well.

The 180 books from Montgomery's personal library, housed at the Archival and Special Collections at the University of Guelph, reveal fascinating additional evidence of her reading habits. Many of them are full of markings, underlines, punctuation marks and arrows, relevant (and sometimes irrelevant) clippings pasted inside their covers or inserted into the book, as Lesley Clement discusses in chapter 13 regarding Montgomery's copy of G.B. Shaw's *Saint Joan*. Some books contain greeting cards and notes sent to her over the years. Nearly all the books are inscribed with her signature (some with her maiden name only) and the date of their purchase or receipt. The clippings alone, like her scrapbooks, could be mined for even more of her reading tendencies, but it is the annotations and marginalia that are particularly significant here.[29] In writing *on* and *in* these texts (effectively speaking *to* the texts themselves), Montgomery attempts to communicate with her reading and her reading self. Her copy of H.G. Wells's *The Outline of History* (1919), received in 1922, is filled with annotations. In the chapter on "The Beginnings of Christianity," Wells recounts the death of Jesus and records his last words: "My God! My God! Why hast thou forsaken me?" In the margin, Montgomery has written, "The most tragic utterance of all history."[30] Her volumes of poetry are filled with small underlines and arrows setting off lines and stanzas. Books she owned or received during the Cavendish period tend to be marked with pen and contain fewer comments than the books from the Leaskdale years and after, when she seems to have read with a pencil in hand and was more inclined to leave notes in order to speak to what she was reading. This interactive approach to reading, especially if cross-referenced with thoughts in the journals, suffuses her life writing with literary and autobiographical meaning.

One of the most evocative examples of this autobiographical meaning, of the new Montgomery of the journal who uses texts to inspire present self-creation, occurs after she reads *An Autobiography* (1920) by Margot Asquith, countess of Oxford and Asquith. After reading another woman's autobiography, Montgomery very literally constructs herself in her journal. She begins by cataloguing her own appearance in great detail and then shifts focus to explore what she sees in her own general temperament. She ends with a catalogue of her faults and graces: "I will begin with myself physically. I am of medium height – about five feet five inches, but somehow usually impress people as being small – probably because I am delicate featured." She describes her hands, her shoe size, and her "pretty, well-turned delicately made wrists." She talks about her hair and her complexion, all the features of her face, and even comments that her "enemies accuse [her] of being 'fond of dress.'" She describes her temperament and her humour, her tendency to "worry too much over certain things," and her many contradictory opinions about when to speak and when to listen, when change is good and when conventions are needed. She quotes an Emily Brontë poem – "I'll walk where my nature would be leading: / It vexes me to choose another guide" – before describing more details of her feelings.[31] In this entry, she writes a character sketch of herself, an oddly specific creation that exists only in her journal.[32] Her self-reconstruction on the page, inspired by reading another autobiographical text, is a wholly different kind of textual layering than the nostalgic rereading she relied on earlier. Her intellectual work and compulsion to read have, in her middle age, inspired her to create a franker portrait of her journal self. This period reveals a new, literature-inspired, autobiographically confident Montgomery who, although she continues to reread and reminisce, is compelled to assert her journal identity after finishing copying the old one. The reading of her youth is still powerfully present and meaningful to her, but she now devotes time to interacting with texts and meeting the autobiographical "I" she has created in Ontario.

The final period of Montgomery's Ontario reading and journaling, from 1926 to 1942, is marked by her awareness of the passing of time and the ways in which her own age serves as a barrier to her former selves. Even her reading reflects her attempts to close off her previous connections with text. Flint suggests that autobiographers who include reading in their work betray their "literary self-awareness."[33] If this is true, then the final period of Montgomery's reading is concerned with coming to terms with her life and her life of reading, with remembering her past and her vibrant relationship with literature, while fostering a new interaction with it. She still spends time rereading, taking perhaps more time with old books than with new ones, but she records a different sort of memory and connection to them. When she picks up *Undine* again in 1927, she asks, "What is there in books like this that never grows old or stale? Yet it is the simplest tale. And a fairy tale at that, which the modern world sneers at. But we all need some kind of fairy tale else we cannot live. What a strange belief that old persistent belief in the land of faery was. It is found everywhere in some guise and lasted for thousands of years – nay, lasts yet in some lands. Verily, there are moments when I cannot believe that it had no foundation whatever."[34] Her concern with fairyland and the literary/folkloric worlds it suggests seems to have broadened from a connection to the book to a more general sadness that the world can no longer support the romantic and imaginative world of *Undine* and tales like it. She also makes this assertion in *The Alpine Path*. As William Thompson argues in chapter 6, Montgomery "casts [her] childhood [and her former connection to 'Fairyland'] into a particular light, unself-conscious and coloured by imaginative bliss."[35] Her continued emphasis on fairyland/tales as part of her/the past suggests that she can no longer sustain the sort of autobiographical and literary energy of the previous years. She is not inspired to write a lengthy memory of her first reading of *Undine*, nor an angry reflection on the present state of fairies; instead, she settles for a sort of literary resignation.

This late period of reading reflects a different kind of homesickness from her previous uses of the term. In 1929 she declares: "I have been re-reading *The Sentimental Garden*. The pictures in it drive me wild with envy – and *homesickness*. Homesickness for an old dream that will never be fulfilled. For *that* is the garden I have always wanted and can never have."[36] Literary homesickness is no longer a pining for her youthful days of reading or of Cavendish; it is not even for a lost literary age but for a time in which there was room for her dreams. Again, there is a sense that Montgomery has resigned herself to the failed potential of the new world in which she lives, a resignation that takes its toll on her psyche, as chapter 13 in this collection discusses more fully. When she rereads Washington Irving's *Alhambra* in 1936, she again resigns herself to a loss. "An old book but still full of charm," she writes. "It used to be one of my dreams, to see the Alhambra. It will never be fulfilled – but I can still dream of it."[37] She can still imagine the place, her opinion of it entirely informed by her continued rereading of Irving's text, but in her journal she admits that the time for some of her dreams might just be past.

This later Montgomery, still writing about and inspired by text, is now prepared to accept the possibility that fairyland is not reachable, even in her beloved books. In 1937, she copies out two lines of one of Nathaniel Benson's poems: "Life isn't worth the lovely songs / The lying poets sing about it." She observes, "Up to four years ago, in spite of everything, I would not have agreed with that. In youth 'When I saw immortal visions / And knew a god's delight' I would have hooted at it," but "now I have no hope and Benson is right. There are some things no one can bear – and that no one should have to bear."[38] Although all these examples read as bitter and reflective, they also suggest the assurance of someone who has a very different awareness of herself, her identity, and even her relationship with books and reading from her earlier self. These experiences with literature are not the reminiscent travels of someone who has just left home, nor are they only the studied responses of a lifelong reader. The journal entries now paint a particular portrait of a woman whose life, including her reading life, has changed drastically.

The final journal entry to include a discussion of books and reading, from 17 June 1939, recounts yet another bout of rereading. "I have been re-reading an old book tonight, *The House with the Green Shutters* [1901]. Such a sad book – such a bitter book ... But it is very powerful and everything is etched bitingly – and it made me feel as dreary as itself." She says that it "was written in the reaction to the *Kailyard School*. But the people in the *Bonnie Brier Bush* are nearer to real people as I have found them, after all for every 'Mrs Thompson' there are a dozen decent loyal souls. I *know* that. Only tonight I cannot feel it. I am putting here an old card Laura once sent me on an olden Christmas. I want to preserve it. I want to keep every bit of her I can. I came across it today in the *Green Shutters* where I had put it as a bookmark. It does not belong *there*."[39] In removing an old friend's card from the book – the card being physical evidence that she once thought it belonged inside *Green Shutters* – Montgomery confronts a past self. In reassessing the text and spending time with her journal to record her present feelings, she confronts her present self. While the card does not belong in the book *now*, it is an artifact of Montgomery's previous engagement with it. That she records this act while discussing the book in her journal reveals yet again the layers of memory and text and self present in her journal space. Here, she bridges some of the connections between her "real" self, the narrating "I" of her present journals, and the narrated "I" of whom she speaks.[40] Later-life reading uncovers Montgomery's new methods for incorporating text and identity.

Montgomery's Ontario reading is thus an arc that both reflects and reveals other aspects of her life and its changes – an arc not unlike the aesthetic shift in Montgomery's fiction addressed by Natalie Forest in the next chapter. Montgomery is a product of many textual and literary influences. As a result, her autobiographical tasks inspire their own bouts of reading and rereading, reflection and creation. Her struggles and successes lead to extended engagements with text, making her journal, with all its varied contents, even more central to her writing and sense of self. Her use of reading as a means of nostalgic escape and self-reflection is exemplified in her pronouncement that "an old book has something for me which no new book can ever have – for at every reading the memories and atmosphere of other readings come back and I am reading old years as well as an old book."[41] She desires to (re)read the "old years" along with her books. Her constant cycling through and recycling of texts and references, her rereading of her own journal, and her need to reread herself and her books make her journal an intricately textured site for a blending of text and memory. If she rereads her past in her books, she continues the cycle and prolongs the experience by writing about it in her various modes of autobiography. She interfiles text and life and writing in an individual and meaningful way. That one of Montgomery's most powerful autobiographical tools is *textual*, not just *experiential* or cultural or historical, is a significant statement about her reading and autobiographical lives and how she records and presents them.

Margaret E. Turner contends that "we read [Montgomery] as she reads herself. Her journalizing, as she called it, is enabled, allowed, and caused by her repeated re-reading of her earlier records: her simultaneous roles of writer and reader are layered upon each other and are, perhaps, ultimately indistinguishable."[42] Turner refers to Montgomery's tendency to write about rereading her old journals, but the idea that she is an expert at reading and layering different texts over one another is apt here. Reading is often understood as a way for women to enter discourse communities beyond their reach, and this is certainly true of Montgomery's reading. However, her rereading, nostalgia, and simultaneous rereading of her own autobiographical work imply that she is also entering into discourse with past selves. As she confronts her autobiographical constructions and their textual lives, her reading and life-writing identities shift between 1911 and 1942. Her "reading autobiography" in the Ontario years is a unique, text-based performance of self that parallels, outlines, and reflects her layering of auto-, bio-, and -graphy: self, life, and writing.

9

(Re)Locating Montgomery: Prince Edward Island Romance to Southern Ontario Gothic

NATALIE FOREST

On 31 January 1920, in Leaskdale, Ontario, L.M. Montgomery writes in her journal that she is having a "damnable day." With "bitter cold – 20 below zero weather – and a sharp east wind blowing; a grey wintery world; chilly house," Montgomery suffers from a headache that "prevent[s] her from indulging in [her] usual solace of imaginary adventures." Incapable of evoking her usual "power" that allows her to "escape from 'intolerable reality,'" she decides to work out philosophical questions in fictional conversations with such fore-writers as John Ruskin and Charlotte Brontë. "Taste ... is the *only* morality," Montgomery's Ruskin declares. "The first and last and closest trial question to any living creature is 'What do you like?' Tell me what you *like* ... and I'll tell you what you *are*."

Following her list of likes, which are predominantly domestic in nature, Montgomery challenges her imaginary Ruskin to "tell me what I am." Her words here are enigmatic. Statements such as "I like to be kissed by the right kind of a man" suggest a challenge to the principles that a restrictive domestic environment imposes, but others, such as "I like housecleaning – I *do*!" carry an unapologetic tone for enjoying her domestic role. Her musings align her with the domestic romance genre with which she has been associated, most prominently, through the series of *Anne* novels, but her ironic tone and the "numbing greyness and monotonous discomfort" that instigate her philosophical search suggest her sense of a gothic presence in her real rural Leaskdale environment.[1] Her need to find herself and her aesthetic interest in nature are indicative of her being influenced by Romanticism, but the "discomfort" that pushes her to examine her individuality tilts her Romantic notions towards what Timothy Findley would later call "Southern Ontario Gothic."[2]

"Gothic" is a transient literary term that habitually attaches itself to other genres – Romanticism, Victorianism, horror, erotica, science fiction – as its qualities evolve into what is contemporarily considered "disturbing." In *Gothic*, Fred Botting explains that in the nineteenth century, the "clichéd" eighteenth-century gothic conventions of "castles, villains and ghosts ... continued more as signs of internal states and concepts than of external threats ... [and] became part of an internalised world of guilt, anxiety, despair, a world of individual transgression interrogating the uncertain bounds of imaginative freedom and human knowledge."[3] Montgomery utilizes elements of both the eighteenth- and nineteenth-century gothic in several of her works, adjusting their inclusion according to her aesthetic intents. When she moved to Leaskdale in 1911, her style was identified with romantic, pastoral environments. Elizabeth Epperly addresses the difficulty in discussing "romance" and Montgomery, seeing her style as a combination of both the popular "romantic" and the literary eighteenth- and nineteenth-century "Romantic," what she refers to as Montgomery's "romanticized realism."[4] In "(Re)Producing Canadian Literature," Holly Pike maintains that "in the 1920s debate over the relative merits of modernist and realist-idealist fiction ... Montgomery comes down firmly against modernism, and sets out her canons of poetry and fiction in the Emily books," including her choice of Romantic poets. Pike further notes that Montgomery rejected the realism being produced by her contemporaries (citing her 1928 journal entry on latrines and Morley Callaghan) because she had her own brand of what she considered realism.[5] Epperly, Pike, and others (such as Lorna Drew, Faye Hammill, Kate Lawson, and Kathleen Ann Miller)[6] all explore the gothic Victorian romance rhetoric of the patriarchal home, adventurous heroines, and anti-heroes in Montgomery's writings. The content of *Emily of New Moon* and the contemporary journal entries suggest, however, that Montgomery's domestic role at Leaskdale encouraged a psychologically based, gothic strain in her romantic/Romantic style of realism – a gothic strain that developed independently of Romantic or Victorian traditions.

Montgomery also argues for the "real" in *Emily of New Moon* (1923), a novel that she defines in the preparatory stages as "a psychological study of one human being's life ... [a] 'real' novel."[7] Benjamin Lefebvre identifies Montgomery's change towards this "real" as her "late style," a style that Margaret Doody characterizes as her dark side.[8] Montgomery's change in style is often attributed to the world wars, legal battles, and her cousin Frede's death. These multiple events doubtless affected her work significantly, as other chapters in this collection examine, but my focus is on the effects that Montgomery's domestic and rural environment in Leaskdale had on her writing. In the previous chapter, Emily Woster suggests that Montgomery's reading habits and process of rerecording her journals while in Ontario also affected her style; she argues, "The nature of this reading-writing relationship then exposes the text-based layers of Montgomery's identity and self-construction."[9] This action of rewriting her journals is a form of revisiting her past styles and constructions of herself.

Montgomery chronicled her journeys back and forth from Ontario to Prince Edward Island in her journals, and each time her style and perspective began to acquire a new brand of gothic – Ontario gothic – in which the explorations of feelings align with Freud's uncanny. In her paper on the uncanny in Montgomery's *Emily* trilogy, Kate Lawson connects Freud's uncanny concepts of the familiar and the unfamiliar with Montgomery's and Emily's unsettling feelings incurred through encounters with home spaces and the supernatural. Freud posits that "the uncanny that we find in fiction – in creative writing ... is above all much richer than what we know from experience."[10] Extending Lawson's line of examination, I argue that Montgomery transcribes experiences identifiable as uncanny into her journals, and subsequently into her fiction, but unlike Freud's theory on fiction, her real life, as she presents it in her journals, is as "rich" in the uncanny as her fiction.

Pre-Montgomery, autobiographically based Canadian works, such as Susanna Moodie's *Roughing It in the Bush*, are echoed in Montgomery's journals through the gothic elements of harsh wildernesses and climates and of psychological survival in an unknown land. Her journal descriptions of her life in Leaskdale reflect the Canadian gothic theme of a stranger struggling in a strange land; however, the threats to Montgomery's sense of self – Ewan Macdonald's mental illness, the Zephyr people, her exhaustive efforts to fit in as the minister's wife – are on a rural and domestic level. She writes out her gothic conditions in a literary style that is a precursor to what Cynthia Sugars and Gerry Turcotte identify in *Unsettled Remains* as "a more recent strain of gothic literature in Canada [that] has been less preoccupied with an overtly externalized and alien sense of gothic otherness that is 'out there' and more concerned with an interiorized psychological experience of gothic 'uncanniness' and illegitimacy."[11] Montgomery's move to Ontario triggers uncanny sensations and gothic sensibilities that at first attach to her Romantic and Victorian inspired "romantic realism" but ultimately instigate a shift towards a modern gothic style of realism, forming a significant link in the tradition of Southern Ontario Gothic that would later appear in the often autobiographical works of writers such as Alice Munro.[12]

The first to draw comparisons between Montgomery and Emily was Montgomery herself. She acknowledges in her journal that "*New Moon* is in some respects but not all my own old home and 'Emily's' inner life was my own, though outwardly most of the events and incidents were fictitious."[13] Faye Hammill suggests that "Montgomery's romantic idealism is ... amplified by an element of protest against the restrictive social order which has forced both her and Emily to take solace in fantasy."[14] Emily's struggle is not just that of the girl/woman writer in search of herself/home, nor is she a mirror for Montgomery. Rather, Emily and her story present an example of the changes in Montgomery's writing style brought on by her newly defined domestic role as wife and mother and her displacement from PEI to Ontario. There are also four short stories – "The Red Room" (1898), "The Old Chest at Wyther Grange" (1903), "The Garden of Spices" (1918), and "The Tryst of the White Lady" (1922) – that contain characters, plots, or settings that identify the texts as inspiration for the *Emily* series. Montgomery drew from her life experiences in the creation of Emily, but she also mined her previously written stories and refashioned them in order to "fit" with the new gothic style of the *Emily* series. In "Brian O'Connal and Emily Byrd Starr: The Inheritors of Wordsworth's 'Gentle

Breeze,'" Margaret Steffler draws striking comparisons between Montgomery's *Emily* books and Wordsworth's *The Prelude*, concluding, "The most obvious and pure inheritor of a Wordsworthian temperament in Canadian children's literature is L.M. Montgomery's Emily Byrd Starr."[15]

Both Montgomery's and Emily's nature descriptions and quest for the sense of self/artist, or *bildungsroman/künstlerroman*, are Romantic, but their efforts to reconcile their roles as both women *and* artists provoke psychological states of darkness that lean towards the gothic. Meena Alexander explains, "Where the Romantic poets had sought out the clarities of visionary knowledge, women writers, their lives dominated by the bonds of family and the cultural constraints of femininity, altered that knowledge, forcing it to come to terms with the substantial claims of a woman's view of the world"; "the inner-outer dichotomy the Romantic poets played with presupposed a centralising self that could not be easily translated into the world of women."[16] Before her marriage and her move to Leaskdale, Montgomery struggled to balance her public success from *Anne of Green Gables* with her domestic position as a woman. In her journals, she equates her success with being bound in "chains ... doubling [her] worries and mortifications." In Cavendish, she was confined to her domestic responsibility as caretaker to her grandmother, and that relationship was psychologically disturbing. "I am well off and tolerably famous," Montgomery writes, "but the conditions of my life are not even physically comfortable and I am beset with difficulties on every side – and all, or mainly, because I must live in subjection to a woman who, always inclined to be domineering and narrow-minded, has had those qualities intensified by age." In the Romantic fashion, she is depressed by her grandmother's "suppression of all individuality."[17] Her grandmother also repressed the Romantic ideal that "viewed a human being as endowed with limitless aspiration toward an infinite good envisioned by the faculty of imagination."[18] Montgomery's state of physical and psychological confinement in the PEI homestead journals reveals the impact of her grandmother's Victorian principles and the beginning of the shift away from the pastoral, domestic romance of Montgomery's Romantic ideals into the gothic realm of the uncanny.[19]

In the home space she shared with her grandmother, Montgomery experienced an overwhelming and confusing collision of both the familiar and the unfamiliar. Her domestic roles of woman, granddaughter, and caretaker were familiar but so was her role of artist and her interest in public fame. At the same time, all these various roles were unfamiliar to her, as she felt oppressed within her domestic ones, and her grandmother's lack of acceptance created unease with her public ones. Montgomery's sense of self, then, became a confusing locus for both the familiar and the unfamiliar that affected her artistic inclinations. For example, six months before the above-quoted passage on her grandmother, she wrote about her familiar and unfamiliar reaction to her rediscovery in "an old trunk" of a "crazy quilt" she had created when she was in her teens. The crazy quilt trend involved collecting scraps, often from relatives' clothing. In finding the quilt, Montgomery "felt many a tug at [her] heart," as the quilt had become the materialization of a "compact of old memories." However, the language of her nostalgic response also identifies with the repression of domesticity: "To my present taste it is inexpressively hideous. I find it hard to believe it possible that I could ever have thought it beautiful ... I expended more 'gray matter' devising ingenious and complicated 'stitches' than I ever put into anything else."[20] What was once a craze in her pastoral environment she now begins to view as patches of domestic stories and labour from the new aesthetic perspective that she is adopting. In chapter 6, William Thompson presents a similar discussion of Montgomery's journals through Judy Nolte Lensink's theory that female diarists "design" literary patterns "similar to a quilt's."[21] Alexander also draws attention to the quilt imagery in Dorothy Wordsworth's 1803 travelogue, *Recollections of a Tour Made in Scotland*, describing cottage land as a "collection of patchwork, made of pieces as they might have chanced to have been cut by the mantua-maker, only just smoothed to fit each other." Alexander reads Wordsworth's description as a metaphor of the female domestic position: the "image of a patchwork garment, cut of bits and pieces and stitched together as time and resources permit, reflects the realities of a woman's life commonly defined by the hold of the domestic." Alexander further positions the patchwork pattern as "stand[ing] in contrast to the seamless creation which so often seems to emerge in authorial self-presentation, the claim that the writer's life emerges through his works. Literary labour in such a transaction is rewarded by publication and the overt status it accords the writer, with the private and hidden portion of life transposed through the work into the realm of the public and visible."[22]

Montgomery's patches are a series of dichotomies – familiar and unfamiliar, private and public, domestic and professional, fictional and nonfictional, beautiful and sublime, light and dark – and the metaphor is carried into her autobiographical fiction when Emily exclaims to her relatives, "You make me feel as if I was made up of scraps and patches!"[23] Montgomery's journals record the tension created by these patches as she "writes out" her frustrations in the same way that Emily writes the letters addressed to her father – both signifiers of an artist's journey, or *künstlerroman*. Similarly, Alice Munro's Del Jordan from *Lives of Girls and Woman*, another *künstlerroman*, is humiliated for her ability to memorize poetry (also a plight of Emily's) and her inability to sew, making stitches "any six-year-old would be ashamed of."[24] In her analysis of Munro's works, Coral Ann Howells observes that "while Munro manages to contain the familiar and the unfamiliar within the same story structure, the realistic text is threatened by glimpses of a darker fantastic subtext which cannot be easily accommodated within the narrative."[25] The journals, letters, and fiction of Montgomery and Emily act as "darker fantastical subtexts," often confusing reality with the fantastic. When her grandmother dies and Montgomery is displaced from their home in PEI, her locus of repression is altered, but not removed, and the gothic presence of her journals is enriched. As Del comments in *Lives of Girls and Women*, "In the beginning, in the very beginning of everything, there was that house."[26]

After Montgomery leaves PEI for her honeymoon and eventually moves to Leaskdale, her record of each return visit to the Island resembles a study in the uncanny. The loss of her grandmother, followed by her displacement from her family home, has encouraged the disconnected feelings of the familiar and unfamiliar in regards to family and place that already existed through the absence of her parents.

On her honeymoon, she visits the home of her ancestors in her desperate search for familial connection. When she discovers the Woolner home of her maternal ancestors in September 1911, she "cannot describe" her "feelings – nor account for them." She "had expected to feel an interest in the place" but "had the strangest sensation of *coming home*." With her first return to PEI after moving to Ontario in July 1913, Montgomery brings with her the gothic rhetoric and diction she is further developing in Leaskdale. She contrasts the "good" "tang of the salt air" with "Ontario's languid air," a very Munrovian description of the stale rural gothic – of the small town, such as Munro's Hanratty or Jubilee, where the disturbing lies in the ordinary and the characters are either afraid to leave, or eager to leave, or both. At Park Corner, it hurts Montgomery to see objects from "the old home"; she finds it "painful" to see them "divorced from the old surroundings of which they seemed a part."

The longer Montgomery was away from PEI, the more "painful" were her returns, and the more gothic were her descriptions. When she returns to Leaskdale from the 1913 visit, she records in her journal the uncanny experience she had on the Island: "Voices were calling me that could not be resisted – voices of the past, fraught with all the past's enchantment. They summoned me imperiously and I obeyed the summons. I slipped out into the darkness of the summer evening and went to find the lost years." The summons led her to her childhood home: "In the fading gray light I could see the old gray house hooded in shadows ... never have I felt keener pangs – never did my heart ache more bitterly with longing and sense of loss ... it was all there – only those cruel shadows hid it." Montgomery realizes that with each visit to the old homestead, both her experience of the uncanny and her blurring of fantasy and reality more and more border on the dangerous. As she writes on another visit to her old home in July 1918, "It was too full of ghosts – lonely hungry ghosts. They would have pulled me in among them and kept me. I would have disappeared from the realm of mortals and nobody would ever know what had become of me ... These pilgrimages to shadow land are eerie things with an uncanny sweetness. I will make no more of them."

Instead, Montgomery negotiates with her feelings by blurring fantasy and reality in her fiction (and arguably her journals). During this same visit to PEI, she is devastated that the "old school woods had been cut down" and mourns for the "thousand little pitiful ghosts [that] were robbed of their habitations and haunts by the felling of those trees." Her language here is gothic in her horrific description of the cut woods as a physical deformity, "an abomination of desolation of stumps," and her wish to "spit" "Garfield Stewart – the author of the outrage – on a bayonet without pity and without remorse."[27] Instead of spitting Garfield, Montgomery uses her fiction to write/right her devastation when, in chapter 19 of *Emily of New Moon*, Emily is able to halt Lofty John's plan to cut down the grove north of New Moon. While Montgomery allows the uncanny sense of loss to bleed into her fiction, in *Emily of New Moon* she is able to control the outcome.

Montgomery also writes her gothic sensation of the uncanny's supernatural into the *Emily* series; as Lawson points out, "Emily's supernatural vision in each of the three novels relates to a house or homelike space that resonates strongly with her imaginative sense of the familiar." She also suggests that Emily shares Montgomery's "costs associated with being a romantic visionary" and that "in her uncanny experiences Emily comes into contact with a dark world beyond ordinary reality where she is 'possessed' by influences and events that she cannot control."[28] Montgomery's time in Leaskdale altered her creative lens, as she viewed her old home in PEI from a new perspective. The pastoral, gothic romance becomes psychologically and domestically gothic. This transformation reflects the shift in perspective that Munro's characters often experience as they are forced to view the familiar from a different angle. In *Survival,* Margaret Atwood suggests that Munro's Del "transfers her imaginative allegiance from the stylized world of gothic grotesques she has dreamed up as an adolescent to the small-town 'here' she despised when she was actually living in it."[29] Del goes into her local downtown for a grocery trip with her visiting, flashy American Uncle Bill. His presence makes the familiar unfamiliar, and suddenly "Jubilee seemed not unique and permanent as I had thought but almost makeshift, and shabby; it would barely do."[30] With each subsequent visit, Montgomery's Cavendish becomes less likely to host Anne Shirley's Green Gables and more suited for Jane Eyre's Thornfield Hall.

Similarly, in *Emily of New Moon*, Emily's uncanny home environments range from the pastoral of the Maywood house in the hollow where she lives with her dying father to the Victorian gothic of New Moon and the gothic romance of Wyther Grange. The Maywood home "was situated in a grassy little dale, looking as if it had never been built like other houses but had grown up there like a big, brown mushroom," and in her pastoral Eden, Emily is "kin to tribes of elfland," names her trees "Adam-and-Eve," and walks with the "Wind Woman." Cousin Jimmy suggests that there are fairies at New Moon,[31] but the house itself is ruled by stern Aunt Elizabeth who rejects modernity and hangs on to the Victorian rules of household domesticity. It is at Wyther Grange that a more modern gothic emerges in Montgomery's writing, as she begins to write the psychological sublime of Leaskdale into Emily's story. When Emily enters Wyther Grange, she feels "like one of the heroines in Gothic romance, wandering at midnight through a subterranean dungeon, with some unholy guide,"[32] and is terrified on her first night by noises in the walls. She is told that the noises are swallows in the chimney and is quickly cured of her fear. Eventually Emily is pushed psychologically into a dark and disturbing place but not by ghosts in the wall. She is forced into maturity through the acknowledgment of her sexuality by Old Kelly, her aunts, and Dean Priest, and her aunts' ruthless gossip of shamed and broken lives.

In her afterword for the New Canadian Library edition of *Emily of New Moon*, Munro describes Emily's Wyther Grange aunts as "dangerous old women" with "a hint of something sadistic, of cruel play ... as there is something threatening about their permissive atmosphere ... the cold freedom, even the material luxury, that surrounds Emily in that house."[33] Irene Gammel also discusses Emily's stay at Wyther Grange as more than a gothic romance interlude. In "The Eros of Childhood and Early Adolescent Girl Series," Gammel argues, "Critics pre-occupied with the intertextual allusions to gothic romance and the resulting panicky *frisson* of Emily's imaginary wandering through subterranean dungeon spaces have been remarkably blind to the fact that behind the seemingly irrational fears lies the material reality of menstrual and premenstrual symptoms."[34]

The Leaskdale manse is a hub of similar internalizations of the gothic notions of 'sensibility' found at Wyther Grange, and like Emily's reaction to her aunts, Montgomery finds the behaviour of some of the small-town Ontarians distasteful. Her journals record various ailments of the mind and body during these years. The recurring bouts of hypochondria, depression, and even hysterics that fester in Leaskdale appear too sensational to be real, but both husband and wife privately suffer them. At Leaskdale, Montgomery works hard to avoid Ewan's becoming the centre of small-town gossip, hiding his self-absorbed nature and manic depression from the public – a secret that becomes unbearable. Her aesthetic sense finds the small-town environment and the people distasteful, particularly the "Zephyrites." She writes that she "loathe[s]" Zephyr and hates the Zephyrites, finding many of them "ignorant" and "not attractive in any way." She finds their religious zeal unappealing and even names the day of her visits to Zephyr "black Thursday."[35] In chapter 3, Steffler traces the influences of Montgomery's childhood experiences with religion and concludes, "She concentrates her abhorrence on Ewan as both a representative and victim of the type of religion practised by her grandmother and imposed on her in childhood."[36] Montgomery also concentrates her "abhorrence" on the Zephyrites, and her uncanny relationship with religion parallels her uncanny relationship to place. Although she is a stranger in a strange land, Montgomery's life and writing begin to adopt the Southern Ontario Gothic elements of social commentary, mental illness, and small-town Presbyterianism that will later define the writings of Ontario natives such as Munro.

Montgomery's younger PEI self *was* subject to gothic romance prose in her PEI journals, especially in her account of her love affair with Herman Leard. Later, as a married woman, she reflects on that romantic encounter: "My own love for Herman Leard, though so incomplete, is a memory beside which all the rest of life seems gray and dowdy."[37] Her language acknowledges a sadness for the transition of the gothic in her life from romance to disturbing and mundane domesticity. Steffler's chapter also suggests that "while Ewan may be temporarily displaced by Herman Leard of the recopied journal, his continued presence remains necessary for other uses, namely as a receptacle for Montgomery's own fears and repugnance of sexuality and of certain Christian and Presbyterian dogmas."[38] The effort of keeping Ewan's depression private and handling his public responsibilities affected Montgomery deeply and altered her perspective on life. When he finally confessed his deepest fears to her, the scene, characterized through horror, religion, and psychological internalization, is pure gothic: "He said he was possessed by a horrible dread that he was *eternally lost* – that there was no hope for him in the next life. This dread haunted him night and day and he could not banish it. Never shall I forget my despair when I discovered this. I had always known it as one of his symptoms – *the* symptom – of religious melancholia. Unutterable horror seemed to engulf me."[39] Ewan's mind and mood so affected the words and tone of Montgomery's writings that the origin of the text of the journal often became blurred, making it difficult to distinguish what on the pages of the journals belongs to Ewan and what belongs to Montgomery. Like the creator and the creature of gothic literature, she becomes "engulfed" by the horror of Ewan's situation, and thus her text and its perception are often inseparable from him. Although there are various interpretations of the ending of the *Emily* series, Mary Rubio's suggestion that "Emily's creativity will sink into grey domesticity within"[40] reflects Montgomery's fear of the state of her own marriage and domestic position, a fear shared by several of Munro's characters, especially Rose from *Who Do You Think You Are*. Montgomery's record of her marriage to Ewan is less in line with the pastoral romance of Gilbert and Anne and more akin to the subject and style of Munro, whose novels and short stories regularly explore domestic relationships plagued by mental illness and social ruin – both dark fears of Montgomery's and identifiers of Southern Ontario Gothic. With statements such as "I was never in love with Ewan – never have been in love with him. But I was – have been – and am, very fond of him,"[41] the journal entries record the real or dark side of marriage in a way that most gothic romances do not.

Montgomery's journals are not necessarily an exercise book from which works such as *Emily of New Moon* emerge, but they do provide a collection of insights into the psychological creation of her private gothic reality that is, in turn, written into her fiction. Munro's explanation for the source of her own autobiographical fiction is similar. Learning "very early to disguise everything," she translates her private interpretation of her environment into her fiction, proposing that "perhaps the escape into stories was necessary." She struggles with the concept that her reality is more gothic or unreal than what she can translate into fiction, explaining in a separate interview that "the part of the country [she] comes from is absolutely Gothic. You can't get it all down."[42] In "Subverting the Trite," Rubio paraphrases interviews with Munro, who comments on the real in *Emily of New Moon*, that "in many ways there's great psychological truth in it." Rubio also selects a passage that supports a Southern Ontario connection between the two writers: "When asked if there are features of Montgomery's fictional world that connected Montgomery's world with rural Ontario, [Munro] replies: 'Oh, very much so. In the family structure, I think ... A connection with the sort of people she was dealing with, the old aunts and the grandmothers, the female power figures ... a sense of injustice and strangeness in family life and of mystery in people that was familiar to me.'"[43] Freud would argue that Munro cannot transfer the uncanny of her life into "literature without substantial modification, because the realm of the imagination depends for its validity on its contents being exempt from the reality test."[44] However, the autobiographical nature of both Munro's and Montgomery's writings often elicits the subjecting of their work to reality testing, changing the approach to their genres. As Woster suggests in the previous chapter, Montgomery's journal identity "is informed as much by literature and text as it is by her own past."[45] The character of Dean Priest combines Ewan Macdonald, Herman Leard, Mr Rochester, Heathcliff, and the male Romantic poets, while the old homestead, the Leaskdale manse, Emily's Maywood home, New Moon, and Wyther Grange reflect Montgomery's spatial recognition of the uncanny. As with Munro, the "absolutely Gothic" reality is present in Montgomery's journals, and she weaves these gothic elements from her journal into her fictional stories.

In her journal, Montgomery refers to her uncanny sensations as "psychological experiences," often premonitions recognized in retrospect or in moments of extreme duress. Such entries sensationalize the "languid" quality of the rural gothic that is her reality. Following the death of Frede, her cousin and dearest friend, Montgomery recalls a recent dream that she believes foretold Frede's death, although she did not make the connection at the time. In the dream, her house is stripped of its belongings and decorations; in a sense, it is stripped of her domestic contribution and construction of her home space. Montgomery recalls commenting to herself in her dream, "Everything has gone and now I have to set to work to furnish my house all over again." When she makes the uncanny connection between her dream and Frede's death, her reflection reveals a dark gothic link between her subconscious and her environment: "But now I know that it meant Frede's death. And has it not come true? Is it not my house of life left unto me desolate – is it not the inmost shrine of my heart narrowed down? Does not everything seem gone from me? Am I not left to furnish my soul's habitation afresh – if I can?"[46]

Although Montgomery's journals serve as an outlet for her struggles, her fiction is an extension of, and a comment on, her life writing. If the act of reading allows her "to (re)live and write in a space of near constant homesickness and longing," as Woster suggests in the previous chapter,[47] then her fiction writing allows her to navigate through the space of homesickness and longing. Following a quarrel over their "Tansy Patch" playhouse, Emily returns to the patch to see Ilse "gaily" recreating the space she has previously destroyed. Ilse's candid manner "rather posed Emily after her tragic night, wherein she had buried her second friendship and wept over its grave. She was not prepared for so speedy a resurrection."[48] It is possible to conceive of Ilse as Frede, playfully mocking from the grave Montgomery's many journal entries that mourn her death. In crossing the lines between life and death, fiction and non-fiction, Montgomery subconsciously consoles herself through the resurrection of Frede in Ilse's recreation of a domestic uncanny space that all four females can share. The "psychological experience" of writing Frede into her fiction is Montgomery's way of making sense of the devastating loss and, like Munro, of uniquely modifying reality into fiction and moving past traditional gothic romance conventions.

Montgomery's journals share material with all her fictional writings, and her fictional writings share material with each other. Similarities exist between the short stories previously mentioned and *Emily of New Moon*. The stories precede *Emily*, but in comparison to the novel, the stories contain variations that indicate Montgomery's experimentation with new versions of the gothic. In her introduction to a compilation of Montgomery's "darker" stories titled *Among the Shadows*, Rea Wilmshurst comments that Montgomery eventually "lightened her approach to the genre and, while not mocking it, certainly took it less seriously." She "took" the romance portion of the gothic "less seriously," but it could be said that she began to take the gothic *more* seriously, as her approach to the gothic became less sensational and more psychologically disturbing. The Brontëan-titled "The Red Room," an example of what Wilmshurst describes as Montgomery's "early attempt at a 'Gothic' thriller,"[49] has settings, characters, and plot elements similar to those in *Emily of New Moon*, such as old spaces, secrets, forbidden rooms, and a girl for a heroine; however, in "The Red Room" – a potboiler heavily influenced by *Jane Eyre* and *The Mysteries of Udolpho* – the gothic elements are sensationalized and romanticized. The young heroine, Beatrice, recounts from memory an experience of stormy nights, old mansions, an exotic woman, dark men, and a murder of passion, with even a reference to "Bluebeard's chamber."[50] Beatrice's ordeal contrasts Emily's experience of rural farms, domestic women, weak men, and questionable spaces; unlike Beatrice's experiences, Emily's are more internally than externally threatening, and Emily eventually conquers her psychological threats. "The Old Chest at Wyther Grange" has a jilted lover, old maids, and secret spaces, and like Emily, the young heroine is inquisitive about old family secrets. Recalling Emily Brontë's *Wuthering Heights* in its title, the story also shares the names Wyther Grange and Starr with the *Emily* novels but again its style of a sensationalized tragic romance lacks the novels' psychological development and exploration.

Montgomery wrote two more stories in Leaskdale, "The Garden of Spices" and "The Tryst of the White Lady," with aspects that will find their way into the *Emily* series. The two stories are in Montgomery's usual style that includes elements of the pastoral/domestic romance, the Victorian gothic, the gothic romance, and even Romanticism. The modifications she makes to the elements, mostly centred on the psychological state of the characters, are samples of her experimentation with a new style. Like Emily, the young Jims of "The Garden of Spices" escapes through the window of the room in which he has been locked by his strict aunt and finds solace in the garden of his badly scarred neighbour, Miss Avery. Miss Avery's face had been burned in an accident with a lamp, and ashamed of her scarring, she has cut her ties with Jims's uncle. The story, encompassing the pastoral, domestic, romantic, gothic, and Victorian conventions of setting, entrapment, escape, physical deformity, secrets, misunderstandings, and love, ends in happiness with Jims's inadvertently reconnecting Miss Avery with his uncle and the two becoming his new parents. In her self-imposed isolation, Miss Avery has created a safe, pastoral/domestic environment of which Jims becomes a part and where he is physically free and guilt free. Her scarring adds to the romance of the tale, and the psychological impact is easily smoothed over with love. Montgomery repurposes elements of this story for the *Emily* series with the story of Teddy and his mother, Mrs Kent. Mrs Kent is insanely jealous and possessive of her son; however, the psychological impact of her scarring (also by a lamp) is much deeper than Miss Avery's, and her story lacks a romantic tone and outcome. As a psychologically disturbed character, Mrs Kent traps Teddy in a domestically gothic environment that he is never consciously free to escape – a parallel relationship to both that of Montgomery and her grandmother and later to Montgomery and Ewan. In another contrast between the psychological makeup of Miss Avery and Mrs Kent, the former purchases a dog for Jims and saves his pet turkey from slaughter, while the latter is jealous of Teddy's pets and is even suspected of killing one.

Finally, the evolution of Montgomery's style and the reality of her gothic life are written out through the physical and psychological disabilities of Roger "Jarback" Temple in "The Tryst of the White Lady" – a story that, when she completed it in 1921, Montgomery called "a fanciful little thing"[51] – and through Dean Priest and Cousin

Jimmy of the *Emily* series. Roger, a Romantic hero prototype for Dean "Jarback" Priest, believes that "most people ... were ugly – though not so ugly as he was – and ugliness made him sick with repulsion"; this repulsion is countered by an obsession with beauty. To further characterize Roger as a Romantic hero, he carries a volume of Wordsworth in his pocket, longs to "escape into the world of dreams where he habitually live[s] and where he [finds] the loveliness he had not found nor could hope to find in his real world," *and* is in love with an apparition of a beautiful, ethereal woman. He eventually falls in love with a young deaf woman and experiences his world of dreams in reality; however, he overhears his aunt suggest that the two are properly matched for their disabilities, and her "horrible practicalities ... filled him with disgust – they dragged his love in the dust of sordid things."[52] Although Roger and his love reunite for a happy ending, he shares Montgomery's aesthetic interest in beauty and her fear of the sublime and ugliness of reality above her fear of the supernatural. Dean, then, is a psychologically darker and more complex version of Roger. As Emily's physically deformed, intellectually brooding, worldly, and not entirely honest older love interest, Dean is a Byronic hero in his cynicism, jealousy, and passion. Comparisons have been made between Emily and Jane Eyre and between Dean and Rochester, such as those by Epperly in *The Fragrance of Sweet-Grass*.[53] Montgomery's descriptions of Ewan's moods and jealousy of her success align him with Dean, but unlike herself, she offers Emily an alternative (although much debated if "better") to the domesticated gothic in Teddy. Through the character of Emily's Cousin Jimmy, Montgomery also addresses her fears that the people of Leaskdale will notice Ewan's mental illness and lead her family to social ruin. Jimmy's prospects as an independent, intelligent man are ruined after he falls down a well, as the "Blair Water people thought Jimmy a failure and a mental weakling."[54] The small-town misunderstanding and consequent social mistreatment of mental disability is a frequent Southern Ontario Gothic trope, such as with Munro's Mary Agnes and Bobby Sheriff in *Lives of Girls and Women*. Ironically, Jimmy, Mary Agnes, and Bobby have the ability to see details and layers beyond the real, inadvertently teaching the "writers," Emily and Del, to view reality through new lenses.

Montgomery not only "delight[s] and exult[s]" in her ability to exist in both her fictional and non-fictional worlds but also "save[s] [her] nerves by a double life,"[55] a precarious mental state examined in greater detail in chapters 7 and 13 by Melanie Fishbane and Lesley Clement, respectively. Montgomery's realism is affected by a lens that may often appear exaggerated or sentimental but is real to her, aligning her with "the great poets of English Romanticism" who by "highlighting the change wrought by the seeing self, the eye/I ... established a distinctive mode of capturing the real."[56] She retains elements of the romance in the various forms discussed in her fiction, but with her domestic existence in Leaskdale, the gothic "real" is increasingly developed. In *Lives of Girls and Women*, Munro's Del decides to write a gothic fiction novel based on her hometown. She struggles with what elements to retain from reality in her fictional account of her rural gothic environment and invents the tale of a photographer whose pictures of people "turned out to be unusual, even frightening." Reflecting on her choices, Del realizes that "the main thing was that it seemed true to me, not real but true, as if I had discovered, not made up, such people and such a story, as if that town was lying close behind the one I walked through every day."[57] This is the exact perspective that Montgomery's journals offer to readers. Montgomery "discovered" the stories of her fiction in her "real" life, and in her journals, it becomes difficult to determine in which "town" she is walking. Montgomery identifies, both consciously and unconsciously, the elements of the gothic she has acquired through her aesthetic lens and psychological experiences and writes these elements into her fiction.[58] At the end of *Emily of New Moon*, Mr Carpenter comments that Emily's writings are "too much like a faint echo of Wordsworth" and that her "titles are as out of date as the candles at New Moon." When he accidentally happens upon the descriptions of himself and the other inhabitants of Blair Water in Emily's Jimmy-book, descriptions that do not seek to flatter but to *describe*, he sees "himself as in a glass and the artistry of it pleased him so that he cared for nothing else."[59] Mr Carpenter stumbles upon both Emily's *and* Montgomery's talent to capture what is interesting in the real, and his comments act as Montgomery's self-acknowledgment of her new creative direction towards the yet-to-be established Southern Ontario Gothic.

Travels to Muskoka: Commodification and Tourism

10

Propriety and the Proprietary: The Commodification of Health and Nature in The Blue Castle

E. HOLLY PIKE

Readers accustomed to the literary depiction of the recuperative effect of nature usually think of that effect as occurring through the unmediated contact with nature portrayed by Romantic poets and essayists such as William Wordsworth, Ralph Waldo Emerson, and Bliss Carman. In L.M. Montgomery's works, the virtues of direct contact with nature and its powers are asserted through the ecstatic responses of her heroines to natural scenes and through the personal responses she records in her journals. As Rosemary Ross Johnston argues, for Montgomery, "landscape is deeply, profoundly, spiritual, imbricated with what Montgomery often refers to as 'soul.'"[1] Making a similar point, Elizabeth Epperly describes Montgomery as a "reader of Ruskin and also of the Romantics who assumed a Presence, or a spirit called Nature animating beauty in the land, [who] found her strength and success in communion with place," a communion that – at least in the early novels – Epperly describes as "apparently effortless."[2]

Montgomery's *The Blue Castle*, set in the Muskoka resort region of Ontario during the 1920s, presents nature both romantically, as might be expected, and prosaically as the source of freedom, health, and happiness in contrast to social systems in which individuals are constrained by rules and governed by marketplace interactions. In these social systems, well-being is replaced by the treatment of disease, nature by domestic organization, and happiness by a sense of propriety. The novel's protagonist, Valancy Stirling, breaks away from the social system in which she has been raised but, ironically, only when she experiences nature as a commodity through the books of naturalist John Foster. Her reading enables her to pursue the wider experiences of which she has been made aware. Acknowledging that the influences of nature may not be immediately accessible to everyone, Montgomery allows her heroine to locate nature's power on her own terms. Through the culturally and commercially mediated experience of Muskoka, which the newly emerging tourist industry markets as a healthy lifestyle destination, Valancy achieves the freedom, health, and happiness that, despite her being surrounded by Muskoka's natural environs her whole life, were previously inaccessible to her.

When *The Blue Castle* opens, the Muskoka region is clearly an established resort area: there are references to the hotels and cottages scattered over the islands and to the summer residents. However, the Stirling clan to which Valancy belongs does not participate in this world and its notions of nature as an escape. Their social world is bound by rigid rules of interaction and decorum, ritualized social events, and limited acceptance of innovation. As year-round locals of the town of Deerwood rather than summer residents, the Stirlings take part in a class system, being part of the "old-family set" rather than the smart set, the intellectual set, or the common run of visitors, and as such, they have not adopted such modern conveniences as "motorcars." Their health problems are ritualized and subjected to set treatment patterns rather than genuine medical intervention. Cousin Gladys's neuritis, Cousin Stickles's neuralgic back, and Valancy's colds are treated without the benefit of medical advice, and sometimes in opposition to medical advice, with traditional or proprietary treatments. Valancy is made to dress warmly and to stay indoors to avoid colds and bronchitis; Cousin Stickles insists on having her back rubbed with Redfern's Liniment every night. She asks Valancy to buy her some Redfern's Bitters because she feels "sorter peaky and piny," insisting on Bitters in contradiction of Cousin James's reliance on Purple Pills.[3] This reliance on proprietary remedies is a manifestation of the desire to keep control of one's behaviour and to maintain adherence to a code that dictates behaviour; that is, it is based on the assumption, like Mrs Stirling's rule about when to start having fires in the fall, that the world, society, and the relations between things are absolute and therefore that any action outside the established patterns is an impropriety. The Stirlings' clearly ritualized treatment of health is noted by Kate Lawson, who observes that Valancy "has experienced illness only as a more rigid reinforcement of the codes that govern her behaviour."[4] The lack of empirical evidence as to the efficacy of their remedies does nothing to prevent the Stirlings from continuing them. Cousin Stickles uses liniment every night with no improvement in her condition; regular use of Redfern's Hair Vigor has not helped the texture of Valancy's dry hair; and Cousin Stickles's husband took Redfern's Bitters "right up to the day he died." Valancy's first overt act of rebellion on getting Dr Trent's letter telling her of her heart condition is to refuse the family remedy of taking a spoonful of vinegar to treat her supposed headache and immediately afterwards to refuse to be rubbed with Redfern's Liniment, which she declares to be "no good." However, as in the refusal to light a fire on the cold October 20th that supposedly led to the death of Valancy's father,[5] empirical justifications for breaches of the rules – such as excessive cold – are not allowable. Any such breach is regarded as an impropriety, an adherence to agency rather than clan tradition or expectation.

Thus, thinking and acting for herself rather than in accordance with collectively accepted norms makes Valancy seem mad to her family; to them, such a deviation from the clan's code must be a sign of disease, as Kylee-Anne Hingston demonstrates.[6] When Valancy starts to act according to her own desires and declares her intention to have a little "fun," her mother echoes the word "as if Valancy had said she was going to have a little tuberculosis." In discussions of her changed behaviour, Valancy is described by her family as "dippy," "stark mad," and a "maniac."[7] From their perspective, only mental illness could account for a desire to behave outside of their norms, and the manifestation of such a desire in action would be equivalent to a physical illness. Following the etiquette decreed by the clan is the only way to claim status in the "old-family set." That etiquette – the word literally means "label" – is an identifying marker just as much as Dr Redfern's face on his medicine bottles is. The clan's notions of propriety, therefore, are in effect proprietary too, a claim of entitlement to a certain standing and to public acknowledgment of that entitlement. Valancy must be treated as dead when she steps outside the clan's notions of propriety because she has forfeited her claim to the "old-family" brand.

Valancy understands that propriety is important, but she is willing to abandon it. Sitting in Barney's car when they have run out of gas escaping from the dance at Chidley Corners, she tells Olive, "I'm afraid I'm hopelessly proper," seeing no possibility for a change in her status. However, Valancy's family considers her "both mad *and* bad," and her behaviour threatens the family's standing, making Olive's fiancé question the genetic source of Valancy's oddity and causing her mother to stay away from church. At Cissy Gay's funeral, Valancy's family sees her as "decorous and proper and Stirlingish," and Abel Gay's comment to Valancy about the Stirlings confirms that certain characteristics are associated with them in the community: "*They* don't like being sassed back."[8]

The importance of labelling is also clear in the case of Dr Redfern's proprietary medicines, which are commodities identified with Dr Redfern himself, bearing a picture of his "smug, beaming, portly, be-whiskered, be-spectacled" face. When Valancy meets him in person, she does not know who he is but thinks that the face is "as familiar to her as her own."[9] Her statement indicates that the proprietary medicines marketed under his name and face have become part of the propriety of her clan – indeed part of her property, in being as familiar as her own face. As she cannot help noticing, Dr Redfern has not cured himself of the ailments for which the medicines he dreamed up are supposedly panaceas: he is bald, despite having invented Hair Vigor, and he fears rheumatism, despite having invented Redfern's Liniment. These realizations come through the agency of an "imp" at the back of Valancy's mind, prompting her recognition of the images associated with Dr Redfern and supplying her with the necessary advertising language to note his failure to benefit from his own medicines. Valancy cannot access the language of the ads directly because she is "paralysed" by the shock of what she has learned from Dr Trent (that his terminal diagnosis was meant for someone else); she is about to be even more shocked by what she will learn from Dr Redfern – that Barney is in fact Dr Redfern's son and heir.[10] Yet the slogans are so integrally a part of her knowledge that her unconscious supplies them as a critique of the originator – and as Hingston argues, of the notion of "cures"[11] – when she is unable consciously to connect the two. Unconsciously, she is aware that her own good health owes nothing to the proprietary medicines on which her family relies and of whose lack of efficacy she now has first-hand proof. Her instinctive liking for Barney's father – she feels "something that attracted her" in Dr Redfern's voice and "there was something about him she liked" – is justified by Barney's later explanation that "his medicines are quite harmless. Even his Purple Pills do people whole heaps of good when they believe in them." Valancy has had a similar thought herself about the Purple Pills when she considers taking them instead of seeing Dr Trent about her heart pain.[12] For members of her family, who do believe in the power of the proprietary medicines, it is possible that they are effective. They could not work for Valancy, who doubts their utility, hates the smell of the liniment, and finds it "horrible stuff." Lawson makes a similar point in arguing of Redfern's medicines that if illness is "shaped by the sick person according to his or her needs, then the 'cure' for illness must similarly be the product of the imagination."[13] Such a "product" could equally be of the literary market or of the tourism market, both products of the imagination and commodities in their own right.

The source of his family's money being patent medicine has caused Barney shame during his childhood and youth among cultured people in Montreal who looked down on him and his father because of their commercial origins. Barney felt more kinship with the educated people he encountered at McGill, not with the people who were interested in associating with him because of his money, a distinction that parallels the existence of various "sets" in Deerwood, which have clear markers of belonging. Barney finds that having the right interests and abilities to belong to the intellectual set is not enough to secure entry: he must also be able to separate himself from the brand markers of his father's remedies. He chooses to separate himself from society altogether and ends up, through his travels in relatively remote areas of Canada, creating his own brand in his pseudonym, "John Foster." What it sells is not that different from what Dr Redfern sells – a remedy that works if the consumer believes in it. The Deerwood librarian "really can't see what people find in [Foster's books] to rave over," but Valancy "felt vaguely that if she had come across John Foster's books years ago life might have been a different thing for her."[14] Since she responds to the point of view he expresses, his books can make her healthier, just as someone who believes in the efficacy of the Purple Pills can be helped by them.

Dr Trent's diagnosis of Valancy's illness – pseudo-angina – supports her family's contention that her behaviour is not normal, although not necessarily in the way they understand. According to an article by Oliver T. Osborne, in his 1916 treatise *Disturbances of the Heart*, "false anginas occur in the young, and especially in the neurotic."[15] The identification of neurosis as the cause of pseudo-angina also connects the disease to the types of illness for which a trip to Muskoka is supposed to be a cure, according to promotional materials such as *Muskoka: Land of Health and Pleasure* (1897), which recommends the area for "the victim of overwork, brought to the verge of nervous prostration."[16] An article by "Wanderer" in *Rod and Gun in Canada* in 1910, describing a trip by canoe from Go Home Bay to Bala as an escape from "that utter and all-embracing tiredness which comes from the demands of an exacting City Editor," rhapsodizes about the recuperative potential of nature: "It was as though Old Dame Nature, that placid, untroubled Mother of us all, had taken us quietly to her bosom, and, as a mother soothes and 'gentles' a tired and fretful child, had quietly and completely cleared away the mists and cobwebs from the mind, soothed the tired spirits, and induced in both mind and body comprehensive and deep-reaching peace and an unconcern for the things of the too busy world ... That's what I call rest!"[17]

The need to have a commercial or brand structure to produce health as evidenced in Dr Redfern's proprietary medicine and Foster's selling of nature is also demonstrated in the promotional material for the Muskoka region. As *Muskoka: Land of Health and Pleasure* makes clear, the health benefits and beauty of the region can be experienced only thanks to commercial development. Its introductory essay compares the Muskoka region to the Swiss Alps or the Scotch Lakes, noting, "The secret of the charm in each instance lies in the contact with nature in her prestine [sic] beauty and under conditions of comfort and even luxury. To wander through a land where the deer and bear make their winter home, where the crane and wild duck start at the flash of the paddle, and yet to whose gateway lines of railway converge, through whose fairy Lakes and Islands palatial steamers wind their way, is indeed to come close to that condition in which ideal enjoyment is possible."[18] Another essay in this publication, "Muskoka as a Fishing and Health Resort," makes a similar point about the importance of commercial infrastructure, stating that "to the Muskoka Navigation Company is due, in a large measure, the pleasure and satisfaction derived from an outing in Muskoka,"[19] since without the steamships, travel to and within the region would be difficult and time-consuming. In *Wild Things: Nature, Culture and Tourism in Ontario, 1790–1914*, Patricia Jasen discusses the rise of wilderness tourism in Ontario as "connected to a mounting concern over the mental and physical degeneration that was common to many western industrial societies in the late nineteenth century," a class of problems for which "neurasthenia was the catch-all term." Jasen also notes the concomitant rise of nationalist attachment to the landscape and of literature about the landscape, much of which "adopted this therapeutic world view, this desire to bury oneself in the bosom of the great mother who soothes away all hurts and cares." The development of Algonquin Provincial Park in 1894, as Jasen indicates, was a response to the overdevelopment of the Muskoka region due to tourist demands; no settlement was to occur in the park, with the object being "true isolation."[20]

That John Foster also presents nature as a restorative is clear in the first passage from his essays quoted in *The Blue Castle*, which in places closely echoes both Wordsworth's "Lines Written a Few Miles above Tintern Abbey" and Emerson's "Essays: Second Series," particularly its section on "Nature," in its description of the benefits "worshippers" receive from nature and the quasi-physical interaction depicted. Foster's words "for the woods, when they give at all, give unstintedly and hold nothing back from their true worshippers" are reminiscent of Wordsworth's "this prayer I make, / Knowing that Nature never did betray / The heart that loved her." Similarly, Foster's "the immortal heart of the woods will beat against ours and its subtle life will steal into our veins" is reminiscent of Wordsworth's description of the passage of physical sensation to the soul: "sensations sweet, / Felt in the blood, and felt along the heart, / And passing even into my purer mind / With tranquil restoration."[21] Emerson likewise echoes Wordsworth's views on the importance of a connection with nature, stating that "Nature is loved by what is best in us" and, with reference to a walk in the woods, "These enchantments are medicinal, they sober and heal us."[22] The Canadian poet and essayist Bliss Carman also asserts that there is "a power in Nature to rest and console us," that "we shall reap good from [Nature] in abundance, if we are wise," and that "the greatest boon we can receive from Nature is health. Our friendship with her should give us sanity first of all."[23] While these Romantic writers envision the benefits of contact with nature as spiritual, they recognize that such spiritual benefit is achieved through the physical senses and that it is necessary to be in contact with the natural world to realize it.

The passage that introduces Foster's books in *The Blue Castle* closely echoes Emerson's essay as well. A passage of free indirect discourse accounts for why Valancy likes these books so much: "She could hardly say what it was – some tantalising lure of a mystery never revealed – some hint of a great secret just a little further on." Similarly, Emerson identifies the feeling that "there is in the woods and waters a certain enticement and flattery, together with a failure to yield a present satisfaction … Nature is still elsewhere. This or this is but outskirt and far-off reflection and echo of the triumph that has passed by."[24] Despite the Romantic assessment of nature presented in Foster's works and the explicit statement in the first passage "quoted" in the novel, that the woods "give us such treasures of beauty and delight as are not bought or sold in any market-place," selling these "treasures of beauty and delight" is exactly what Foster does. As Valancy thinks, "a Foster book about woods was the next best thing to the woods themselves."[25] Just as Muskoka itself is an escape from the city, made available by commercial development, books about the woods – specifically, the Muskoka woods – provide that escape for those for whom escape is not physically possible. It is clear that the books provide a similar tonic to the neurasthenic that an actual sojourn in the woods does; indeed, it is through reading Foster's books that Valancy gets the strength to consult a doctor about her chest pain and ultimately to defy her family.

Even though Valancy does not know that Barney is John Foster, her life with him strengthens her physically in the same way that reading his books has strengthened her mentally and has created her desire to live on his remote island. Once she is living with him, she finds out that he "knew the woods as a book,"[26] a statement that depicts the woods as a source of knowledge and potentially of inspiration but also puts the woods themselves into the category of commodity. According to Donald Stephens, like John Foster, Carman describes "an elemental relationship with nature, a nature that cannot be completely understood,"[27] and just as the novel claims that Foster has "put Canada on the literary map of the world,"[28] Stephens claims that Carman, "popular in Canada and the United States" in his lifetime, is one of the group that constituted "the first firm step in Canadian poetry."[29] Foster echoes elements of the essays in Carman's *The Kinship of Nature*, published in 1904, although, as Epperly notes, the immediate inspiration of the John Foster passages in this "Ontario fairy tale" is Montgomery's 1911 pieces in *Canadian Magazine*, which themselves reflect Carman's influence.[30] Carman's "Behold the rituals of the forest! The aspiration of the maples taking shape, after the traditions of their ancestors for a thousand generations, in one form, the aspiration of the pines in another" is similar to Foster's "Behold the young wild plum-tree which has adorned herself after immemorial fashion in a wedding-veil of fine lace," both passages endowing the trees with agency and addressing the reader in elevated language.[31] Carman's essays share Foster's mix of first-person narration and second-person address as well as description of and meditation on natural scenes. It is tempting to identify Carman as an inspiration for Foster also because he was a featured speaker at the Muskoka Assembly in August 1924,[32] an event that was surely widely publicized during the months that Montgomery was writing *The Blue Castle*. From the perspective of Carman and Foster, the woods have both a significance of their own and also one that is created by the person who describes them and therefore creates a commodity.[33] As John Foster, therefore, Barney has proprietary right in the woods similar to the right that his father has in his medicines, since he has dreamed them up in the incarnation in which Valancy and his other readers experience them. As the owner of an island in Mistawis, he also has property rights in the woods, although he realizes that most of what he contemplates and enjoys cannot be owned: "Most of the scenery belongs to the government, but they don't tax you for looking at it, and the moon belongs to everybody."[34] While government does not tax citizens for looking at the scenery, there is ownership of it and of ways of seeing it, such as the way of seeing devised and circulated by John Foster.

Valancy's "cure" in the Muskoka woods can be partly attributed to her and Barney's eating and sleeping outdoors as well as indoors, making their domestic space a composite of nature and culture, a state signalled by Valancy's recognition of her "Blue Castle" on her first sight of Barney's island, seeing the cabin with the surrounding trees and the sunset behind: "the two enormous pine-trees that clasped hands over Barney's shack loomed out like dark turrets."[35] The freedom to treat the outdoors as part of the domestic space places Valancy's "Blue Castle" among what Stacy Alaimo calls "hybrid landscapes ... which confound and confuse the boundaries between nature and the domestic,"[36] and therefore allow Valancy to exist outside "conventional structures and social arrangements,"[37] escaping the excessive propriety of her clan's indoor life and being rejected by her family because of the impropriety of her escape. Thus, for Valancy, her ideal home and the site of her healing are depicted as equally indoors and outdoors – not within the domesticated landscape of her family home, where even the view is of failed commerce and advertisements,[38] but within the landscape that provides the inspiration for Foster's commodified cultural products.

Valancy's suitability for life in the woods is demonstrated in the ways that Barney describes her, which echo the narrator's and Foster's descriptions of the woods. In the central scene in which Valancy and Barney escape from the dance at the Corners, Valancy, riding in a car for the first time, sees the landscape from a different perspective: "The thistles looked like drunken fairies or tipsy elves as their car-lights passed over them." Later in this scene Barney agrees with Valancy that moonlight in the woods is special: "It always makes me feel so clean, somehow – body and soul," a significant statement given that "Moonlight" becomes his name for her after their marriage. The implication is that he associates her with cleanliness of body and soul, an implication that is confirmed both when he calls her "you nice little thing! Sometimes I feel you're too nice to be real – that I'm just dreaming you" and again at the end of the novel when he tells her, "You made me believe again in the reality of friendship and love." Valancy has cured him of the disillusionment and the "little, bitter, cynical laugh" she was aware of when she first met him.[39]

In comparing Valancy to moonlight, Barney also compares her to an "elf maiden" and a "wood sprite," a comparison that he has already thought of in Abel Gay's garden: "Was this elfin girl the little, old-maidish creature who had stood there two minutes ago?" The narrator has previously made that point in describing Valancy in her green dress and hat – "she really looked like a wild elf strayed out of the greenwood" – and again in describing her improved health and appearance – "Valancy might never be beautiful, but she was of the type that looks its best in the woods – elfin – mocking – alluring."[40] Several of the descriptions of the woods refer to fairies: Mistawis is "like a scene out of some fairy tale"; "Valancy learned the different fairy-likenesses of the mosses"; "The undergrowth ... was a little fairy forest cut out of marble"; "fairy-like blendings"; "islands fairy-like in a green haze"; "wood-pixies must have woven it"; "stepping from one world to another – from reality to fairyland."[41] These references both prepare for the fairy-tale ending and reinforce the Romantic idea that the woods have mysterious powers, as well as invoking one of the Muskoka lakes, Fairy Lake. Painter Alan Tierney's expressed wish to paint Valancy as "the Spirit of Muskoka" after seeing her with "a shaft of pale spring sunlight .... athwart her bare black head," with "a fillet of linnæa vine about her hair" and her arms overflowing with a "feathery fountain of trailing spruce," strengthens the identification of her with the woods and with nature in general, indirectly justifying her achievement of full health while living with Barney. As Barney points out, Valancy's beauty is not the conventional beauty of her cousin Olive, but, just as nature is supposed to communicate directly with those who seek it, Valancy's face now allows her soul "to shine through it."[42] Thus Valancy's beauty in the Muskoka woods, as validated by Tierney's desire to paint her, is an aspect of the "continued agency" that Linda Rodenburg argues in chapter 11 Valancy gains by "creat[ing] a place of her own in the woods."[43] It is also significant that, if granted his wish, Tierney would create another commodity – a painting – from the imaginative material of the Muskoka woods and from Valancy's improved health and changed appearance since choosing life in the woods.

Living with Barney and sharing his activities expose Valancy both to nature as described by John Foster and to a way of living that builds her physical strength through exercise and relieves the neurotic stress of her unhappy life with her family. While she claims that "John Foster's books were all that saved my soul alive the past five years" and therefore credits him with her survival, either one of the lifestyle changes, according to Osborne in his *Disturbances of the Heart*, would have been enough to cure her pseudo-angina. The passages from Foster's books that appear in the novel before Valancy marries Barney, referring to courage and hope, apparently form the attitude that allows her to defy her family: "Fear is the original sin"; "Who could endure life were it not for the hope of death?" These quotations remind her that fear is damaging to the psyche and that anything one endures will have an end. After her marriage to Barney, she no longer needs the support of this philosophy, and the excerpts she quotes are about the beauty of nature, particularly its elusiveness and delicacy.[44] There is nothing in these passages suggestive of healthy living either mentally or physically, nor does Valancy need such support given the improvement in her living conditions – meals according to her own tastes, fresh air, vigorous exercise, and mental stimulation – exactly the commodities that Muskoka is supposed to provide visitors. Chapters 30 and 31 describe some of Valancy and Barney's activities: "wandering at will through the enchanted Muskoka country," canoeing, berry-picking, gathering waterlilies, trouting, sleeping outdoors, swimming, snowshoeing, and skating. Despite all these activities, Valancy "had not even a cold" and "her heart bothered her very little." Her improved appearance is also described in terms that explicitly indicate improved health: "Her eyes were bright and her sallow skin had cleared to the hue of creamy ivory ... she was really fat at last – anyway, no longer skinny."[45] Whether it is because of happiness and freedom or because of physical activity in itself, it is clearly the activities and lifestyle that support Valancy's exploration of nature and that actually improve her health, just as the Muskoka promotional material promised.

The Commodification of Health and Nature

For Montgomery, too, the Muskoka region represented rejuvenation and escape. It was at Bala, in the heart of this tourist area, that in 1922 she had the extended daydream she recounts in various versions, resurrecting her cousin Frede and pairing off her friends according to her sense of their suitability rather than their actual relationships. Recording her imaginings in her journal, as Rodenburg suggests in the next chapter, "enables her to control and construct the place of the Muskokas envisioned through her tourist gaze."[46] In stating in her journal that she does not try to account in her dream how they manage about the mosquitoes, she also refers to it as a "fairy dream," echoing the language she will later use in descriptions in the novel. It was not until 1924 that she actually started to write *The Blue Castle*, but these descriptions of her daydream suggest their influence on the imaginary world of the novel. Montgomery clearly found Muskoka beautiful apart from the dream world she creates. The name, to her, is "music – charm – wonder – it suggests them all." In language similar to that of the advertising brochures, she writes, "The hot, noisy world was far away – cool silence was all around me – the gods of the wild wood welcomed back their own."[47]

10.1 Dreaming, Bala

Montgomery used the scenery of Muskoka to imagine a new life in which Ewan was not a minister and Frede was still alive, nullifying the major stress and the major grief of her experiences in Ontario – a happier world than the one she actually inhabited. Perhaps because of the pleasant daydream she created while at Bala, she also enjoyed writing *The Blue Castle*: "I am finding much pleasure writing my new book *The Blue Castle* and getting ready to write Emily III," she notes in a journal entry dated November 1924. In March 1925, she finished revising the novel: "I am sorry it is done. It has been for several months a daily escape from a world of intolerable realities." These "intolerable realities" included Ewan's mental health issues during this period. Like the Stirlings' self-medication, Montgomery's medication of Ewan was frequently carried out without medical advice, using non-prescription drugs including bromides, veronal, blue pills, and chloral, a mixture of sedative, hypnotic, and liver/digestive treatments. In the weeks prior to their Bala trip, Montgomery records in her journal that Ewan "had a return of headache and melancholia" and "has been very dull and moody of late" but observes several days into their stay that "Ewan has been rather dull, too, bothered by headache and depression but seems better now."[48] The first time that Montgomery notes that she is working on *The Blue Castle* (10 April 1924) immediately follows a period in which she records "the worst attack [Ewan] has ever had" and discusses her conclusions about his condition based on what she has read: "I have read a great many books on melancholia and neurasthenia in these past five years and it always seems to me that his attacks are more like neurasthenia or, indeed, hysteria than melancholia," a belief partially supported by one of the doctors they consulted. Ewan's problems recurred throughout the period in which Montgomery wrote and revised *The Blue Castle*, and she continued to treat him experimentally, including with "thyroid" pills, which she intended to discontinue in order to monitor the results.[49] In this same entry, she notes her pleasure in writing, explicitly linking the pleasure of recalling Muskoka with escape from Ewan's condition. Similarly, there is a link between her assessment of Ewan's condition as neurasthenia and the early marketing of Muskoka as a location to recover from neurasthenic symptoms.

As Lawson asserts, "The language of illness – 'anodynes,' 'pain,' 'opiate' – begins to permeate [Montgomery's] writing about *The Blue Castle*, suggesting that this new book was not only an *escape* from the world of Ewan's illness and her worry, but also an *immersion* into the domain of sickness" and therefore "simultaneously the anodyne genre that treats it and an expressive symptom of the malady"[50] and the source of the imaginative creation of Valancy's achievement of freedom through the experience of illness. Clearly the world of the novel represents escape and relief. It focuses on a life of nature worship, lived in a beautiful landscape. The story has the happy ending of the kind with which Montgomery was most comfortable. The minor characters allowed her to use her gift for humour. And not least, the plot and the setting allowed her to recreate the happy daydream that in her imagination restored her lost Frede, the one person with whom she felt, as Lesley Clement argues in chapter 13, that her "public personae" were unnecessary.[51] Looked at this way, it is easy to see why writing *The Blue Castle* would be "a daily escape."

For Montgomery, in visiting Muskoka as a tourist and experiencing there the imaginary recovery of a lost friend and a pleasant mental recreation while admiring the natural scene, the promised commodity had been delivered. She experienced relief from her troubles, romantically enjoyed the scenery, and felt at one with the natural world. In turn, she used this experience and some of her journal and epistolary record of it to produce another commodity, the novel *The Blue Castle*. The novel does not give an explicit empirical reason for Valancy's improvement in health and happiness. The references to "fairy" and to her imaginary "Blue Castle" keep the story firmly in the realm of fantasy, even though it is possible to account for Valancy's health through lifestyle changes or through psychological change. Either way, according to the philosophy expressed by Barney when they are stranded in the car on the way back from the dance, Valancy purchases the change in her condition: "If you buy your experience it's your own. So it's no matter how much you pay for it." Valancy is also described as paying for her happiness on the night Barney is out in the storm, on the night she gets her foot stuck in the train track, and on the day she learns of Dr Trent's mistake.[52] In these passages, the price of happiness is pain, and Valancy has apparently already had enough pain in her life to purchase both the happiness of her naturally and imaginatively created Blue Castle represented by the pines above Barney's cabin and the "nearest thing to the Blue Castle of your dreams" Barney can think of, the Alhambra. The money from Redfern's proprietary medicines, given to them as a wedding present, and the money from John Foster's selling of Muskoka will support Barney and Valancy's tourist experiences of "the beauty of the world" and will purchase the picture of Valancy as "the Spirit of Muskoka" that was previously rejected because they are "outlaws."[53] The public acknowledgment of Barney's right to the Redfern and John Foster brand names that establishes the propriety of Valancy's marriage thus restores Valancy to the "old-family set" and allows her to supplant Olive as the prime representative of the clan's brand, reinforcing the notion that the proprietary is the governing principle of the society Montgomery depicts in *The Blue Castle*. Epperly notes that the "apparently effortless communion with Nature, Beauty, and thus Home that characterizes the early novels becomes a site for fiercer opposition if not greater effort for the heroines through the years."[54] That statement is certainly borne out in relation to this novel, as Montgomery apparently raises the possibility of that direct connection with nature not being a birthright of the willing heroine but a commodity that must be purchased.

11

Bala and The Blue Castle: *The "Spirit of Muskoka" and the Tourist Gaze*

LINDA RODENBURG

> Whether we travel to foreign lands or just across the room, we all journey and from our journeying define ourselves.
> ~ Susan L. Roberson, introduction to *Defining Travel*

In July 1922, L.M. Montgomery travelled north 130 kilometres from her home in Leaskdale, Ontario, with her husband and two sons, to vacation in Bala, a small community in the Muskoka Lakes region that she initially describes in her journal as "a dear spot." For her, it has "the flavor of home"; she compares the "roar of its falls" to "the old surge roar of the Atlantic on some windy, dark-gray night on the old north shore." In Bala, she dreams of building a summer cottage on an island; she sits on a veranda and spends the afternoon "liv[ing] it all out in every detail." Indeed, in the thirteen days she spends in the Bala area, she finds locations as "lovely as [her] dream-built castle"[1] that inspire her to write *The Blue Castle*, a novel through which, Mary Rubio argues, she "was able to reinforce all the prevailing ideologies [of the domestic romance] which her conventional readers expected while at the same time embedding a counter-text of rebellion for those who were clever enough to read between the lines." *The Blue Castle* reflects Montgomery's experience in the Muskokas and represents, according to Rubio, a "room of Montgomery's own" in which an ordinary woman – Valancy Stirling – becomes extraordinary as a result of her ability to assert control over her own location.[2]

The Blue Castle, then, is Montgomery's adult novel of female empowerment, one that grows out of her exposure to and experiences in a new environment. What was it about this act of travelling, and this particular vacation-spot, that enabled Montgomery to write such a novel? Can contemporary literary tourists visiting Bala today, specifically its museum set up to honour Montgomery and her work, make productive and nuanced connections to this particular story and to Montgomery as an author? I draw on Yi-Fu Tuan's distinctions between place and space, John Urry's formulation of the "tourist gaze," and the theoretical works on tourism of Erik Cohen and Dean MacCannell to argue that Bala offers the possibility for a tourist experience today that links back to Montgomery's journey to the Muskoka region, relates to the novel this travel inspired, and encompasses contemporary Montgomery-related tourist sites. Critical readings of Montgomery's experiences and those of her main character, Valancy Stirling, *as* tourists lead to alternative conceptualizations of the tourist that can – like *The Blue Castle* itself – both reinforce dominant expectations and undermine them. If visitors to Bala read these entries from Montgomery's journal and this novel in critical relation to the contemporary "text" of the Bala Museum, their visit to Bala has the potential to enable an integrated reading experience that allows not only access to a recreational experience but *also* participation in Montgomery's questioning nature and Valancy's "Spirit of Muskoka."[3]

Montgomery's love for the Muskoka region is clear from her journal entries for the July 1922 trip. She recognizes a spirit in this region that appeals to her for two reasons: it reminds her of her original home in Prince Edward Island, and it speaks to her as a writer strongly affected by place. Six days after her arrival in the region, Montgomery begins writing in her journal. Rooming at Roselawn, a boarding house in Bala situated on the Muskosh River and run by Miss Toms, while taking meals close by in the home of Mrs Pykes, "a lady cumbered with much serving," Montgomery describes the area in detail. The "lawn runs down to the river where the bank is fringed by trees. It is beautiful at all times but especially at night when the river silvers under the moon, the lights of the cottages twinkle out in the woods along the opposite bank, bonfires blaze with all the old allure of the camp fire, and music and laughter drift across from the innumerable canoes and launches on the river."[4] In this passage, Montgomery draws on what

11.1 Montgomery on veranda of Roselawn, Bala

she knows to re-create and negotiate this location, constructing it in a way that enables her own agency. This agency is exhibited in her ability to determine what is beautiful about the Muskoka region, as she writes about this location on her own terms.

Montgomery's ability to take control of this location through writing reflects the negotiation of what Tuan would call an unknown "space" to create a "place." In *Space and Time*, Tuan posits that "'space' is more abstract than 'place.' What begins as undifferentiated space becomes place as we get to know it better."[5] When Montgomery likens the Muskoka bonfires to her own previous knowledge of "the camp fire" and interprets the sights and sounds of the evening on her own terms, she makes it explicit that she feels validated and empowered even by the name "Muskoka! Music – charm – wonder – it suggests them all." Bala "is a dear spot – somehow I love it," she states unequivocally. Her only complaint seems to be the "terrible beds."[6] For her, this unknown space quickly becomes a place: she is able to know it, have power and control within it, "endow it with value,"[7] and even love it on her own terms because of her ability, in part, to write about her experience in her journal.

In chapter 8, Emily Woster discusses Montgomery's self-construction in her journals, particularly as these relate to textual annotations in her books. Montgomery's ability to link Bala to Prince Edward Island, bringing together her stories of the two through her journaling, demonstrates her penchant for a particular type of self-fashioning, which Woster argues is highlighted in this period in Montgomery's life. Woster observes that Montgomery's "nostalgia eventually gives way to more direct self-confrontation and self-construction" between 1919 and 1930 as "she more consciously documents her present rather than past through the textual occupations of the moment." This documentation of the present, however, necessarily involves negotiations of spaces and re-creations of places through her writing, as she brings what she knows together with what she reads to assert power over her locations through further acts of writing. In this period, as Woster observes, Montgomery "reveal[s] a new 'identity pattern' in the journal that is informed as much by literature and text as it is by [Montgomery's] own past."[8]

To create this identity pattern, Montgomery maintains control over the value systems in this particular location, as is evident in the ways in which she writes about both the Muskoka region as a place and her relationships within it. For example, in her journal she discusses her continuing relationship with John Mustard, her former high-school teacher, who was vacationing in Muskoka at the same time as Montgomery and her family. Mary Beth Cavert describes Mustard as one who "bored [Montgomery] as a suitor in Prince Albert, Saskatchewan almost 30 years earlier."[9] When Mustard insists on remaining behind with her when the others go fishing, Montgomery admits to feeling "rather disagreeably conscious of the last time [they] were alone together – that evening in the twilight in Eglinton Villa, Prince Albert, when he asked [her] to marry him." However, neither refers to the past in their present location, and Montgomery retains the control of interpretation when she states that "the world has changed so much since that last time we were alone together that it is rather hard to think it ever happened." She further asserts her control over the social situation – and their relationship in this new location – by refusing the fleeting urge to discuss the circumstances of the "affair" and also by determining that the reason she "never refer[s] to them – he never refers to them ... is the same in both cases." She is adamant that she understands his reasoning and the nature of their ongoing relationship and this enables her to define it, even though Mustard does not utter a word.[10]

This control of the relationships central to her place in the Muskokas enables Montgomery to dream in ways that were not common in her everyday life. Seemingly spending much of her time alone while on this vacation, she writes that some of her old dreams, which regularly seem "lost" to her in her everyday environment, re-emerge in Bala as "immortal." She states explicitly, "I find that I can dream even yet in Muskoka."[11] Cavert summarizes Montgomery's daydream: "On an evening of magic where the river reflected the light from the moon, cottages and flickering bonfires, she imagined a summer cottage and boat dock on a beautiful island. She peopled it with her dearest kindred spirits." Most importantly, as Cavert points out, "The centerpiece of this dream was talk – the frequent 'soul-satisfying talk of congenial souls.' This was a restorative and crucial element to any daydream for Maud Montgomery, for it was the thing she craved the most."[12] Conversation and positive, trusting relationships – and here her imagining of them – emerge as central to Montgomery's construction of place.

Montgomery revels in asserting what Urry theorizes as the "tourist gaze," the ability to look at the world in a new light due to "a basic binary division between the ordinary/everyday and the extraordinary."[13] Far from being overwhelmed by her experience of this new location as a tourist, Montgomery draws strength from her time in recollection, stating, the "continuous panorama of lake and river and island made me think of Robert Louis Stevenson's lines, 'Where all the ways on every hand / Lead onward into fairyland.'"[14] Her ability to dream in this place is, by her own admission, extraordinary. It enables her not only to write about Bala but, ultimately, to imagine it in ways linked to the worlds imagined and created by other writers. In her journals, she demonstrates that she can find the way to her own version of this extraordinary fairyland while daydreaming alone on the porch at Roselawn. She envisions an ideal location, complete with her own island-based cottage. Here, she creates a story and a location filled with furnishings *"de luxe"* and with detailed relationships between people; in this location, she clearly has a prominent voice. She imagines herself within the place "talk[ing] – the soul-satisfying talk of kindred spirits, asking all the old, unanswered questions, caring not though there were no answers as long as we were all ignorant together."[15] The lack of answers does not denote a lack of control for Montgomery; her voice is clearly empowered here, and her journal writing enables her to control and construct the place of the Muskokas envisioned through her tourist gaze.

There are many kinds of tourists, however, and Cohen's "Phenomenology of Tourist Experiences" reminds us that people see locations in various ways. Cohen delineates five modes that "span the spectrum between the experience of the tourist as the traveler in pursuit of 'mere' pleasure in the strange and novel, to that of the modern pilgrim in quest of meaning at somebody else's centre." In this segment of Montgomery's journal, we see her reaching out to establish what Cohen describes as the "existential mode," which involves commitment to "an 'elective' spiritual centre" and "comes phenomenologically closest to a religious conversion, to 'switching worlds.'"[16] Bala becomes another world for Montgomery, a fairyland where she can write new stories apart from her own realities at the Leaskdale manse. In the Muskokas, she becomes a different kind of tourist than Ewan, the boys, and Mrs Mustard, who – while she is daydreaming on the veranda – have gone fishing. Fishing fits into what Cohen refers to as the "recreational mode," which occurs when the tourist seeks and attains "the pleasure of entertainment," or perhaps even the "diversionary mode," a kind of escape from daily routine "into the forgetfulness of a vacation."[17] Montgomery's experience involves a more substantial relationship to her location. However, existential tourists can never have full access to worlds other than their own, as even these tourists must return home. They cannot subvert the binary and move to the alternative centre but will live in two worlds: the world of their everyday life, where they follow their practical pursuits, but which for them may often be devoid of deeper meaning; and the world associated with this new centre, to which they will depart on periodical pilgrimages to derive spiritual sustenance.[18]

Montgomery's recognition that she cannot live in the worlds she imagines brings her pain. A few days after creating her imagined place filled with kindred spirits, she takes a tour of the area and finds the locations she visits as "lovely as her dream-built castle of last Monday ... so lovely that it hurts [her]." She knows that she must return home. Back at the manse in Leaskdale, she writes, "The vacation has been – as most vacations are – a compound of pleasures and discomforts. But the pleasures far outweighed the discomforts and we were sorry to come away – then when we got home we were glad to get home. It was so nice to see my own green lawn and maple trees again – my garden, my flowers, my house." Montgomery takes ownership of her home as a place and prepares to switch back into her role in that world. However, even six years later, when passing through Bala, she expresses her fondness for it: it is "full of pleasant memories ... I've always wanted to go back."[19]

At the manse, Montgomery returns to her normal life, but it is the world of the Muskoka region – the dream, the fairyland – that enables her to write *The Blue Castle*. Rubio posits that when Montgomery returned home, her attempts to finish the novel were initially stymied by Ewan's unstable mental health and additional upheaval in her domestic routine, but ultimately her "spirits soared and her pen started flying again." Writing about Valancy's life in the Muskokas was a "release from her cares and worries,"[20] as Montgomery continued to enact Cohen's "existential mode," switching between worlds to finish writing *The Blue Castle* in under a month. In the process, she created a character in Valancy who finds the inner strength to switch worlds, moving beyond her own initial experience as a tourist to re-create and live in a place that Montgomery is only able to visit. When Montgomery finished her revisions of the novel in March 1925, she regretted that the existential vacation it inspired had to come to an end: "I am sorry it is done. It has been for several months a daily escape from a world of intolerable realities."[21] In its completion, *The Blue Castle* represents the ultimate expression of Urry's "tourist gaze": Montgomery's ordinary life exists in a binary relationship with the extraordinary life of Valancy Stirling. Whereas Valancy elects to put herself and her own dreams at the centre of her chosen home to establish a new place in her "blue castle," her creator, according to Rubio, "closed off this book [and] resolutely returned, with dignity, to her own personal prison."[22]

The Blue Castle was published in 1926, between the second and third books of the semi-autobiographical *Emily* series, and four years after Montgomery's visit to the Muskoka region. The story is set in Deerwood, a small, lakeside town that clearly mirrors Bala: Deerwood has many geographical similarities, such as Elm Street, site of the fictional Stirling family home, which remains in Bala today, as well as conservative values akin to those of Bala of the early 1920s. Considered one of Montgomery's only adult novels, *The Blue Castle* is also her only work to be set exclusively outside of Prince Edward Island. The story centres on Valancy, a twenty-nine-year-old woman "relegated ... to hopeless old maidenhood" by her family, the Stirling clan. Valancy feels disempowered because she "had never had a chance to be anything but an old maid. No man had ever desired her."[23] She knows her position within her family – she is well aware of the systems that devalue her, reminded of them daily through her family's refusal to call her by her name. Instead, they call her "Doss" and relegate her to a secondary position within the family.

Like Montgomery, Valancy seems to find some freedom and sense of empowerment in being alone. However, her family does not permit her to stay alone in her room: "People who wanted to be alone, so Mrs Frederick Stirling and Cousin Stickles believed, could only want to be alone for some sinister purpose." Her family's vigilance allows Valancy little reflective time on her own, and she is initially unable to create an empowering "place," in Tuan's sense, on her own terms. In fact, "the only thing she liked about her room was that she could be alone there at night to cry if she wanted to." Within her home, she is "cowed and subdued and overridden and snubbed in real life"; however, she does manage to create an imaginary place that contrasts with her limiting home life. As a result, "Valancy had two homes – the ugly red brick box of a home on Elm Street, and the Blue Castle in Spain. Valancy had lived spiritually in the Blue Castle ever since she could remember. She had been a very tiny child when she found herself possessed of it. Always, when she shut her eyes, she could see it plainly, with its turrets and banners on the pine-clad mountain height, wrapped in its faint, blue loveliness, against the sunset skies of the fair and unknown land."[24] Valancy is at home in this land as a regular visitor, and her imaginary travels to it clearly reflect Cohen's "existential mode." Montgomery writes of Valancy's ability to make strong connections with "kindred spirits," mirroring the author's own experiences; as a result of her relationships with others in this fertile place, Valancy is able to question the norms of the Stirling clan.

Through her writing of Valancy's constructed dreamland, Montgomery enables Valancy to escape the Stirling home to a diversionary place in which she feels empowered and has control over the value systems. Indeed, Valancy knows the "Stirlings would have died of horror if they had known half the things that Valancy did in her Blue Castle. For one thing, she had quite a few lovers in it."[25] Each night, she travels to Spain, where her negotiation of the binary division between her limiting experiences in her daily life and the extraordinary experiences available in the exotic locale of her imagined Blue Castle reflects Urry's "tourist gaze."[26] However, the established norms are clearly still present in Valancy's imagined place: while she has numerous lovers, there is "only ever one at a time," and she does not "deliberately murder these loves as she out[grows] them. One simply fade[s] away as another [comes]."[27]

Valancy finds validation for her dreams through reading the books of John Foster, which seem to her to contain "some tantalizing lure of a mystery never revealed – some hint of a great secret just a little further on."[28] Like her Blue Castle, however, the worlds of these books initially enable diversionary tourism at best; on the eve of her thirtieth birthday, they represent only temporary escape. In order to subvert the traditions of the domestic romance, it is not enough for Valancy to imagine or read about new places; indeed, as Rubio argues, for Valancy to create a place that can represent a "room of Montgomery's own," she must move from her position as an ordinary woman to an extraordinary one. This transition involves both a challenge to the norms of her home life and a journey to explore the freedom – and face the fear – associated with Tuan's unknown and unexplored "spaces."[29]

As Tuan notes, interactions with locations are complex, and new locations can enable personal growth, provided one takes the time to negotiate them on one's own terms.[30] Valancy takes the opportunity to negotiate her newfound freedom once she has left the Stirling clan behind. Caroline Jones argues in chapter 5 that "freedom leads Valancy into traditional romantic love ... but the stronger discovery may be Valancy's own inner mother, willing and able to love, nurture, and accept herself unconditionally."[31] This self-love enables Valancy to move beyond the position offered her within her family home to establish a new role for herself as an empowered woman who can negotiate her location on her own terms. Perhaps this is the ultimate difference between Valancy and Montgomery: in Valancy, Montgomery writes a character who is able to do more than she herself can do in actuality. Valancy creates her own location of empowerment within her marital relationship, collapsing both elements of the tourist gaze to ensure that the once-extraordinary becomes central to her ongoing, ordinary existence as Barney's wife.

Valancy's original, traditional family life initially prevents this collapse from occurring. Familial relationships are central to the construction of her place; they limit her behaviour – she should be "decorous and proper and Stirlingish" as a member of the family because, as Abel Gay points out, "*They* don't like being sassed back."[32] Indeed, as both Laura Robinson and Holly Pike suggest in their chapters, Valancy's challenges to the value systems of the conservative Stirlings and accepted gender roles are linked by her family to mental illness and disease.[33] At the outset, these challenges represent a limited escape from her family's control over her. For example, when she defies her family at dinner – "she had merely *said* the things she had always *thought*" – she returns to her own room not to cry but to laugh and acknowledge that "dinner *had* been fun."[34] Although she does not travel far in this instance, she does defy her family's expectations in a way that reflects Cohen's most limited mode of tourist experiences: she is in "pursuit of 'mere' pleasure in the strange and novel."[35] She is finally able to "laugh at her clan as she has always wanted to laugh" before returning to enjoy time alone in her room on her own terms. It is telling that, at this moment, Valancy begins to look out the window and feel connected to the world beyond her family home, the natural world central to Foster's books. She feels the "moist, beautiful wind blowing across groves of young-leafed wild trees [as it] touched her face with the caress of a wise, tender, old friend" and acknowledges a connection to "the shadowy, purple-hooded woods around Lake Mistawis." She continues to find the strength to defy her family, shortly thereafter leaving to "keep house" for Roaring Abel and care for Cissy Gay, asserting to her horrified mother, "I am going to look for my Blue Castle."[36]

Much of what occurs in *The Blue Castle* reflects the tradition of the domestic romance, as Valancy is a relatively young woman – although cast as an "old maid" – who is initially denied agency and the ability to define herself. Her story demonstrates what Nina Baym discusses as central to this genre: "the failure of the world to satisfy either reasonable or unreasonable expectations [which] awakens the heroine to inner possibilities." As the novel unfolds, Valancy develops as other heroines of domestic romance whom Baym describes, with "a strong conviction of her own worth as a result of which she does ask much from herself. She can meet her own demands and, inevitably, the change in herself has changed the world's attitude toward her."[37] What occurs, however, is more than a change in attitude; Valancy does not return home to her established life but instead re-creates a new place for herself that moves beyond established norms. In leaving her established place to care for another, she moves beyond Cohen's "recreational" and "diversionary" modes of tourism toward the "existential": she commits to an "elective spiritual centre" in her friendships with the socially unacceptable characters of Cissy and Abel and, eventually, in her relationship with the outcast Barney Snaith. In choosing to live with Barney as his wife – even prior to discovering that he is, in fact, the writer John Foster and the creator of the worlds she so admires – she rejects her family's value systems to create a place of her own in the woods she previously could only glimpse from her bedroom window. Thus, as Rubio argues, Montgomery, through Valancy's experience, "has validated female experience, given voice to female emotion, and helped remove women from imprisonment within silence and pain." In enabling Valancy in this way, "Montgomery both works within the traditional literary genre of domestic romance and yet circumvents its restrictive conventions when she critiques her society"; a reader who can read "between the lines" will know that Montgomery is creating room for acknowledging women's stories that were often unwritten, and unheard, in her time.[38] Here is Rubio's "counter-text of rebellion": Valancy is able to change society's attitude towards her and to do so *without* returning home.

Montgomery creates a new life for Valancy in *The Blue Castle*, moving beyond her own "existential" tourist experience in the Muskokas to imbed her character in a new world in which Valancy controls her relationships and is able to re-create a sense of Tuan's "place" that enables her continued agency. Thus, she is able to find her "Blue Castle" and unpack the "mystery" of John Foster's books and identity. Unlike Montgomery, who must return home to Leaskdale, Valancy is able to build a life on Lake Mistawis. In fact, when she leaves her new home to become a more traditional tourist with Barney, on her "real honeymoon," she demonstrates best her ongoing ability to negotiate spaces to create places: "Despite the delights before her – 'the glory that was Greece and the grandeur that was Rome' – the lure of the ageless Nile – glamour of the Riviera – mosque and palace and minaret – she knew perfectly well that no spot or palace or home in the world could ever possess the sorcery of her Blue Castle."[39]

Valancy's actualized Blue Castle is appropriately located in the Muskoka woods, and the pine trees link her imaginary Blue Castle directly to Montgomery's own Muskoka-based "dream-built castle": Montgomery's love of Bala is instinctual because of its similarity to Prince Edward Island and the shared, recognizable "flavor of home – perhaps because of *its pines* which are plentiful hereabout."[40] This natural location, then, is notable for both its effect on the author and the story she creates in *The Blue Castle*. In the previous chapter, Pike describes not only the significance of this natural location but also the history and importance of its commodification as a site for personal rejuvenation and empowerment, arguing that "the woods have both a significance of their own and also one that is created by the person who describes them."[41] As I discuss earlier, Montgomery codes her environment and her experience and demonstrates her control over her relationships, transforming unknown spaces into known places into which she can insert her own story as well as that of Valancy as female heroine. In the process, she asserts control over, while participating in, the commodification of the location of Bala through the creation of a novel for her readers' consumption. Montgomery is clearly aware of the power of storytelling and how stories might enable readers to assert control over places of their own. As Pike discusses, the stories of John Foster enable Valancy to connect with the natural world on the terms of a consumer, and – as such – they become a "remedy that works if the consumer believes in" the stories themselves.[42] Thus, the commodification of place through stories directly relates to Valancy's ability to assert control over her experience, which can be linked to Montgomery's ability to write about this empowered woman's experience in the Muskokas in her own time.

How, then, does the story of *The Blue Castle* function in relation to the world of Bala today? Do the stories of Montgomery, through her journal entries here discussed and *The Blue Castle*, mediate the continued commodification of the "story" of Montgomery in Bala? Indeed, like the story of the pine-filled woods, the story of Montgomery's visit to Bala has no significance on its own but is created by those who experience it and seek to make sense of it on their own terms, adapting their own versions of the tourist gaze to negotiate spaces and create their own places on their own terms in the contemporary moment. This experience entails the negotiation of what Lorraine York discusses generally as Montgomery's "literary celebrity" in relation to Bala. According to York, what Montgomery "has created has become so famous that it has attained celebrity status in its own right and has circulated through various popular cultural channels while keeping Montgomery's own reflected celebrity alive and thriving."[43] This reflection invites examination of how Montgomery and her stories continue to inform Bala today. A visitor to the small Ontario community will find that "Bala's Museum" – subtitled "with Memories of Lucy Maud Montgomery" – fits well with York's discussion of sites centred on this Canadian literary icon and her works, as it conflates the celebrity of the character of Anne with the larger story of Montgomery, Bala, and *The Blue Castle*. The site is described on a plaque erected in 1993 during Bala's 125th "founding anniversary": "Bala midwife Fanny Pike and her husband, Charles, a CPR track walker, built this home in 1909. Originally one room, later additions allowed the house to be run as a tourist home. Its most famous guest was Canadian author Lucy Maud Montgomery, who had meals here with her family. That two week Bala holiday in 1922 was the inspiration for LMM's book, *The Blue Castle*, published in 1926." The museum, privately owned and operated by Jack and Linda Hutton since 1992, was designated an historic site by the Township of Muskoka Lakes Council in April 2013; its website indicates that it "has become known as one of the best LMM museums in all Canada, attracting LMM fans and scholars from all around the world (41 countries so far)."

The Huttons have accumulated a wide collection of Montgomery memorabilia, ranging from photos and written material to a large number of Montgomery's books, to a vast array of mostly *Anne of Green Gables*–related souvenirs including dolls, tea sets, and even an ashtray.[44] Thus, the museum participates in what Poushali Bhadury calls the "storm of commodification ventures (that are the) generator of a virtual Canadian subindustry" in literary tourism related to Montgomery.[45] Like the stories represented in sites highlighting Montgomery – particularly in relation to *Anne of Green Gables* – which Bhadury discusses, the story of Montgomery in Muskoka is a commodified one in multiple ways. At the site, for $4.99 per person or $16.99 per family, tourists can view this wide assortment of "artifacts," including the "silver tea set given to LMM as a wedding present in 1911 ... The basket in which Maud kept her personal correspondence ... One of the best collection [sic] of her books, including rare and first editions ... Handwritten excerpts and photos from LMM's Bala diary ... The boat that sank under actress Megan Follows in the TV movie 'Anne of Green Gables' ... [and the] Avonlea schoolhouse in miniature."[46]

Like the exhibits at the L.M. Montgomery Institute in Prince Edward Island discussed by York, where "bedspreads and lacework share cultural space with the author's writings, as objects of celebrity devotion," this disjointed assortment of artifacts provokes the question of what kind of experience is available to a tourist visiting a literary site of this nature.[47] How can such sites negotiate the relationship between Montgomery-as-author, Montgomery-as-product, and the books themselves? Certainly, the museum navigates between the "real" and "fictional" in similar ways to those outlined in both Jeanette Lynes's discussion of "Consumable Avonlea" and Bhadury's argument that the Green Gables site in Prince Edward Island is a "simulacral space," a "product of the imagination striving from legitimacy and entrance into the 'real' world to satisfy consumer desires."[48] The Bala Museum is perhaps an even more complex simulacrum: it draws on Montgomery's tourist experience to highlight the legitimacy of the relationship between the author and the Muskokas, yet it offers a tourist experience that links more explicitly to the fictional character of Anne. What is missing from the Bala Museum is not only the older Anne that channels elements of Montgomery herself – and Montgomery in Ontario – but also the less marketable, or at least less marketed, character of Valancy, along with significant reference to *The Blue Castle*.

The Huttons' book, *Lucy Maud Montgomery and Bala: A Love Story of the North Woods*, closes with the following apostrophic address: "In a way, Maud, you have never left Muskoka. As long as people continue to read *The Blue Castle*, a part of you will always remain here with us in Bala. Thank you for writing such a beautiful book. It continues to speak to us on so many different levels after more than 70 years."[49] The Huttons have travelled across Canada and beyond to bring together items which, for them, represent the "experiential mode" of travel, in which "a tourist seeks meaning from the aesthetic experience of the authenticity of the life of others,"[50] namely, Montgomery as author, primarily of the *Anne* series. As a result, like the fishing trip enjoyed by Ewan, the boys, and Mrs Mustard in 1922, a visit to the Bala Museum encourages an experience that can be classified in Cohen's "diversionary or recreational modes," as there are many items present in this house that a Montgomery enthusiast might find of interest. The authenticity of the resulting experience as somehow related to Montgomery in Muskoka, however, is undermined in some ways by the disjointed nature of the narrative here, as Montgomery's personal belongings sit side-by-side with photocopies of her journals, editions of her books, and countless representations of her characters from books, movies, plays, and other media.

Can Bala's Museum offer tourism in the "existential mode," connecting visitors today with the "Spirit of Muskoka" that caused Montgomery to ask questions and to challenge social norms through the story of Valancy Stirling? I would argue that these interrelated stories – of Montgomery, Valancy, and the contemporary tourist – rely, like the stories of John Foster, in their efficacy on the consumer's belief in them. The Huttons certainly believe, but whether their museum enables tourists to access a meaningful connection to Montgomery and her stories that moves beyond simple entertainment depends, I would suggest, on the nature of the tourist. Despite the passion and commitment with which this museum has been built, the product – the museum – sets up the possibility for Urry's "tourist gaze" to be enacted: there *is* a binary relationship between the ordinary world of Bala today and the extraordinary world represented in Bala's Museum that becomes obvious immediately when the visitor enters the museum and has the opportunity to don costumes like those worn by characters in the *Anne of Green Gables* television movie (1985), complete with hats with attached "Anne braids." An "alternative world" is on offer here, and the possibility for entertainment is present; however, the authenticity of links between a tourist's performance of a Prince Edward Island-based "Anne" in 2015 and Montgomery's experience of Muskoka in 1922, reflected in *The Blue Castle*, is questionable.

That said, the contemporary theorist Dean MacCannell links the "authenticity" of tourist sites specifically to their ability to facilitate pedagogy, textualizing a story that educates the nation about its historical past. What validates a site is not the strength of its markers but the possibility of "fixing" them with replication – a site "becomes 'authentic' only after the first copy of it is produced."[51] As Bhadury, York, and others discuss in detail, there is no doubt about the fixity and replication of Anne-related memorabilia, and such items are juxtaposed with Muskoka and *The Blue Castle* through both the Bala Museum website and the Huttons' book. Thus, one could argue that the emerging story of Montgomery in Muskoka succeeds in its own way despite the disjointed nature of its component parts. MacCannell further argues that contemporary touristic places are produced through a process validated by this commodification. The Bala Museum effectively follows the model that he outlines through the production of postcards and a book, not to mention the large assortment of products available for purchase in the museum gift shop. This process begins "when the site is marked off from similar objects worthy of preservation," which happened when the site was designated as a local historic site in 2013.[52] The second and third phases, "framing and elevation" and "enshrinement," are highlighted through the ongoing perpetuation of the site as a tourist destination – through signage, tourist brochures, and stories. One could argue that this essay actually participates in the legitimation of this site by not only putting it into a larger academic frame of reference but also reading it alongside other literary tourist destinations. The fourth phase is the mechanical reproduction of the site through further markers, including the postcards already mentioned and the doll house replicas housed within the museum. People can participate in the mechanics of reproduction through re-enactments encouraged on-site, including taking part in a raspberry cordial tea party like that of Anne and Diana in multiple renditions of *Anne of Green Gables*.[53] Such acts of reproduction are followed by MacCannell's fifth phase: social reproduction, in which "groups, cities, and regions begin to name themselves after famous attractions."[54] This volume's appendix identifies such reproduction in Ontario; in PEI, the reproduction is even more extensive.

It would appear that this process validates Bala's Museum precisely *as* a site labelled "Memories of Lucy Maud Montgomery," *as* a disjointed place celebrating a simulacral relationship between and among Bala, Montgomery, and her books. However, as the philosopher Henri Lefebvre argues, disjuncture most accurately reflects the nature of "everyday life"; therefore, Lefebvre searches for a different set of spatial codes from the dominant one that forces things to be encoded separately and systematically. He posits that the "first thing that [an alternative] code would do is recapture the unity of dissociated elements."[55] This code can be established through reading the journals of Montgomery in relation to *The Blue Castle* and the site of Bala's Museum. For those whom Rubio might call "clever enough to read between the lines," this code also enables the creation of an interrelated counter-text reflecting Valancy's imaginative and empowered "Spirit of Muskoka" and Montgomery's "soul-satisfying," questioning nature.[56]

Visitors to the Bala Museum must actively enact a tourist gaze and participate in creating a place from the dissociated artifacts at this site.

This process requires tourists to adopt a critical perspective antithetical to that of the passive museum-goer or recreational tourist; they must decide what they will include or interrogate from the myriad representations of "Maud," Anne, Montgomery's novels, and their various manifestations to recreate actively the story of Montgomery in Muskoka. "The Spirit of Muskoka" involves the tourists' acknowledgment of the power of the imagination and the importance of "fairyland"; there is ample opportunity to question "authenticity" and to place, instead, critical imaginings at the centre of the tourist's own integrated counter-text, created at the intersection of the stories in Montgomery's journals, *The Blue Castle,* and "Bala's Museum: With Memories of Lucy Maud Montgomery." Like Valancy, today's tourist should listen to the voice of "the imp" that questions the nature of place in order to discover the ever-changing, empowering "Spirit of Muskoka" that Montgomery so loved.[57]

Life in Toronto: Professional and Cultural Links

12

Advocating for Authors and Battling Critics in Toronto: Montgomery and the Canadian Authors Association

KATE SUTHERLAND

The Canadian Authors Association (CAA) was founded in Montreal in 1921, and a Toronto branch was established shortly thereafter. L.M. Montgomery was active in the Toronto branch from its inception throughout her years in Leaskdale and Norval, and, with her move to Toronto in 1935, her involvement deepened, including serving a term as second vice-president. Her involvement with the CAA was just one aspect of Montgomery's literary life in Toronto, but it stands as something of a microcosm of the latter part of her career and thus provides an illuminating lens through which to examine broader themes such as her relationships with fellow writers and critics and her place in Canadian literature.

The Montreal meeting in March 1921 out of which the CAA emerged was organized by a group of writers and academics including Stephen Leacock, Pelham Edgar, J.M. Gibbon, and B.K. Sandwell. The intent was to bring together Canadian authors and educate them about copyright in order to galvanize opposition to a new copyright bill then working its way through Parliament.[1] The bill was intended in part to protect the interests of Canadian printers, but it did so at the expense of writers. The licensing provisions it contained were of particular concern in that they appeared to leave Canadian writers wholly without copyright protection for work first published outside Canada.[2]

The organizers received an enthusiastic response to their invitations to the Montreal meeting. With more than one hundred authors in attendance (and hundreds more expressing support in absentia), a motion calling for the establishment of a national association with local branches was resoundingly approved, a slate of executive officers elected, and a constitution passed. The objectives of the new association were articulated in its constitution:

1. To act for the mutual benefit and protection of Canadian Authors and for the maintenance of high ideals and practice in the literary profession.
2. To procure adequate copyright legislation.
3. To assist in protecting the literary property of its members, and to disseminate information as to the business rights and interests of its members as authors.
4. To promote the general professional interests of all creators of copyrightable material.
5. To encourage the cordial relationships among the members and with authors of other nations.[3]

Within months, local branches of the CAA were formed in Montreal, Ottawa, Toronto, Winnipeg, Edmonton, Calgary, Vancouver, Victoria, Halifax, and Saint John, and expansion into other cities continued steadily.[4] There were two categories of membership: "creator[s] of copyrightable material ... of recognized position in [their] profession as author, composer, or artist" were accorded regular membership, while those "in sympathy with the objectives of the Association" but not yet considered to be qualified for regular membership could join as associate members.[5] The category for which an applicant qualified was left to the discretion of local executive committees.

The original purpose of fighting for Canadian copyright laws serving the interests of authors remained central in the CAA's early years, but efforts to that end were largely unsuccessful, at least in so far as the 1921 act and a 1923 amendment to it were concerned.[6] The CAA won only minor concessions for authors. Nevertheless, in her detailed history of the CAA, Lyn Harrington concludes that the battle was not fought entirely in vain: "After seven years of altruistic struggle and expense, countless hours of unpaid effort, what had the authors achieved? They were organized into an articulate body, no longer too isolated and timid to speak up for themselves and their convictions."[7]

Thus empowered, the CAA sought to serve the interests of Canadian authors in other ways, including the general promotion of Canadian literature, the encouragement of the production of Canadian literature through mentorship of young writers, and the facilitation of literary community. The promotion of Canadian literature was most visibly effected through the vehicle of Canadian Book Week, a long-running annual event first held in November 1921. Mary Vipond summarizes the event: "Book Week was simply a massive, multi-faceted publicity campaign. At the instigation of the CAA, Canadian magazines reviewed Canadian books, schools held literary competitions and awarded Canadian books as prizes, bookstores displayed Canadian books in their windows while authors autographed them inside, service club luncheons and church services alike were addressed by leading literary figures with one common message: buy Canadian books."[8]

Montgomery did not attend the founding meeting of the CAA in Montreal in March 1921. Her biographer Mary Rubio notes that at that time, living in Leaskdale, assisting her minister husband, and raising two young sons, she was too busy to do so; but "she followed events with great interest,"[9] and she was on hand for the first meeting of the Toronto branch shortly thereafter.[10] Five years before, in 1916, she had joined the Authors League of America prior to initiating legal action against her first US publisher, L.C. Page and Company. Although that gruelling litigation would not reach a final conclusion until 1928, by 1921 Montgomery had chalked up one legal victory against Page with the assistance of a lawyer obtained through the Authors League. A lack of effective copyright protection for Canadian authors was one of the factors that rendered her vulnerable to the exploitation by Page that culminated in their legal battle. In part, Montgomery endured that lengthy battle despite its enormous personal and financial cost because she felt an obligation to stand up not just for her own rights but also for those of her fellow authors.[11]

Against that backdrop, it is no surprise that she was quick to see the value of a parallel Canadian organization to advocate for authors in her home country on the issue of copyright reform as well as other literary matters. Indeed, Montgomery was explicitly named in the CAA's submissions to Parliament as an example of a popular Canadian author who would be harmed by the passage of the 1921 Copyright

Bill.[12] Publishing some of her stories first in Canada had put her at a disadvantage in her dealings with an unscrupulous US publisher under US copyright law; if the Canadian bill were to be passed in its original form, the alternative course of publishing first in the United States (adopted by many successful Canadian writers) would deny her copyright protection in Canada.

Montgomery was also in sympathy with the broader aims of the CAA, as evidenced by the content of her public speeches and by the various activities in which she engaged to assist fellow writers.[13] She encouraged readers to buy Canadian books, and she praised the books of lesser-known Canadian authors in her speeches and reviews. She took pleasure in the fact that the profits generated by her books enabled her publishers, McClelland and Stewart, to take chances on the work of new, young Canadian writers, and she wrote blurbs to promote their books. She maintained a lively correspondence with a number of up-and-coming writers, offering them encouragement and advice. Finally, as Lesley Clement explores in depth in the next chapter, she relished the intellectual stimulation that participation in literary gatherings in Toronto and elsewhere provided.

Clearly Montgomery was well suited for an active role in the CAA, and she was an enthusiastic participant in the activities of the Toronto branch from its inception, despite then living some distance away in Leaskdale. For example, on 16 November 1921, on the eve of the inaugural Book Week, she reports in her journal, "I have been very busy, and have sat up till twelve or one every night writing letters and publicity articles for the Canadian Book Week which begins Saturday." She travelled to Toronto the following day to take part in the event, sitting at the head table at a dinner in honour of Nellie McClung held at the Arts and Letters Club on the first night and attending a series of speeches, plays, and receptions over subsequent days.[14]

On 23 April 1923, she wrote of going to Toronto to attend that year's CAA convention where, at another dinner at the Arts and Letters Club, she experienced the novelty of her first sight of Canadian women smoking in public. On that occasion, she has this to say after being updated on the status of the CAA's ongoing copyright fight: "We had a breeze over the newly passed Copyright Bill. Nobody can understand it. I believe it will kill our young Canadian authors altogether and in the end our Canadian literature. Under the terms of it publishers will be afraid to accept the work of unknown authors."[15]

Montgomery's CAA involvement continued after her move to Norval in 1926, from where it was easier to travel to Toronto. In her journal, she documents giving an address to the CAA on 11 February 1928, and, later the same year, again playing a prominent role in Book Week: "Yesterday I went into Toronto and at night Dr Charles Roberts, Arthur Stringer, Bernard Sandwell and I opened the annual Canadian Book Week by speaking in Convocation Hall to an audience of 2,000 people, after another thousand had been turned away. I had never faced such a big audience before and for a moment I came all out in goose-flesh. But they received me so rapturously that I forgot to be nervous and told my stories of the old north shore as to friends."[16]

Montgomery found these jaunts to Toronto a welcome respite from the stresses and sometimes boredom of her domestic life as a mother and a minister's wife. After a trip to Toronto on 14 February 1931 to read a chapter from her new book, *A Tangled Web*, at the CAA, she confides: "I had little heart for it but I found that I enjoyed the evening for all. A little incense does hearten one up! And a little conversation with people who are interested in something besides local gossip." She often felt that her writing was undervalued or even actively disapproved of at home and so relished being lauded at such events for her talent and success by her readers – "After the affair was over I was literally mobbed by hundreds of girls wanting autographs" – and especially by literary peers: "I did not find it unpleasant when Dr. Logan of Halifax came up to me and said, 'Hail, Queen of Canadian Novelists.'" On occasion, Montgomery rued that other obligations prevented her from participating even more fully in CAA affairs. She particularly regretted missing out on a trip to England in the company of fellow CAA members in June 1933: "The Canadian Authors' Association is going to England – leaves Wednesday – at least most of them. I wanted to go too, more than I've wanted anything for years but several reasons made it impossible."[17]

When Montgomery moved to Toronto in 1935, she no doubt anticipated greater opportunity to participate in the literary culture that she had so enjoyed on visits. Rubio writes: "She had wanted all her life to be part of an intellectual community of people who loved books, and now she was on the verge of getting her wish." Further, with her husband retired and her sons grown, she was released from parish duties and some of her domestic responsibilities and could put the time and energy thus freed up into literary service: "Maud looked forward to putting her organizational skills and her celebrity to use in a new context. She was public-spirited, and as an ardent Canadian nationalist, she wanted to foster the growing field of Canadian literature."[18] She likely expected that her work with the CAA would be a central part of her life in Toronto as a prominent and successful author.

To a considerable extent, this proved to be the case. Her involvement with the Toronto branch of the CAA deepened, including a term as second vice-president. Minutes of the executive committee meetings show her regularly in attendance, making and seconding motions, and participating in decisions about branch membership and activities.[19] She also continued to attend CAA events, sometimes on the podium and other times in the audience. Her Toronto years, from 1935 until her death in 1942, were difficult ones marked by illness (her own and her husband's) and anxiety. She worried about her sons' difficulties in university and their questionable romantic entanglements and, most dominantly, about the possibility that her elder son, Chester, had inherited his father's mental illness. Her work on the CAA executive and her attendance at CAA and other literary events provided distraction from that illness and worry. Her journals from those years are peppered with references to meetings and events that, whatever her prior expectations, ultimately lifted her spirits.[20] A poignant example can be found in an entry dated 28 January 1937, following the death of her beloved cat Lucky: "I went to a meeting of the Authors' Association tonight and 'forgot' for a little while. But when I came home – there was no Lucky. Who could have believed that the passing of a little cat could leave a house so empty – so desolate? But I have so little companionship. Ewan is wrapped in his hypochondriac fears and symptoms – I am alone – alone." In October of the same year, her concern about Chester's behaviour and mental state now intensifying, she writes: "I went to the opening meeting of the Authors' Association this evening and found it rather pleasant. A lady told me she had met a family in BC who had 'read all my books and all Hardy's'! What a conjunction! I walked home from the car line in the crisp cool night. Thank God I can escape now and then from reality again. I could not go on if it were not for these occasional moments."[21]

However, Montgomery's experience on the CAA executive was by no means uniformly positive. She was often frustrated by lack of progress at meetings. She sums up 22 September 1937: "In the evening I went to an Executive meeting of Canadian Authors' at Mrs. Junor's. Much talk and little done as usual." In a similar vein, on 18 October, she reports: "This evening I went to an executive meeting of the CAA. The men smoked and argued till a quarter to twelve over the program for book week and got nowhere. My head ached and I was glad when it ended." She had long felt that "the Association is not what it should be and is not doing the work it should be."[22] Rubio writes: "According to Eric Gaskell, later the national executive director of the CAA, Maud brought many ideas to these CAA meetings," including suggestions to improve "management, organization, and fund-raising within the CAA."[23] However, even as second vice-president, she does not appear to have had the power to put her ideas into effect.

Her efforts may well have been stymied by some of the men whom she encountered within the CAA, members of Canada's developing literary old boys' network who had openly expressed disdain for Montgomery's writing. Interaction with these men could thoroughly sour her enjoyment of CAA activities. Chief among them was William Arthur Deacon, a powerful critic who was shortly to become literary editor of the *Globe and Mail* and president of the Toronto branch of the CAA. In a journal entry dated 16 September 1935, Montgomery says of Deacon: "I am on the [CAA] executive this year and heartily wish I were not. One of the men on it is no friend of mine and has gone out of his way many a time to sneer at my books in the nastiest fashion. So it is not pleasant for me to be associated with him."[24] Deacon had gone very public with his criticism of Montgomery some years previously, writing in a "Survey of Canadian Literature" published in his 1926 essay collection *Poteen*: "Lucy Maud Montgomery of Prince Edward Island shared the quick popularity of [Ralph] Connor in a series of girls' sugary stories begun with *Anne of Green Gables* (1908). Canadian fiction was to go no lower; and she is only mentioned to show the dearth of mature novels at the time."[25] This pronouncement had been a surprise and a serious blow to Montgomery. Certainly she had weathered bad reviews before, but on the whole, her work had been well received by critics.[26] Just two years earlier, in a more broad-ranging survey, John Logan and Donald French had identified 1908 as "the real beginning of the Second Renaissance in Canadian fiction," in part because it was the publication date of *Anne of Green Gables*; of the novel, they said that it "may confidently be labeled a 'Canadian classic.'" They had expressed praise for Montgomery's entire oeuvre and, far from dismissing her work as being for children only, had described *Emily of New Moon* as "an adult's story of youth" by virtue of the "analytic psychological method" that Montgomery employed in depicting her heroine.[27]

Montgomery could be forgiven for assuming that she had earned a solid place for herself in the pantheon of Canadian letters. But stark condemnation and dismissal by a high-profile critic such as Deacon in a critically acclaimed and briskly selling book dented her hard-earned literary reputation. And Deacon, although he was clearly trying to make a splash by going against the popular grain, did not prove an outlier. With the growing embrace of realist and modernist fiction, other critics soon piled on. Although her books remained popular with readers, more and more often they were dismissed by critics as sentimental, poorly written, and of interest only to children if at all. Little wonder then that Montgomery did not enjoy her interaction with Deacon in the CAA, particularly since his disdain for her work seemed to extend to her person. She recounted being snubbed by him at a Press Club lunch at which he was seated next to her but did not speak one word to her, leaving her to dine in silence.[28]

Other CAA members critically dismissed and personally slighted Montgomery as well. The esteemed University of Toronto English professor Pelham Edgar barely made mention of her when tasked with proposing a toast to her and four others at a CAA dinner given in their honour: "He orated freely about Sir Charles Roberts who fitly represented Canada's poetry, Sir Ernest MacMillan who had rendered great services to music and Sir Wyly Grier, a worthy representative of Canada in arts. Remained only Dr Hardy and myself. Dr Hardy is a noted educationalist and had I not been one of the five I know Prof. Edgar would have made as fulsome a speech about him as about any of the others. But to have done this and then merely mentioned my name – for Prof. E. would have died any death you could mention rather than admit *I* represented Canadian literature – would have been *too* pointed, so the good Edgar selected his horn of the dilemma and impaled himself thereon. He merely said, 'The other two who are included in this toast are Dr Hardy and Mrs Macdonald'!!"[29]

Despite its frustrations and occasional indignities, Montgomery generally enjoyed her CAA work and valued it enormously. Thus, it was a great blow to her when, through some backroom manoeuvring, she was ousted from the executive in 1938. She laid the blame squarely at the feet of Deacon.[30] In a journal entry dated 8 April, she recounts: "I have had two bad days. It has been stormy and cold. Tonight I went to the Authors'. The election of a new executive was held and I was elbowed out. It is not worth while going into details. Deacon had it all planned very astutely and things went exactly as he had foreseen. I at once withdrew my name from the list of candidates. It does not matter in the least to me that I am not on the executive. Deacon has always pursued me with malice and I am glad I will have no longer to work with him. He is exceedingly petty and vindictive and seems to be detested by everybody who knows him. All this would have hurt me once but now it doesn't matter at all."[31]

There is no public record of how the ousting of Montgomery was effected nor of what precisely Deacon's role in it was, but Rubio fills in some of the gaps: "In 1937, Maud had been the second vice-president of the Toronto branch of the CAA, and had things progressed normally she might have ascended to the presidency ... [but] Deacon saw this power vacuum after Kennedy's death [then national executive secretary of the CAA] as a chance to sweep the 'old guard' out of the Toronto CAA executive. Maud was one of his targets. It was widely known that he was not a fan of Maud's writing. He liked to be in charge, and he liked even more to be 'seen' to be in charge, as his biographers note. The leadership vacuum gave him the opportunity to work behind the scenes to shake up the executive slate and dump Maud in the process." There were those who could see the value that Montgomery had brought to her work with the executive and who regretted her departure. Perhaps in recognition of this as well as of her successful literary career, in 1940 she was awarded an honorary membership, "the highest distinction of the CAA."[32] But after her painful ousting, she was never to regain her prominence within the organization.

The conflict between Montgomery and Deacon within the CAA is a tale worth telling simply on the basis that both are important figures in Canadian literary history and both are fascinating personalities. But a detailed consideration of this episode is also a valuable undertaking for the insight that it can afford into the latter part of Montgomery's career, as well as for what it reveals about Deacon and the inner workings of the CAA and how it thereby illuminates Canadian literary culture in the interwar period.

What prompted Deacon's strong animus toward Montgomery? What grounded his determination to remove her from the executive of the Toronto branch of the CAA? Rubio points to evidence that "like many men of his generation, Deacon held a patronizing attitude towards women."[33] Yet this attitude did not manifest in a general denigration of women writers. He publicly championed several novels by women, including Martha Ostenso's *Wild Geese*, Laura Salverson's *The Viking Heart*, and Mazo de la Roche's *Jalna*.[34] And there were a number of women writers whom he mentored in private correspondence.[35] Further, he was a close friend of prominent feminist Emily Murphy and even praised her as a pioneer for women's rights in a memorial published in the *Mail and Empire* on her death in 1933.[36] I do think that sexism was a key factor in Deacon's dealings with Montgomery, but it operated in complex ways. It was not a simple matter of dismissing Montgomery's work because of her gender but rather because of the presumed gender of her readers ("girls' sugary stories") and, relatedly, because of the genre of fiction she wrote (popular, sentimental, provincial). Fully exploring how this dynamic affected Deacon's personal interaction with Montgomery requires a closer look at the gender and genre politics in play within the CAA and in its relationship with its external critics.

Large numbers of women were involved in the CAA from its inception, including in positions of power. Indeed, Carole Gerson points out, "By the 1930s women comprised the majority of [its] members."[37] In 1939, Madge Macbeth was the first woman to be voted in as national president, and she was re-elected twice to serve a record three terms. This is not to say, however, that the CAA was a bastion of equality. At the outset, the organizers of the founding meeting in Montreal in 1921 were horrified to find that more than half of the authors who had agreed to attend were women ("They could make the time for travel").[38] In subsequent years, the ascension of women to leadership positions sometimes provoked bitter opposition, not least in the case of the historic election of Macbeth to the office of national president. Those who sought to block her bid for the presidency were motivated by a range of factors, but her sex was unquestionably one of them.[39] A group led by Charles G.D. Roberts nominated Deacon as an alternative, and Deacon, although he had already pledged to support Macbeth, agreed to run, leading to a nasty six-week campaign at the conclusion of which Macbeth prevailed.[40] That was not the end of the matter, however. Deacon remained resentful, and his unhappiness and that of other members of the Toronto branch over the outcome manifested in a very disrespectful reception for Macbeth when she travelled from Ottawa to make a speech at the annual CAA dinner. Kathryn Colquhoun describes the scene: "[E.J.] Pratt was in the chair and he, and Prof De Lury, spoke so long, that she didn't get a chance to say a word. A lot of people thought that it was a put up job, as Pratt had charge of things as chairman. Then, when she was [re]elected National President, none of the executive, Pratt, Deacon or Edgar, attended the Convention."[41]

There are echoes in this campaign and these incidents of the treatment that Montgomery received within the CAA – the public slights delivered to her by Deacon and Edgar and the machinations to prevent her from advancing further in the CAA power structure. Perhaps the role played by Deacon in both scenarios also provides some indication that, while he was generous in mentoring some women writers from a position of power, he was not so keen to have women serve in positions of power parallel to or above him. Certainly he was not prepared to let women such as Montgomery and Macbeth stand in the way of his personal ambition.

The foregoing offers some insight into gender politics within the CAA in Montgomery's time: but what of the gender dimension to external critiques of the CAA and of the way in which that in turn affected gender relations within the CAA? Daisy Neijmann highlights two factions of the Canadian literary scene during the interwar period and describes how the CAA, rather than serving as a forum for debate between them, came to be identified with only one side: "The association's vigorous and largely conservative nationalism, as well as its attention to writers' professional and financial interests and its apparent disregard for the quality of its membership's work, which was perceived to cater to a morally and culturally conservative readership ... soon incurred the scorn of younger, more radical writers such as [Raymond] Knister, [Frederick Philip] Grove, and [Morley] Callaghan, whose isolated attempts at more 'universal' and innovative writing aimed to jolt Canadian literature out of its staid, Victorian mould, into the twentieth century." Neijmann identifies a gender as well as a genre dimension to the opposition between these factions: "It represents in many ways a debate between writers of a more popular Canadian literature, much of it written by women, and those of intellectual, cosmopolitan, and experimental writing."[42]

Rubio and Elizabeth Waterston offer a more detailed articulation of the link between gender and genre in the context of the shifting winds of literary fashion in this period: "Romantic, affirmative women novelists like Mazo de la Roche, Marian Keith, and Marshall Saunders – and L.M. Montgomery – had been dominant throughout the first part of the twentieth century. Their dominance was now giving way (at least in the eyes of literary critics) to a new cadre of darker (male) realists, including F.P. Grove and Morley Callaghan."[43] Gerson asserts: "The assumption underlying the reception of women writers in Canada during the critical canon-forming decades between the wars was that women's writing was expected to conform to a Romantic/sentimental/domestic model. Those who followed suit and did not practice modernism were then easily dismissed, while those who engaged with modernist methods were seldom taken as seriously as their male counterparts and have been consistently under-represented in the canon."[44]

Thus, Rubio points out that Montgomery's style and subject matter were such that she was never going to attain acceptance under the modernist aesthetic in ascendency in the 1920s and 1930s: "The new post-war Modernist critics called for a tough, hard-edged, pared-down style, as well as gritty subject matter, including tortured people, war, criminality, and sex. Maud's writing – humorous, domestic, and localized in a rural region – fell short on all counts."[45] And Gerson makes clear that, even if Montgomery had changed her writing, she would have been unlikely to have thereby garnered the approval of the modernist faction.[46] The fate of Icelandic Canadian writer Laura Salverson is instructive in this respect. In her later work, she embraced the realist and, to some extent, modernist credo, only to have her work censored by her publishers and to experience diminishment of sales and of critical acclaim, and she still failed to gain any attention in the male-dominated modernist realm.[47]

A vivid demonstration of the conflation of gender and genre in the criticism levelled against the CAA from outside can be found in F.R. Scott's poem "The Canadian Authors Meet." In it he pokes vicious fun at the "poetesses" of the CAA personified by one "Miss Crochet" whose "muse has failed to function" and characterized en masse as "virgins of sixty who still write of passion."[48] Gerson notes that it is no surprise that Scott would choose to ridicule the CAA in this highly gendered way at a moment in time when it was increasingly dominated by women and aligned in the eyes of young academic critics with sentimental styles and subject matter primarily identified as female.[49] A parallel although less public example of the subjection of the CAA to ridicule by virtue of its association with women writers can be found in the incident described in the next chapter of "a 'rare night at Arts and Letters monthly dinner' featuring 'a debate in burlesque' on a resolution to abolish the Canadian Authors Association and about women as authors" at which "Doug Hallam, in drag" impersonated recent CAA honouree Nellie McClung.[50]

What, then, were members of the CAA to do if they wished to remain personally and institutionally relevant in the face of such criticism? One strategy would have been to reform the CAA, sweeping away the old guard, in particular the senior women and the writers and supporters of sentimental fiction and verse whose presence made the ridicule of Scott and others resonate, and to draw in up-and-coming young writers who were increasingly garnering acclaim with gritty, realist fiction or experimental poems. This, I would argue, was the course adopted by Deacon.

Deacon's biographers Clara Thomas and John Lennox indicate that, upon becoming president of the Toronto branch of the CAA in 1937, he "had several objectives for the reconstruction of the branch which was then, he thought, part of a 'pretty dead organization,'" including "the consolidation and increase of membership, particularly of young writers" and "the creation of a new sense of purpose and direction." Further, they note, "As his term continued he was more and more apprehensive of the inhibiting effect of what he called the Old Guard – Pelham Edgar, W.G. Hardy, B.K. Sandwell – on the association's ability to change and adapt."[51] Deacon's correspondence suggests that his plans to divest the old guard of their power were speedily put into motion. In a letter dated 7 October 1937 to a young male writer who had been critical of the CAA, Deacon attempted to persuade him to join by taking the following tack. He conceded that "there are maiden ladies in the membership" but signalled that that might shortly change in that a "palace revolution is going on at the present moment" whereby "older people of established fame are standing aside for those in mid-career."[52] Montgomery was not Deacon's only target, but it seems clear that pushing her out of the executive in 1938 was part of a strategy to steer the CAA away from its identification with popular, and sentimental, and Victorian literature, in effect to de-feminize it in a bid to curry favour with a new guard, and to thereby protect Deacon's position in the vanguard of Canadian literary criticism.

I would argue too that, in so doing, Deacon was not merely propagating his own literary tastes but also in some measure covering what he perceived to be his deficiencies. Thomas and Lennox note that, although "Deacon consistently denigrated [Montgomery and Connor] for their sentimental optimism, his own fantasies about Canada and Canadians ... ran on the same track"; even though he championed Callaghan and other controversial young writers, "he was never as radical in his literary opinions as he thought himself to be." In particular, "he always remained somewhat baffled by the work of the modernist poets and more than a little defensive about all poets and critics he felt to be of the academic world."[53] That defensiveness may account for the vehemence with which he denigrated Montgomery and threw in his lot with her realist and modernist critics. Perhaps just as Deacon had become an emblem for Montgomery of the forces conspiring to push her hard-won literary reputation into decline, she had become an emblem for him of the literary past that had to be cut loose for Canadian literature, and for himself as its most prominent booster and critic, to thrive. Hence their seemingly out of proportion antipathy to one another.

Montgomery's involvement with the CAA was just one part of her literary life in Toronto, but it serves as an effective lens to magnify and sharpen our understanding of the forces at play in the decline of her critical reputation in the latter part of her career, a central aspect of her Toronto years. For those familiar with Montgomery's personal story, and for those who value her work, it is heartbreaking to contemplate her having to confront those forces in the midst of all of the other difficulties she endured in the final years of her life. As Rubio notes, "Once her critical descent started, Maud's loss of status would continue steadily until her death. Not until near the end of the twentieth century, long after she was dead, would literary critics dismantle and discredit the norms that the entire generation of academic critics had worked so hard to establish in the 1930s, norms that pushed popular fiction – and almost all women's writing – completely out of the canon and off the map of literary culture."[54] But Montgomery's resurgence would eventually occur, and a fuller understanding of the literary landscape including the gender and genre politics of her time assists in making sense of the trajectory of her career and of the evolution of her posthumous reputation.

13
Toronto's Cultural Scene: Tonic or Toxin for a Sagged Soul?

LESLEY D. CLEMENT

I do like Toronto. I almost think I would like to live there. I have always said and believed that I could never wish to live anywhere save in the country. But I now begin to suspect that what I meant by "country" was really "Cavendish." I would rather live in Cavendish than anywhere else in the world. But apart from it, I really believe I would like very much to live in a place like Toronto – where I could have some intellectual companionship, have access to good music, drama and art, and some little real social life.
~ L.M. Montgomery, *Selected Journals*, 1 November 1913

When L.M. Montgomery left Cavendish to establish her new home in Ontario, she left behind a community stamped indelibly with her trademark – just how indelibly she had yet to understand. Cavendish and indeed the entire province of Prince Edward Island were just beginning to negotiate how to adopt the orphan Anne without being engulfed by her red-headed presence. Throughout the preceding chapters, we have seen various Ontario communities, large and small, domestic and public, secular and religious, imaginary and real, in which and through which Montgomery sought home. For Ontario to become her new home, and not just a place to live, it would have to provide opportunities for social, intellectual, and cultural companionship while respecting her privacy and granting solitude for reflection and creation. This chapter examines a perhaps irremediable tension that steered her quest for a community, a quest that frequently attracted her to Toronto, "tonic" for a "sagged" soul, as she writes in 1919.[1] Because of her celebrity status whereby she was constantly "lionized" – which Montgomery concedes was "not a disagreeable sensation"[2] – and because of the sense of speciousness that this lionization engendered in her, this tension was never resolved.

Passing through Toronto during his Canadian tour of 1907, Rudyard Kipling tagged Toronto as "consumingly commercial."[3] In *The Municipality of Toronto: A History* (1923), J. Edgar Middleton attributes this commercialism to American influences, seeing in Toronto's "outward semblance ... an American city ... with plays and films from the United States ... exactly such as one may see in Detroit or in Chicago." Despite this façade, Middleton continues, struggling as so many others to define his country's distinctive properties, Toronto is a "Canadian" city, "British in the North American manner ... perfectly equipped to interpret Great Britain to the United States, and the United States to Great Britain."[4] Published the year before Middleton's history, Katherine Hale's chapter "Toronto – A Place of Meeting" in her *Canadian Cities of Romance* leaves the American and British elements out of the mix to focus on indigenous and immigrant groupings and regroupings until the original settlements in the Valley of the Humber grew into a metropolis, "humming on its commercial way," with "crowds on the pavements, crowds in the trolleys, crowds in the shops." Hale rhapsodizes about the surprises that Toronto conceals, mentioning The Grange (the Art Gallery of Toronto) and the Royal Ontario Museum of Archaeology,[5] opened to the public in 1913 and 1914, respectively.

Into this maelstrom of commercialism and evolving culture, Montgomery journeyed to meet with her publishers and to do the family's shopping for items unavailable in the smaller centres of Leaskdale or Uxbridge and, later, Norval. Increasingly, as her residence in Ontario became more publicized, she was invited to Toronto to give recitations and speeches or to be the guest of honour at an organization's or friend's social function. Her hosts often entertained her with excursions to the theatre. Business and domestic obligations and opportunities for "some intellectual companionship" and "some little real social life"[6] were often accomplished in a whirlwind trip of several days. Although Montgomery regarded these excursions as respite from the familial and pastoral duties of Leaskdale or Norval, she herself became a product of

13.1 Dorothy Stevens, "The Whirlpool of King and Yonge"

the cultural industry in which she participated. In *Literary Celebrity in Canada*, Lorraine York begins with the question, "Are authors of literary works, then, no more than consumable trademarks once they enter the culture of celebrity?" Through an examination of Montgomery's awareness of and attempt to manipulate and control factors such as media scrutiny and the potential value of artifacts and places associated with her name, York argues that the author was "canny and clear-eyed about her fame" and "knew what it was to negotiate the public and the private in the face of wide publicity."[7] Quoting from a letter that Montgomery wrote to G.B. MacMillan in 1909 about the fabrication of biographical details in a false interview and conflation of the public and private spheres ("I don't care what they say about my book – *it* is public property – but I wish they would leave my ego alone"[8]), York situates Montgomery's "simple, pragmatic division between the public product, the writing, and the private entity, the writer" within "the celebrity culture that was taking shape in North America during the years she experienced her success," a culture that "militated against any such easy division."[9]

This penultimate chapter of *L.M. Montgomery's Rainbow Valleys* examines a final valley through which Montgomery journeyed. As she travelled to and from and finally took up permanent residence in the Valley of the Humber, Montgomery became more and more cognisant of the damage – and her powerlessness to stay the damage – that subsisting as a consumer product had inflicted on her "ego" (the conscious self that translates the external world, including one's public personae, to the private inner self) and her "soul" (the animating core of one's being that provides the will to persist). This is not to suggest that she was "the innocent small-town Canadian literary star described by Clarence Karr," a perception that York challenges, but rather that, even though "Montgomery was unusually articulate about and aware of the conditions and ironies of her celebrity," her Ontario years and her connections with Toronto's cultural scene generate a further irony. York observes generally that celebrity "signals the meeting and exchange of the public and private realms, and such a condition is itself productive of uneasiness," which she identifies as "one of the conditions most prevalent among the literary celebrities" whom she examines in her study.[10] But, as Montgomery says to MacMillan, the "fake" interview produced more than "uneasiness"; it "jarred on [her] horribly."[11] The jarring of "overlapping, competing spheres of cultural production" – "the very essence of ... literary celebrity," as York maintains[12] – ultimately wore down her ego. Her pursuit of tonic for her sagged soul in the cultural products of Toronto – of which she was one – reveals itself to be a toxic illusion. The cultural products to which she was drawn – primarily elocutionary and theatrical performances, later supplanted by the cinema – reflect and profile Montgomery's growing consciousness of herself as a consumer product in an illusionary and ultimately insubstantial world of literary fame.

In Cavendish, Montgomery had already experienced being a celebrity when Governor General Earl Grey personally requested a meeting with the author of *Anne of Green Gables* on his visit to the Island in September 1910, a request that Montgomery found somewhat "unwelcome."[13] Several months later, after a similar vein of resistance from her, she was convinced by her publisher, L.C. Page, to visit Boston. Montgomery states: "Hitherto my literary success has brought me some money, some pleasant letters and an increase of worries and secret mortifications. I had experienced only the seamy side of fame. But now I was to see the other side." Overcoming her feelings of insignificance and fear that she was being mocked, she found herself "besieged with invitations" in Boston and discovered a "certain requirement of [her] nature, which has been starved for years," including "gay, witty companionship and conversation ... necessary for [her] normal well-being." But her lengthy descriptions of her Boston lionization also capture the tedious demands on a public figure, and she apostrophizes facetiously, "Anne, Anne, you little red-headed monkey, you are responsible for much!"[14] Thus, from the time that *Anne of Green Gables* became an immediate best-seller in the summer of 1908, Montgomery experienced conflicting responses to her success, exacerbated, Mary Rubio concludes, by her "fragile temperament [that] found sudden fame disorienting."[15]

Because Montgomery lacked a long-standing supportive community of friends and family, her residence in Ontario intensified the disorientation generated by her fame. The Reverend Ewan Macdonald, as Rubio observes, would soon "sense that his powerhouse of a wife was hoping he would do well as a minister so that they could eventually move to a bigger community ... ideally in Toronto, where her book life was" but where he "would have been totally out of his milieu."[16] Meanwhile, Montgomery was carving out a separate life for herself in what she felt to be a more compatible and stimulating environment than the Leaskdale parish. While she was still in Cavendish, two Toronto journalists, Florence Livesay and Marjory MacMurchy, "had sought her out." She would occasionally cross paths with Livesay again; the "well-connected" MacMurchy welcomed the newly wedded couple to Ontario with lunch in Toronto as they were en route to Leaskdale.[17]

Montgomery was barely settled into the Leaskdale manse when she went to Toronto on 5 December 1911, at Marjory MacMurchy's invitation and as her house guest, for a reception that the Canadian Women's Press Club hosted for her and "Marian Keith," the pen name of Mary Esther Miller MacGregor from Galt, who also had recently married a Presbyterian minister. The reception the next day at the King Edward Hotel was, Montgomery writes, "pronounced by all a great success. In reality it was the wearisome, unsatisfying farce all such receptions are and, in their very nature, must be."[18] With MacMurchy and the president of Toronto's Women's Press Club, Jane Wells Fraser, Montgomery also attended the theatre, which in one form or another would become a favourite cultural pastime for her. The Charles Frohman production they attended at the Princess, *A Single Man* by British playwright Hubert Henry Davies, starring American stage actor John Barrymore, was typical of the frivolous British comedies staged and toured by large American syndicates in Toronto theatres. As B.K. Sandwell asserts in his oft-quoted "The Annexation of our Stage" (1911), "Canada is the only nation in the world whose stage is entirely controlled by aliens." He denounces the commercial ambitions of Broadway producers such as Frohman, whose control over what is produced, in Sandwell's view, has hindered the growth of Canadian theatre and drama. His suggestion that Canadian audiences, when given the opportunity, prefer performances of "the best English standard"[19] aligns with Montgomery's assessment of *A Single Man* as "a silly backboneless affair." She was obviously seeking something more substantial to sustain her than frivolous comedies and vacuous receptions. She was therefore "heartily glad to get back home" to Leaskdale: "Some outings I like. But they are such as I plan myself and are not of the conventional kind at all."[20] She optimistically clung to the notion that she had some control over the cultural products she consumed.

Over the next three years, Montgomery records in her journal attending only two other plays in Toronto, including a "silly and superficial" musical comedy she saw with "the MacMurchy girls" in the last week of October 1913. During this visit, she herself became the entertainment when she delivered her first public speech – as opposed to a prepared recitation or reading – and she admits to being for many months "in a blue funk at the idea." Her speech on her home province captivated her audience of eight hundred members of the Women's Canadian Club and received praise from those in the audience and the local press. Montgomery cites several of these newspapers in her journal, selecting passages that compliment her clear articulation despite her lack of elocutionary training; another describes her stature, eyes, hair, and complexion; and another finds her "a vari-talented woman who did not quite all go between the covers of 'Anne of Green Gables.'" This strange image of a woman not fully wedged inside or confined by her own literary creation prompts Montgomery to respond that "I have no intention however of rushing into a career of platform speaking."[21] Although certainly not a full-time career, putting herself on public display would become the norm throughout the next two decades. Rubio writes that with the success of this event Montgomery "embarked on a new career as a riveting platform speaker."[22] The numerous journal entries focusing on the readings, speeches, and stories she delivered are generally accompanied by accounts of the enthusiastically favourable responses of the audience and media to her content and performance. These two days that she spent in Toronto were a time of "no cares, no worries. I didn't have to watch over everything I said, lest it might be reported to my own or my husband's discredit." All these factors contribute to her declaration quoted in this chapter's epigraph: "I do like Toronto. I almost think I would like to live there."[23]

Because of her celebrity status, however, Montgomery had to heed not only what she said in the parishioners' presence but also, although eighty-five kilometres away, what she did and where she went in Toronto. Her giving a speech on her home province would not offend even the most orthodox Presbyterian or Methodist, but theatre was an entirely different kind of cultural product. When she attended the theatrical hit of the 1914 spring season, J. Hartley Manners's *Peg o' My Heart* at the Royal Alexandra, the society page of the *Globe* reported that "Mrs Ewan Macdonald, who has been staying with Mrs Norman [Mary] Beal, Hilton avenue, returns to her home in Leaskdale today. The authoress, who has been enjoying the theatre, says she sees all sorts of resemblances to 'Anne of Green Gables' in winsome 'Peg o' My Heart.'"[24] Robertson Davies conjectures that plays like *Peg o' My Heart* "struck a note that was resonantly and entirely of its time. It offered on the stage not what was observable fact, but a dream of what the audiences wished were true, spiced with enough contemporary fun to give it a spurious air of reality."[25] Montgomery's enjoyment of "one of the most charming little comedies I've ever seen" – despite or perhaps because of its "spurious air of reality" – was tainted by the *Globe*'s reporting her presence at the play: "All 'the parish' will see it and what will the Zephyrites think!! Verily, that I am a brand, not yet plucked from the burning!" This seems an early example from the Ontario years of Montgomery's fabrication or skewing of details for the kinds of self-dramatization discussed more fully later in this chapter. Although she claims that it was "some wretched newspaper reporter" who saw her and inserted this report,[26] its appearance in a society column that depended on submitted material and inclusion of a quotation from Montgomery and information about her hostess suggest that the notice was more likely provided by Mary Beal, an Uxbridge (Hypatia Club) friend, now living in Toronto, whom Montgomery met soon after arriving in Leaskdale. This suspicion is reinforced by the other newspaper clippings from society columns preserved in the Black and Red Scrapbooks housed at the University of Guelph Library's Archival and Special Collections that describe teas hosted by Mary. "My soul loathes afternoon teas," Montgomery exclaims after yet another of Mary's teas. "And this is in the year of grace 1919! How long does it take a world to learn how to live?"[27] These rounds of vacuous social events are reflected in Montgomery's creation of Robin Stuart, Jane's mother in *Jane of Lantern Hill*, whose finery – clothes and jewellery selected by Jane's detestable Grandmother Kennedy – cannot camouflage the young Toronto socialite's unhappiness and consequent growing thinness. By the time that Montgomery began writing this novel in 1936, her experiences with Toronto's cultural scene had been displaced by participation in its social scene. Jane's mother is depicted as a bird in a cage from which she envisions no escape, caught in a round of dances, parties, and afternoon teas where the women come and go speaking of old Mrs Kennedy as "an utterly sweet silver-haired thing, just like a Whistler mother."[28]

Montgomery's concern over what the "Zephyrites" might think was well warranted. For several years, the topic of theatre censorship had been entertaining readers of Toronto newspapers, especially the *Globe*, then edited by the ordained Presbyterian minister J.A. Macdonald, with front-page coverage of and outraged editorials over the theatrical legal battles of "the man in the green goggles." A Methodist minister, John Coburn, disguised with green goggles and false whiskers, had assumed for himself the role of official theatre censor, attending performances he thought required his vigilance and then waging legal battles throughout 1912 and 1913 against productions he deemed profane. These legal battles ensured that the city's appellation "Toronto the Good" was carried well into the twentieth century – albeit in absurd fashion. Even after a court ruling on 7 June 1913 that "restricted the church again to its traditional role of pulpit-critic, not legal guardian, of drama in Toronto,"[29] and even after the Methodist Church relaxed its strictures in 1914 on church members attending theatre,[30] theatre remained the target of official and unofficial censorship. The "tyranny of organized virtue," as Robertson Davies describes both the religious and secular restrictions on anything suspected of being "irreverent," held sway well after the Second World War over those fearful for their own and others' souls.[31] With any tyrannical regime, scrutiny of those who are publicly visible, as Montgomery was throughout her years in Ontario, is paramount.

When Hart House Theatre opened in 1919, Toronto audiences were finally exposed to serious drama, although certainly not less contentious theatre, much of it written and produced by Canadians. On Saturday evening, 19 November 1921, Montgomery records that, with Mary and Norman Beal, she attended "a couple of plays" at Hart House mounted by the Community Players of Montreal: "Good amateur acting is always enjoyable, all the more so from the absence of stage mannerisms and too-great skill. There is more reality about it."[32] In their introduction to *Later Stages: Essays in Ontario Theatre from the First World War to the 1970s*, editors Ann Saddlemyer and Richard Plant remind us that "for many people in the 1920s, 'professional' was synonymous with corrupt commercialism and the foreign domination, particularly American economic control, of our theatre."[33] Montgomery's response to the plays' "reality" came after an afternoon spent at a talk given by Basil King, another lionized Island novelist (who had, however, been living outside Canada, mostly in Boston, for more than two decades). King's talk in the Robert Simpson's auditorium was followed by a "big reception given by the Press Club to the Authors' Association," where a meeting with a friend of Frede brought Montgomery to tears: "There in that swarming mob ... I felt like a maggot in a swarm of inane maggots – at least they seemed inane in that personality smothering mass – coming and going and repeating endlessly, 'I love your books' – 'Was "Anne" a real girl?' – etc. etc."[34] Montgomery captures the spuriousness of her situation in this atypical (for her) image of the parasitic relationship between lionizers and lionized. York notes the aversion she experienced to this parasitism when she visited Cavendish in 1929: "Hot dogs and tea rooms: these were, in Montgomery's eyes, horrors of commodification, displaced objects of consumption for what was really up for sale: Montgomery herself."[35] By the early 1920s, she already sensed just how devouring these commercial relationships could be on body and soul of consumer and consumed alike.

Although Montgomery does not identify the plays she attended that Saturday evening at Hart House and whose realistic production she appreciated, advertisements and reviews confirm that they were Marjorie Pickthall's *The Wood-Carver's Wife* and George Calderon's *The Little Stone House*. Augustus Bridle's detailed laudatory review for the *Toronto Daily Star* the following Monday focuses primarily on Pickthall's play, which, one of his several headlines declares, is a "Canadian

Play: Poetic Tragedy without Stagecraft." He notes the "tension" the audience experienced as a result of Pickthall's intense, powerful language. Although he asserts that the play "is much too detached from common human experience" to make a major contribution to Canadian drama, Rupert Caplan's "integrity of delineation" of the woodcarver compensated for the play's having "almost no more action than in a tableau just come to life." Bridle then conjectures why the audience "began to laugh at [Calderon's] sombre Russian play" when "there is as much comedy in *The Little Stone House* as in the average epitaph. But the audience wanted something human after the tense atmosphere of the *Woodcarver*, and the Russian play has it ... This is tragedy that lurks on the edge of humor, and is therefore the kind that stimulates and entertains." Pickthall's play is about a woman's discovering the complicated facets of herself as wife and model for her husband's craft; Calderon's play is about a mother's "refus[ing] to give up her sacrificial idea of a dead son whose memory she worshipped in order to reclaim her living son in the starving convict."[36] These plays in tandem seem to have provoked in Montgomery a personal response to loss, memory, and the illusory position of the artist, which then prompted the uncharacteristic image of herself in a symbiotic, parasitical relationship with her admirers.

The twelve days between 18 and 29 November 1921 that Montgomery spent in Toronto exemplify the extent to which she was becoming the consumed, herself the cultural product, not just the consumer, and her sense of the toxicity to her sagged soul. The first Tuesday was a "full day – full of something at least," she writes enigmatically. In the morning, she gave a reading and brief talk followed by "writing a hundred autographs" at Moulton College; she then shopped, lunched, and took in a movie (*Quo Vadis*) with Mary Beal; later in the afternoon, she gave "readings in the auditorium of the Simpson store" to "a bumper audience. The room was packed and half as many more couldn't get in ... After it came the usual autographing and handshaking." She kept up this pace through the entire week and into the following: an audience of eight hundred girls at Jarvis Street Collegiate; "some charming women and some very foolish ones" at an IODE meeting in Parkdale; thirteen hundred boys and girls at Oakwood; fifteen hundred high-school girls at the School of Commerce ("everything seemed vanity and schoolgirls the vainest of all"); one of Mary's "At Home[s] ... the usual thing"; autographing books in Hamilton; a luncheon hosted by her publishers at the National Club; readings at Sherbourne House "to a mob of school teachers who may have been very nice individually but were bores *en masse*"; six hundred Sunday School pupils at Dunn Avenue Methodist Church; a Business Women's Club luncheon, where she was a guest along with Emmeline Pankhurst, followed by "the Press Club reception of Lady Byng" – and then home that evening to her "darling boys again." Between the trip to Hamilton and the luncheon at the National Club, Montgomery admits to being "so drugged by the rapid succession of the crowded days that I haven't really thought of home at all. But now the effects of the drug have worn off and last night my hunger for Stuart and Chester seemed absolutely physical in its intensity."[37] Celebrity has failed to sate the appetite for meaningful human interaction.

Whereas the Hart House plays give her a sense of the "tragedy that lurks on the edge of humor," the other theatrical event Montgomery attended, again with the Beals, provides her with undiluted mirth. This was the vaudeville production *Biff-Bing-Bang* of the touring Dumbells, a troupe of demobbed Canadian soldiers, which she finds "incredibly funny and well done, and I laughed as I haven't laughed for years." She particularly admires the "stunning beauties" among this troupe of female impersonators: "The ladies of *Biff-Bing-Bang* were wonderful creations, with their snowy shoulders, jewelled breasts and rose bloom cheeks. The only thing that gave them away was their thick ankles!"[38] Montgomery responds to the carefree gaiety of this entertainment, and her description, couched in humorous terms, also conveys her keen visual sense that leads to her scrutinizing of shoulders, breasts, cheeks, and even ankles. The "man in the green goggles" would not have been amused.

Although Montgomery had no aspirations as a thespian, elocution was an avocation that attracted her and would not have outraged any orthodox parishioners in Ewan's two-point callings of Leaskdale/Zephyr or Norval/Glen Williams. Many women in her novels pursue elocution as either a pastime or a career – from Anne Shirley through Sara Stanley to Ilse Burnley. Unlike her undiluted mirth over the female impersonators of *Biff-Bing-Bang*, however, Montgomery's responses to actual women displaying themselves publicly are complex, reflecting the rapid changes and ambivalent and often conflicting attitudes of the early decades of the twentieth century. The twelve days of intense lionization discussed above began with an event that, had Montgomery known the full story, would perhaps have tempered her portrayal of the guest of honour. She records that, on 18 November, she and Mary Beal attended a Canadian Authors Association dinner honouring Nellie McClung at St George's Hall, home to the Arts and Letters Club. Although Montgomery was not the guest of honour, she sat at the head table. She writes: "Nellie is a handsome woman in a stunning dress, glib of tongue. She made a speech full of obvious platitudes and amusing little stories which made everyone laugh and deluded us into thinking it was quite a fine thing – until we began to think it over."[39] Another person who gives an account of this evening, someone who did have time to think it over, would have disagreed: M.O. Hammond, a charter member of the Arts and Letters Club (of whom Sandra Gwyn writes, "the earth had seldom produced a more honourable and upright character"[40]) describes McClung in his diary on this occasion as "happy, breezy, bright" with "plenty of stories from real life, good humor and philosophy."[41]

Hammond also records the sequel to this evening in an entry for 26 November that narrates a "rare night at Arts and Letters monthly dinner" featuring "a debate in burlesque" on a resolution to abolish the Canadian Authors Association and about women as authors.[42] In her history of the club, Margaret McBurney summarizes Hammond's diary entry: "In the midst of the debate there was a noisy interruption from the gallery, where Doug Hallam, in drag, was impersonating McClung and attempting to hang a banner over the railing. A 'sergeant-at-arms' rushed up to arrest 'her.' He brought 'her' downstairs, and forced 'her' to take a drink."[43] A testament to this event is a sketch by Arthur Lismer of Hallam impersonating the abstemious McClung and a long poem commemorating the event, both of which are in the Arts and Letters Club file at the Thomas Fisher Library.[44] Although Montgomery would have had no knowledge of these specific misogynist antics, Augustus Bridle, the founder of the Arts and Letters Club, was notorious for his outspoken exclusionary views on women,[45] views that represent "the mediaeval mind" – such as Montgomery attributes to Ewan several months later – that relegated women to a place outside the citadel walls of the baronial St George's Hall. Montgomery contrasts Nellie McClung's speech to Basil King's, "full of good ideas, with no superfluities or frills or gallery plays."[46] As an aspiring public speaker, Montgomery clearly has bought into the myth with which York concludes her study: "Canadians, and Canadian women in particular, are more modest about their fame, less affected by it ... and, therefore, more authentic and unspoiled as celebrities. As the growing body of theoretical work on celebrity has amply maintained, however, this claim of authenticity holds both powerful and unstable cultural currency."[47] While the men at the Arts and Letters Club force "Nellie McClung" to imbibe, Montgomery's pen skewers a woman she deems an inauthentic woman flaunting the celebrated status bestowed on her. Montgomery's own approach is much more humble and self-effacing: "If I had had the proper training in early life I think I could have made a fairly good speaker. But it is too late now and I don't want to bother with it anyway. I have one work to do and have no time to take up another. Besides, the country is lousy with amateur speakers."[48]

When Montgomery attends Margot Asquith's lecture at Massey Hall a few months later on 27 February 1922, her response is yet more complex: "She was not worth listening to and I had not expected she would be but I was extremely anxious to see her, after reading that amazing biography of hers. She was not worth looking at either. I never saw so witch-like a profile; and she was so flat you couldn't have told her front from her back if she had been headless. Nevertheless, she was – Margot Asquith! She is a personality. You may hate – despise – deride – but you cannot ignore her."[49] Despite Asquith's androgynous appearance that obviously repels her, this grand orator provides Montgomery with an opportunity to learn how to talk "Little Things" without, as Asquith does, betraying the "Intimacies of Great Folk" (the *Globe*'s headlines for the article covering this event). The *Globe* reports that early in Asquith's speech, "she remarked that she had been told to be careful of her words in Toronto, but, with a touch of her insurgent and flamboyant youth, Margot declared: 'I cannot be careful of what I say, though,' and received the applause of the audience." The *Globe*'s reporter generally commends the orator's choice of topics and magnetic delivery, the one exception being when she performed rather than delivered "her dissertation on prohibition ... Margot illustrated with several anecdotes, which, although immensely amusing to the audience, were of an almost vulgar nature, in that each of them depicted an individual half stupid with drink."[50] Margot would have done well to remember that she was not only addressing a Toronto audience but also performing in Massey Hall, which had been built fewer than thirty years before, with "no proscenium or wings – the Hall was not a theatre, after all," by Hart Massey, a staunch Methodist, who "disapproved of drink, tobacco, cards, theatre, dancing, and other forms of self-indulgence."[51]

As a public speaker, Montgomery would need to adhere to topics more compatible with her own temperament and palatable to her audience – Prince Edward Island and its lore, her writing of *Anne*, her ascent of the Alpine Path, and advocacy for Canadian literature. Like the essays, letters, and interviews that Benjamin Lefebvre includes in the first volume of *The L.M. Montgomery Reader*, these public talks are "evidence of a more public Montgomery" and "complement and complicate the poetics of self-representation that scholars have traced in past published sources."[52] Rubio notes that, after readings that Montgomery gave to the Chatham branch of the Women's Canadian Club in 1920, the confession of her insecurity and surprise over the thunderous reception she received is one of the few times, even in the privacy of her journal, that she reveals "some of the really 'secret' aspects of her inner life": "Her life is truly a game of smoke and mirrors."[53] The journal entry Rubio refers to would have been written when Montgomery was reading Asquith's *An Autobiography* as it is dated just two days before the long entry that Emily Woster discusses in chapter 8 in her exploration of the "autobiographical meaning" and "self-creation" of Montgomery's reading. Montgomery "literally constructs herself in the journal," Woster concludes.[54] Asquith was a woman who had become a celebrity by airing secrets – hers and others' – in public. Montgomery's readings of both Asquith's text and performance reveal the potential dangers of celebrity when not just the public personae (which York's

Literary Celebrity in Canada discusses) but the ego get caught up in "a game of smoke and mirrors," especially when the rules of this game are dictated by a commercially controlled and often misogynist cultural environment. With the erosion of the ego's filter, the public personae begin to collide with the soul, leaving the soul vulnerable.

Later in life Montgomery turned more and more to the movies as tonic for her sagged soul, as pure escape, although often faulting them for being a travesty of the book or history on which they were based and with which she was intimately familiar. Many of the new movie houses had taken over the old vaudeville theatres. Toronto architect Robert Fairfield writes that these theatres were "the commercial ambitions of a few syndicates in the United States and Canada that brought mass-produced entertainment to the twentieth-century urban market, packaging it with the kind of theatre buildings they thought would lure a mass audience through the turnstiles. The result was a commercially inspired make-believe theatre architecture, aimed at creating an atmosphere into which one could pleasurably escape from the grinding realities of everyday life. In the years to come deluxe movie houses and motion picture palaces were to move those make-believe creations into new realms of extravagantly romantic fantasy."[55] One of the most extravagant theatres was the Runnymede, at 2225 Bloor Street West, Montgomery's neighbourhood theatre after her move in 1935 to "Journey's End."[56] The Runnymede's atmospheric style with a celestial ceiling earned it the reputation of being "Canada's Theatre Beautiful."[57] During her Toronto residency, the final years of her life, Montgomery records visiting this (and other) movie houses several times a week for the kind of escapism that Fairchild describes. For example, on 25 June 1938, "I went alone to see *Tom Sawyer*. Enjoyed it and enjoyed my walk home afterwards. My worries and problems remain the same but I felt now that I can grapple with them and forget them by times. And I am able to escape into my 'dream lives' again and come back refreshed and stimulated."[58] Whereas she once wove these "dream lives" out of her imagination, often spurred by her active engagement with literature and history, they now need the stimulant of the screen to provide the desired tonicity. They are conducive to neither the kind of self-constructive autobiographical meaning that Woster discusses in chapter 8 nor the creative process whereby, Montgomery writes, "I am *outside* of [the story] – merely recording what I see others do. But in a dream life I am *inside* – I am living it, not recording it."[59] The darkened movie house made her invisible to public scrutiny, but it also inhibited fruitful self-scrutiny, its cultural product promoting the escape from any reality but that projected visually on the screen.

Unlike these movies, the few plays that Montgomery attended from the mid-1920s onwards – and one in particular – provided her with an opportunity to develop a clearer understanding of the toxicity of celebrity in a "consumingly commercial" cultural environment. Hart House Theatre was not the only effort to combat the commercialization of the dominant American syndicates; there had been a number of endeavours to develop antidotes to the Americanization of the Canadian stage, primarily touring British companies, which floundered during the First World War. From these various companies, one emerged after the war: "Maurice Colbourne's London Company was unquestionably the strongest and most important influence in the province ... Colbourne first came to Ontario in 1926 to help organize the English Repertory Theatre in Toronto and to champion Shavian drama as a bulwark against the crassly commercial American theatre ... As a result, many audiences were given their first taste of 'modern' drama through productions that, in terms of the excellence of the acting and staging techniques, were uniformly well above those usually provided by the American touring system."[60] Montgomery attended a Colbourne production of *John Bull's Other Island* at the Royal Alexandra Theatre in late February 1929 with the Barracloughs from Glen Williams, but she was more focused on describing her enjoyment of "the excursion in spite of [her] languor and headache" than the play itself: "Shaw's play was quite good but not nearly so good as *St Joan* and the accent of the English cast made it difficult to follow the dialogue."[61]

Montgomery had attended a remarkable production of Shaw's *Saint Joan* nearly five years previously, on 9 October 1924, of which she declared, "never did I have such an evening of enjoyment."[62] Extensive media coverage was given to the premier of Shaw's play on 28 December 1923 at New York's Garrick Theatre, a Theatre Guild production starring Winifred Lenihan; the London staging with Sybil Thorndike, for whom Shaw had written the play, which began its run 26 March 1924; and the Theatre Guild's touring production, which replaced Lenihan with Hamilton-born Julia Arthur, and successfully travelled throughout North America for two years after opening in Toronto at the New Princess Theatre on 6 October 1924. The stories of Shaw and Arthur, as aired in the press – like the story of Saint Joan herself, for whom church and various French and English factions are willing to negotiate "a king's ransom" and who must be totally consumed to ensure there are no relics to incite an idolatrous following[63] – address the "consumingly commercial" vagaries of lionization. Montgomery would certainly have been aware of the vicissitudes of Shaw's status as an international celebrity, the deepest valley occurring during the First World War because of his controversial anti-war newspaper articles, published collectively as *Common Sense about War* (1914). Shaw ascended from this valley in the 1920s with the success of *Saint Joan* and consequent honour of the Nobel Prize for Literature in 1925, which he initially declined but then accepted, although donating the money to the Anglo-Swedish Literary Foundation, a newly formed organization more in need of money than himself, he declared. The title of a long article by Lawrence Mason, drama critic for the *Globe*, sums up well the playwright's return to public favour: "'Saint Joan': Why Has This Particular Masterpiece, among Shaw's Many, Reconciled Thousands to Him after a Lifetime of Dislike?"[64]

From beginning to end, Julia Arthur's story was fodder for magazines and newspapers, tabloid and mainstream. Most pertinent to Montgomery's story is Arthur's coming out of retirement in her mid-forties, fifteen years after her marriage to the fabulously wealthy Bostonian, Benjamin Pierce Cheney Jr, with *The Eternal Magdalene*, which played in both Hamilton and Toronto (March 1916) after a mixed reception in the United States where it was deemed by some too old-fashioned.[65] In the role of Saint Joan, Arthur reached the pinnacle of her career at the age of fifty-five. The Toronto drama critic Hector Charlesworth contends that with Arthur "the play became a new thing, noble, moving, and at every moment appealing."[66] Her biographer, Denis Salter, describes the strengths that Arthur brought to the role: Joan's "sturdy conviction formed the ruling passion of [Arthur's] conception, while around it were seemingly myriad qualities – of courage, fire, resiliency, simplicity, and determination – which she brought so intensely and yet so naturally together that some audience members felt that both she and they had become pure disembodied spirit in an act of worship." Through the "publicity interview" that Arthur gave Geraldine Steinmetz for *Maclean's* magazine (January 1916) – in which Steinmetz suggests that "Canadians were excited because one of *their* artists … was now making a newsworthy come-back" – and the five-part serialization of her memoirs for *Hearst's* magazine (March–July 1916), "an exciting legend was fashioned from her career," carrying her through another decade of performance and lionization. Throughout the later years of her career, but especially while touring *Saint Joan* in Ontario, Arthur – like Montgomery – made the rounds as guest of honour and guest speaker at various service and cultural organizations. Canadians, Salter concludes, "shared vicariously in her success as an international star. 'We all feel a sort of reflected glory about Miss Arthur's fame,' observed a member of the Women's Canadian Club."[67]

Montgomery's own copy of Shaw's *Saint Joan* (Constable, 1925) shows that it is a text, like those that Woster discusses, with which she communicated over a number of years. Montgomery inscribed her copy of *Saint Joan* with her name, the date 1925, and her signature cat icon; she marked passages with arrowheads and question marks; she inserted and pasted in performance photographs from periodical clippings and images of Shaw's Dublin birthplace and magazine reproductions of George William Joy's *Jeanne d'Arc endormie* (1895) and Jules Lenepveu's *Jeanne d'Arc au sacre de Charles VII* (1874) – thus conflating the man, his product, and visual and dramatic representations of it between the covers of one book. The Black Scrapbook also preserves a noteworthy artifact, inserted almost a decade later, a letter to the editor addressing the debate over the relevance of the play's Epilogue to Joan's "second martyrdom": "Here is the real tragedy of Joan, and of Mankind. Our saints, like our Christs, must be kept on pedestals and in stain-glass windows, to be worshipped but not to be met with."[68] Literary celebrities such as Shaw and Montgomery experienced a similarly tragic fate as that of Joan: an isolating lionization.

In previous chapters, William Thompson and Emily Woster discuss Montgomery's journals as self-constructions, but her journal descriptions of attending the production of *Saint Joan* and several interactive readings of the play move beyond self-fashioning to self-dramatization. Montgomery inserts herself into this narrative as if she were living a tragic play of the misunderstood and isolated lone lion. In *Writing a Life*, a companion to the journals, Rubio and Waterston begin with the observation that Montgomery "was fettered by her own popularity" and "caught, perhaps unawares, in another trap: her own facility in creating narratives. To keep her secret journal going, she unconsciously adapted her life to her narrative skill. Gradually she began to make life-choices shaped to fit the kind of story she was prepared to tell in that journal."[69] The back story of Montgomery's communication with *Saint Joan* – as performance and text – sets the stage: it begins with Montgomery's journey to North Bay on Tuesday (7 October 1924), where, on Wednesday, she gave a series of readings and lectures, including "to the girls in the Convent school in the forenoon ... The Reverend Mother and Sister St John were very sweet and interesting women." After several other speaking engagements, she took the night train back to Toronto; however, because of a six-hour delay, her plans to catch the morning train from Toronto to Leaskdale changed. "Now, mark! Had I caught that train home I would not have had a wonderful pleasure."[70] To whom is this passage addressed? To her journal, her understanding "friend and confidante," as Thompson discusses more generally in chapter 6?[71] It seems much more consciously crafted than Rubio and Waterston suggest, addressed to a posthumous audience witnessing the vicissitudes of L.M. Montgomery.

Montgomery was not as enamoured with Julia Arthur as the reviewers were: "Joan was never such a pink-and-white golden haired, brilliant, beautifully clad person. Only when I shut my eyes and listened to her wonderful golden voice did I get the conviction of the Maid." Because Arthur was renowned for her coal-black eyes and hair, and because Montgomery voices this same objection about many of the Hollywood actresses in the movies that she attends, another variation on her perception of inauthentic celebrated women, her response to *Saint Joan* seems shaped primarily to provide an apposite medium for her lament, "Oh, if Frede could only have been sitting beside me while I saw that play." She concedes that "Shaw's play is a ripe and wonderful thing; but I don't think his Joan is the real Joan either. That Joan is still an enigma."[72] Since she is an enigma, Joan's story, like Frede's – and Montgomery's – can be told and retold – romantically, lyrically, satirically, farcically, comedically, tragically – and never be totally consumed. As Margaret Turner concludes, Montgomery's process of reading and writing and responding "does not advance her or us toward an integrated subject, but rather keeps the multiple versions of the I that she constructs and lives active, relevant, and fluid."[73]

Montgomery decides to attend the play only after her physical hunger has been assuaged – "the first food I had eaten since supper the evening before" – but her hunger for Frede's companionship remains unsatisfied. Two days later, Montgomery records, "I have been re-reading Frede's letters. I have not read them since the winter she died. But I have been so hungry for her lately – especially since seeing *Saint Joan* – that I had to get out the letters. Last night when I went to bed I thought I would read just one. Then I said 'Just one more' – and that went on till twelve o'clock. It was always 'just one more.' I was like a famished creature pleading for just one more bite of food." What is it about *Saint Joan* that sends Montgomery on this binge of letter reading? She goes on to say that, with Frede, the façade of "laughter and satisfaction" characterizing her public personae was unnecessary; with Frede, her joy "was not pretence – it was reality," or, as Mary Beth Cavert writes in chapter 2, when together, these two cousins "could be their true selves and confess feelings they could never express anywhere else."[74] In his *Saturday Night* review of the touring production of *Saint Joan*, Charlesworth captures the tragedy of Joan, whose ego can no longer provide a buffer against the jarring of the public personae against her soul: "After all there could be no more dramatic spectacle than that of an heroic soul striving to be true to itself in a maze of misunderstandings and antagonistic motives, – far more dramatic than battles and visions and escapes."[75] Although the "antagonistic motives" are not so clearly delineated in life as they are in art, this too is the tragedy of Montgomery as crafted in her journals: a woman who fights for the integrity of her soul in a commercial milieu that eventually consumes her, whether that consumption be of a ravenous public whose appetite needs feeding or the sputtering flames of a celebrity's public personae, as Kate Sutherland describes in the previous chapter.

On 7 November 1925, the *Globe* reprinted excerpts from a sketch of Shaw by his first authorized biographer, Archibald Henderson, which had appeared several months before in the *New York Times*: "When I began to write about Shaw, more than twenty years ago, he was virtually unknown to fame. When people thought of him ... they thought of a ghastly little celebrity dancing in a vacuum, a comical jack-in-the-box ludicrously popping up at intervals to cry himself and his wares."[76] With this perception of literary personalities, then, it is not surprising that the remainder of Montgomery's journal references to Shaw are rooted in metaphors of consumption that interrogate the degenerative cost of fame when celebrity depends on exhibiting only those personae that the public is willing to consume. Whether as "L.M. Montgomery" or "Mrs Ewan Macdonald," her personae must be consistently self-effacing and optimistic; however, a close reading of the journals reveals self-absorption, pessimism, and a deteriorating strength to fight on in an increasingly alien world. The final mention of reading Shaw comes in November 1933: "Lately I have been having a debauch of George Bernard Shaw. Today I reread *Androcles and The Lion*. Shaw is very brilliant. I think he must be a reincarnation of Voltaire. And yet – satirically true as he is, his writings lack the essential truth after all. And he is too conscious of G.B. Shaw. He is always saying in effect, 'Oh, am I not clever. You *must* think me tremendously clever. You can't deny it. Listen to this and this.'" Montgomery may see Shaw as the public saw him, "a ghastly little celebrity," and he may, as she alleges, produce "brilliant fireworks, not a permanent coruscation," but "he tastes good" because his soul is that of a reincarnated Voltaire, which is what his plays rather than public personae reveal.[77]

In *Literary Celebrity in Canada*, York remarks upon the effect that the signage of the "iron bower" over the entrance to the Cavendish cemetery – with "Resting Place of L.M. Montgomery" writ large – must have on its resident community: "One wonders how families of others who rest there feel about Montgomery becoming the synecdoche for all of the Cavendish ancestors. It seems a strange kind of celebrity vampirism visited upon a community-host."[78] If Montgomery were to answer (as Joan does Cauchon in her tragedy's Epilogue), she might say, "Your dead body did not feel the spade and the sewer as my live body felt the fire" – a passage Montgomery marked in her copy of *Saint Joan*.[79] Rubio and Waterston's conclusion to *Writing a Life* takes us back to the novels, a cultural product whose legacy, like Joan's, withstands the consuming flames: "Montgomery exits from her journals suffering and silenced, perhaps believing they contained the true and only story of her life. But she was far from defeated – and far from silenced."[80] An examination of her final journey through the Valley of the Humber and her exposure to its cultural products reveals the tragic consequences of the erosion of the ego that leaves the soul vulnerable to conflicting demands on someone who has herself become a cultural product. It also reveals, however, a vulnerability that led to Montgomery's final line of characters: the wife, mother, and grandmother Anne; the sister Rilla experiencing vicariously the pain of a brother who does not go unthinkingly to war; the artist Emily, whom Teddy Kent envisions as "Joan of Arc – with a face all spirit – listening to her voices";[81] the emotionally starved and psychologically abused Valancy Stirling and Robin and Jane Stuart; and the recalcitrant Pat, whose "home for generations [is] wiped out [by fire] ... all its memories, all its possessions ... in ashes!"[82] And like Emily – "a chaser of rainbows" – who produces *The Moral of the Rose* after *A Seller of Dreams* has been consumed by the flames, and after "the delight and allurement and despair and anguish of the rainbow quest,"[83] each of these characters, in her own way, maps a narrative arc characteristic of Montgomery's own Ontario years: she travels westward and seeks a new home for herself far from Prince Edward Island.

Epilogue

14

Dear Grandmother Maud on the Road to Heaven

KATE MACDONALD BUTLER

Dear Grandmother Maud on the Road to Heaven,

I hope I have addressed you in an acceptable and respectful manner. I have thought long and hard about the most appropriate way to address you since we never had a conversation in person, although over the years we've had hundreds of conversations in my imagination. I wonder if I should have called you Grandma or Grandmother Macdonald or Grandmother Lucy Maud or Nanna. I notice that you refer to your own grandmother as Grandmother Macneill, and I wonder if you would have wanted your grandchildren to address you in a respectful but less formal manner. I wonder also if it would please you to know that the language of today is not so formal anymore. Somehow I feel most comfortable addressing you as Grandmother Maud. There is no doubt in my mind that you would make your thoughts on this subject quite clear to me and the other grandchildren. There are seven of us, you know, four boys and three girls.

    My beloved father, Stuart, often told me while I was growing up that I was named for his Aunt Kate of whom he was very fond. Who could that have been? Could it have been Kate Montgomery, your half-sister, the daughter from great-grandfather's second marriage to Mary Ann McRae? Perhaps it was Katie Macneill, Uncle John Macneill's fourth child and your first cousin. It seems unlikely that I would be named for Kate Montgomery since she had little contact with my father and cousin. Katie Macneill died in 1904 at the age of twenty, long before Stuart was born, although maybe it was through your warm stories and memories of Katie Macneill that he developed his own affection for her.

My father died in 1982, and I'll never know the true significance of the other Kate in Dad's life. There are so many questions I wish I had asked him, and I still miss him very much. I wish I had listened more attentively to his stories because, like you, he had the gift of storytelling. You were so well informed and immersed in the family histories of both the Montgomery and Macneill clans. Your journals are filled with descriptions of family gatherings, aunts, uncles, favourite foods, habits, furnishings; I love your appreciation of your own family history, and I wish I had paid more attention as a teenager to my father's stories, many of which he must have heard from you. Isn't that typical of youth that they don't have the time or patience to listen to their elders and don't know how invaluable their parents' and grandparents' oral histories are to their own fundamental sense of being?

I have many memories of social gatherings at my parents' house on Glenvale Blvd, in a Toronto neighbourhood with a very similar feel to your neighbourhood on Riverside Drive. When Stuart was in the mood and had a receptive audience around the dining-room table, he was a dramatic and articulate storyteller. His favourite topics for discussion included his days as a child in Leaskdale and Norval. He had many fond reminiscences of Norval: his favourite stories involved the forks of the Credit River and the fun he had there with his tent and canoe. I had a sense from his stories that his summers in Norval were some of the happiest times of his childhood, and I hope you still remember those times with Stuart in a special way.

His university days were full of devilry, and, as I'm sure you are well aware, he was quite a prankster. One memorable story he told us many times happened during his years studying medicine at University of Toronto. Stuart had a fun-loving pal who will for now remain nameless, but I will tell you he was from a very prominent Prince Edward Island family and was a great friend of my father for the rest of his life. They got the notion into their heads that it would be fun to take the old grey mare that belonged to the milkman up the stairs of Knox College and deposit her in the room of Isaac Usher, a fellow student and friend. When Isaac had finished his classes for the day, he came back to residence to find that half of his room was taken up by an old grey mare and the other half by a sizable pile of manure. The interesting thing about horses is that they will go up stairs, but they won't go down, and the pile of manure grew and grew and grew. I don't know if Dad and his friend were ever found out for this prank, or if it was even true, but someone paid for the cost of lowering the mare out the window by way of a crane. Did you ever hear this story, Grandmother? I have always wondered if you were the anonymous benefactor who paid for the crane.

Dad had many more hilarious stories of his university days, and I wonder if you knew about them. I'm guessing that you probably didn't find them quite as funny as his children did. I have a photograph taken of you and Father on his graduation day, you beaming with pride, and he looking like he was ready to take on the world. Were you there for the pigeons? Another of father's dining-room stories occurred on the day that picture was taken at graduation. According to my father, on the steps of Convocation Hall, each of the graduating students had a pigeon under his gown. At the end of the last dignified speech by the president of the university, Stuart and his classmates simultaneously opened their gowns and released the birds, which flew en masse back to their home in the tower over the startled heads of the university's finest. It was a good thing that all the faculty members were wearing mortar boards and gowns that day. I would love to have heard your version of that story.

Stuart went on to marry Ruth Eliza Steele, my mother, a graduate nurse at St Michael's Hospital he had his eye on for several years. My mother never met you or Grandfather Ewan, but she has told me many times how touched she was by Stuart's devotion to you during the last years of your life and his daily visits to your home on Riverside Drive.

I am writing this letter in the year 2013 to tell you some stories of how you continue to make a profound impact on the world today, even though you left us in 1942. This may seem like another of the yarns that you and my father loved to tell, but I promise you that I am not exaggerating. I hope you would be pleased to know that you have been acknowledged several times as one of Canada's greatest writers of the twentieth century by readers' polls across the country, and you have

14.1
Stuart's graduation,
University of Toronto
(1940)

been designated as one of Canada's top twenty heroes of all time. I want to tell you, my dear grandmother, that all of your books are still in print, and although in your lifetime there were Swedish, Dutch, Polish, Norwegian, Danish, Finnish, and French translations, your books have now been translated into more than twenty-five languages, including recent translations into Arabic, Slovak, Romanian, Chinese, and Icelandic.

Your readership still crosses the boundaries of class, gender, age, race, culture, and time. *Anne of Green Gables* played a key role in Japan's creative recovery in the 1950s, and your novels were hot sellers as part of the black market in an iron-curtain Poland that prized writing about love of home. I hope you will be proud that your hidden talent as a photographer has also been acknowledged publicly with your keen eye for your subjects, be they places of natural beauty, people, or your beloved pets. In the 1890s, you took many snaps (as you called them) and were experimenting with developing glass-plate negatives and films. I think of the fun you might have had with a digital camera and the ability to upload your personal pictures onto a social networking site, a phenomenon that has taken over the world now. So much of what you wrote in your journals was about the daily happenings of your life, your family, and your trips to Prince Edward Island, and I truly can envisage that you would have gotten a kick out of electronic media, Facebook, Instagram, and today's challenging multi-media world. Of course, it is so difficult to presume to know your inner thoughts ... someone who kept so much of her interior life private. Maybe you would have disapproved of Facebook for the same reasons I am uncomfortable with the lack of privacy in general on these social networking sites.

There is a complex cultural industry that has been created as a direct result of you and your books. Tourists from around the world visit museums dedicated to the preservation of your memory. Plaques mark your residences from infancy to death, and historical groups have restored some of the homes in which you lived. Publishers, archivists, librarians, academics, historians, research groups, movie moguls, television executives, theatrical stage producers, artisans, online fan sites, merchandisers, and intellectual property and entertainment lawyers continue to ensure that your name will never be forgotten.

As your heirs, we have made it our primary goal always to respect your wishes – often this involves some speculation – and, at the same time, to ensure that your works continue to be made available to the public and, also, to consider new projects and initiatives that are brought to our attention without denigrating the spirit of your writing. You'll be pleased to know that the *Anne* and *Emily* novels continue to be introduced to new generations through the printed word, film, and television series, on the dramatic and musical stages, in multimedia formats, and even on three-dimensional merchandise. I do think about how other famous writers' estates are managed. I have heard, for example, that both the T.S. Eliot and James Joyce estates are perceived by some as being difficult and restrictive and that the Ernest Hemingway estate authorized the posthumous publication of a novel that Hemingway himself didn't want published because he considered it to be second rate. I recently read that his grandson has authorized the reissue of a new version of *A Moveable Feast*, removing some unpleasant family material from the original published memoir. J.D. Salinger is known to have repeatedly said that there will be no movie made of his most famous novel, *The Catcher in the Rye*, but it is not an impossible scenario to imagine that his literary executors might be tempted one day to sell movie rights. I'm not kidding when I say I lie awake in bed thinking of how you would have wanted your family to act on your behalf, and we continue to respect what we hope would be your wishes and to act responsibly.

Often, the public image of a famous person is different from the private person. Dear grandmother, you were a very complicated person who kept many of your most intimate thoughts well hidden but also wrote some of them down in your private journals. In your will, you left specific instructions for my father to arrange for the publication of your unpublished journals, which, you'll be pleased to know, have been published in a five-volume edition by Oxford University Press. *The Selected Journals of L.M. Montgomery*, painstakingly edited by professors Mary Rubio and Elizabeth Waterston, has opened up a new adult readership for you and your work and allowed us an edited version of parts of your private life. And now the Prince Edward Island years have been fully captured in the two-volume *Complete Journals of L.M. Montgomery*. I have bittersweet memories of spending time with my father at the family home, where he would sit at the dining-room table, poring over the contents of these old, worn, rather shabby black ledgers with handwriting in longhand that was totally undecipherable to me. Sometimes he would read aloud from them to us kids – my brothers, Deke and Rod, and myself – and we could see and hear from his voice how important these journals were to him. We were all aware that they should be treated with the utmost respect. He talked about editing and publishing them himself, but as the years went on, it seemed their presence was a mixed blessing for him. He was a devoted doctor, and while he was a talented writer, I think he was too overwhelmed at the prospect, for reasons he never explained. He may have felt more at ease tackling some of your fiction manuscripts, and he did authorize the publication of two collections of short stories, *The Doctor's Sweetheart* and *The Road to Yesterday*, published after your death.

As your legal heirs and literary executors, we contemplate many opportunities, and we take this responsibility very seriously. Caring for your legacy of creative material has been very different from managing real estate or a family business. Inheriting a literary legacy is a different sort of gift, because it is covered by copyright laws, and the duration of copyright is finite. Unlike the gift of a physical property, copyright doesn't last forever. Your heirs realized a number of years ago that one of the most important responsibilities we had was to protect your name, as well as some of the characters and settings from your novels. We formed a company and registered some valuable trademarks, including the trademark "L.M. Montgomery." A trademark may be a word or words, symbols or designs, or a combination of words and designs. For example, we have registered a trademark for your L.M. Montgomery cat and signature design, which is such a distinctive symbol associated with you. Given your great love of cats, I know that you would approve. We have also considered your personality or character rights. For example, if a biographical film is made, "L.M. Montgomery" trademark, personality, and character rights will be negotiated into any film contract. Another important decision we made was to join with the Government of the Province of Prince Edward Island in 1994 to form a company to pursue our common interests in preserving your legacy and the integrity of the characters and images you created that continue to be associated with Prince Edward Island. The Anne of Green Gables Licensing Authority Inc. owns "Anne of Green Gables" and other related "Anne" trademarks in Canada and around the world and oversees the licensing of their use. I sometimes wonder if you would be pleased or shocked – or perhaps a little of both – to learn that the name "L.M. Montgomery" is a trademark belonging to your heirs. With the phenomenal interest in your life and your works, we felt that this would be the best way to ensure the integrity of your legacy and to respect your memory.

You are also an incredible inspiration as a business woman, and I am especially proud of your reputation as a heroine on the legal front. Your creation of Anne Shirley was so powerful, as you well know, that her distinctive "Titian red" hair played a major part in a lawsuit with the L.C. Page Company in Boston, a lawsuit that began in 1920 when you were forty-six and ended in 1928. I know you refused to knuckle under to the Boston publishing house that was cheating you, and you sued them, were counter-sued by them, and, after almost nine years of trials, hearings appeals, and judgments, you won your cases outright. There is a delicious irony for me, Grandmother, in the spirit with which you won your lawsuit, for lawsuits about Anne and her books are not just matters of the past. I'd love to write to you privately about these – how cases from the past prepared the scene for the struggles of the late twentieth and early twenty-first centuries, more than 125 years after your birth. There are some uncanny similarities.

The history of your first publishing experience is a fascinating story in itself. I know that you tried four times to get *Anne of Green Gables* published before L.C. Page and Company finally accepted it in 1907. It had languished in a hat box for many months after its early rejections, and when you rediscovered it, you decided to send it out one more time. When L.C. Page accepted it, you were offered a contract that was not very author friendly. The first edition cover of *Anne of Green Gables* shows that Page was aiming the book at a general audience and not just the children's market. The portrait of red-haired Anne on the first edition cover shows a very sophisticated Gibson-girl image. The later *Anne* books published by Page have similar red-haired portraits in mahogany or brown frames on a beige or a light green background. As a licensor myself, I can see how savvy Lewis Page was in establishing a brand name and brand look for what would become the highly successful and extremely marketable *Anne* stories. In fact, exhibitions have been mounted and academic papers published on these book covers.

I am confident that you would be proud to know that your family eventually did regain many of the rights that publishers and others around the world had acquired long ago or, even more recently, have claimed to your works. Mostly this reversion has happened through amicable negotiation and renegotiation of contracts, although we have not shied away from the possibility of litigation. All of this cost us a lot of energy, anxiety, and expense, but in the end, we were successful in regaining control over many of our rights that you had given up or – in the case of film rights – were tricked into signing away. I have been reading in your diary your reaction to the 1934 RKO film version of *Anne of Green Gables,* from which you did not benefit financially because Page turned around and sold film rights right after they secured the rights from you. I'm quoting your 29 November 1934 diary entry here: "'Marilla,' played by Helen Westley, was in no respect whatever my tall, thin, Puritan Marilla. She was, indeed, my perfect conception of 'Mrs Rachel Lynde' (who was not in the picture at all). But her performance, judged on its own merits, was capital. 'Matthew' was very good also, though he had no beard. 'Gilbert,' at least in the earlier scenes, was much too crude and 'Diana' was a complete wash-out. However, on the whole, the picture was a thousandfold better than the silent film in 1921." What I find so interesting from your diary entries is that this problem continues. We have licensed some of the stories you wrote so many years ago, and we face similar problems to those you did. Characters have been deleted, some have been amalgamated, and some have been invented; story lines have been distorted so much that one often wonders whether this interpretation is based on the Montgomery novel at all. I can't tell you how I enjoyed your reply when asked how you liked the characters: "I am pestered to death by questions as to 'how I like it' and 'what I feel like' seeing my characters 'come to life' like that. I liked it well enough but I had no sense of seeing my characters come to life because they were *not* my characters as I saw them, with the exception of 'Anne.' The whole picture was so entirely different from *my* vision of the scenes and the people that it did not seem *my* book at all. It was just a pleasant, well-directed little play by somebody else."

Perhaps you would not be surprised to hear that there are debates concerning the use of the name "Anne of Green Gables." Often, Grandmother, I feel that I have swung back to the 1920s and your own case against a business world intent on profiting from Anne and your other characters. I take comfort from your words about your struggles. Your

Anne is considered the quintessential symbol for good-hearted innocence and imagination, but it is sometimes difficult to control the use and potential misuse of your creations. Some people first learn of Anne and your other characters through one of the many adaptations. We are glad when these lead them back to the originals.

Just think, if *Anne of Green Gables* were first published in 2008 and if you lived in today's plugged-in world ... would you be on Facebook, have a Twitter account, possibly your own website and blog? Would you have thousands of virtual friends, pen pals, and kindred spirits? I think it is a pretty safe bet that you would since you were interested in what the public thought about your writing and you kept detailed scrapbooks of your life, including book reviews and items of interest, both on the personal and world fronts.

I anticipate that we, as your heirs, will continue to struggle with new proposals that may use artistic licence to interpret your work, be it fiction or non-fiction. Some of these proposals will contribute to my lying awake at night and imagining how you would have wanted to respond. Sometimes it is quite challenging to manage your literary estate, but we try our best to do so with integrity and sensitivity.

Your vision is one of imagination and creativity that has captivated the world for over one hundred years and will likely do so for many years to come – be it on a Kindle, or a PDA (personal digital assistant), or maybe on electronic reading devices that contain all your works, including all your family photographs, in a miniscule computer chip. Change is inevitable, I know, and I welcome the new world of communication, most particularly if it respects and acknowledges the rights of creators and makes both classic and contemporary literature available to the readers of today. I have great faith that your name will continue to be a household name in another hundred years' time.

Yours respectfully,
Kate Macdonald Butler

Appendix

Montgomery's Ontario Legacies: A Community Presence in the Twenty-First Century

RITA BODE AND LESLEY D. CLEMENT
with the assistance of Kristina Eldridge and Chloe Verner

In the triangle formed by two prongs of Riverside Drive and a third by Riverside Crescent in west-end Toronto is a small green space appropriately named Lucy Maud Montgomery Park. A plaque commemorates Montgomery's residence here just further down Riverside Drive in the house that she purchased when she and her husband left Norval for Toronto. Perhaps the green space itself and the proximity of the Humber River, in the midst of an urban environment, serve her memory as much as the plaque does. On the other side of the city, in east-end Scarborough, Lucy Maud Montgomery Public School welcomes students from Junior Kindergarten through Grade 8. The school's website states: "Lucy Maud Montgomery's goals are inspired by our commitment to excellence." It is a slightly odd statement since one would think that it would be the other way around – her goals inspiring the school's striving for excellence – but, in another way, the statement attests to Montgomery's immediacy in the local imagination. She *is* present, her works taking both popular and critical inspiration from the continuing and enduring attention that they evoke. The school's vision statement, moreover, "building the foundation for a lifetime of learning," carries apt meaning for Montgomery's cultural contributions.

While Charlottetown's Confederation Centre and the University of Prince Edward Island's Robertson Library have much of interest for Montgomery's readers, the largest and most comprehensive archival resource for Montgomery's work in Canada is housed by an Ontario university. The University of Guelph's L.M. Montgomery Collection is an invaluable repository of Montgomery's journals, scrapbooks, photo albums, and a broad array of significant memorabilia. Furthermore, much of the Guelph collection has been digitized, facilitating access for the international community of Montgomery scholars.

Montgomery's impact nationally and internationally is evidenced by the extensive list of cinematic, dramatic, and wide-ranging print adaptations that Benjamin Lefebvre provides in his introduction to volume 2 of *The L.M. Montgomery Reader*. Montgomery's reach into twenty-first century Ontario continues to be impressive and extends to entertainment- and family-oriented museums, garden walks, local plays inspired by her life and work, visual art, and historic and educational sites. The Bala Museum in Muskoka lets visitors re-enact scenes from Montgomery's novels, an activity that appeals to the dramatic in young and old alike. A walk through the Lucy Maud Montgomery Heritage Garden in Norval reveals many of the flowers and plants that she mentions in her fiction. The vibrance that Montgomery and her writings brought to her Ontario communities lives on in the theatrical events that commemorate her life and work. The Historic Leaskdale Church has been the site of performances of *Emily*, a musical based on the *Emily* books, as well as of the one-woman show *Maud of Leaskdale*, which draws on Montgomery's journals of the Leaskdale years and has had three successive summer runs. In Norval, the Spirit of Maud Theatre Company presents dramatic adaptations of Montgomery's fiction and life-writing in St Paul's Anglican Church Parish Hall, the same community space where Montgomery directed amateur theatricals performed by the Young People Guild's Norval Dramatic Club and Olde Tyme concerts.

Montgomery also holds a place today through Ontario's visual arts. In 1974, to commemorate her one hundredth birthday, the Uxbridge-Scott Historical Society commissioned Leaskdale artist Arnold Hodgkins to paint a portrait of Montgomery in her Leaskdale years. In the painting, entitled *A Moment with Maud*, Hodgkins appropriately depicts her with pen and book in hand against a background that suggestively refers to both Montgomery's ties to PEI and her Leaskdale years. The portrait now hangs in the front hall of the Historic Leaskdale Manse. More recently, Uxbridge artist Wynn Walters has been working on a life-size bronze sculpture of Montgomery, seated on a garden bench. Entitled *Maud in the Garden*, it will be installed, upon its completion in 2015, in the L.M. Montgomery Commemorative Garden at the Historic Leaskdale Church.

The Walters statue of Montgomery was commissioned by the Lucy Maud Montgomery Society of Ontario (LMMSO), the organization responsible for the restoration of the Historic Leaskdale Manse and Church. The society, with its tireless and enthusiastic leadership, and its committed members and donors, continues to ensure that Montgomery's Ontario legacy endures in vibrant material ways. What follows is an exchange that took place on 15 November 2013 at the Historic Leaskdale Church (formerly St Paul's Presbyterian Church), across from the manse on Durham Regional Road 1. Students Kristina Eldridge, Trent University, and Chloe Verner, Lakehead University Orillia, talked to long-time executive members Tess Dempster, Kathy Wasylenky, and Melanie Whitfield about the society's commitment to preserving and furthering Montgomery's Ontario presence.

How did the Lucy Maud Montgomery Society of Ontario come about? What prompted it?
It started with Wilda Clark in the early 1960s. Wilda was a retired Uxbridge teacher who recognized the significance of the Montgomery sites in Leaskdale. She wrote hundreds of letters to the Ontario government urging a designation as a provincial site of historical interest for the church and manse. This was granted to the manse in 1965.

Wilda was also active within Leaskdale in raising awareness and gaining support of Montgomery's contribution to the community. She drew in members of a local women's church group to form a committee that took upon itself the mandate of preserving and protecting the church and manse and promoting Montgomery's artistic work. The members published a small book that gave Montgomery a real personality through personal memories of her as a local community member. This group also worked over the next two to three decades to have the manse designated as a National Historical Site, which was finally granted in 1997.

When did the committee become the Lucy Maud Montgomery Society of Ontario?
First we became the Leaskdale Manse Museum Committee. Uxbridge Township bought the manse in 1992, but it continued to have tenants until 2002. Our plans began with possible restorations of the manse's exterior. When St Paul's decided to relocate to a nearby site, purchase of the church building and adjacent property became a possibility. In November 2004, we became an independent incorporated society and assumed the name Lucy Maud Montgomery Society of Ontario, and when St Paul's made its move in 2006, we purchased the property, calling it the Historic Leaskdale Church. Through the generosity of many donors, we were able to hold a "Burn the Mortgage" celebration in November 2011 as part of our centenary celebration of Montgomery's arrival in Ontario.

Interior restoration for the manse began early in 2010 and was completed the following year, again in time for our centenary celebration. The township transferred ownership of the manse to us in September 2013. Our mandate moved increasingly towards restoration, and our focus is now on educational programming and hosting Montgomery-related events.

What are the significant requirements that the Leaskdale properties had to meet to attain designation as historical sites?
There must be proof that the site has local historical significance, more so than others in the area. Since 1864, there has been a church on this property, donated by George Leask. The current brick church replaced a wooden structure in 1906. The manse was built in 1886. In the case of these Leaskdale properties, however, the historical significance comes from the people associated with the sites rather than anything unique about the age or architectural features of the buildings. Montgomery's involvement in the community through missionary societies and youth groups and her literary output while residing in Leaskdale are what give these properties historical significance. Montgomery captured these years – people, places, and events, including those related to the First World War – in her journals.

The church and manse both have provincial heritage status. The manse also has National Historic designation, which requires demonstration of significance for all Canadians and the world. At first, because there was already a site associated with Montgomery in Cavendish, PEI, there were obstacles to having the manse declared a National Historic Site. Thanks to the persistence of Wilda Clark and her committee, Montgomery is now the only Canadian with two National Historic sites honouring her name and reputation.

How were the restoration projects tackled?
The success of any restoration project depends on funding and research. We had township grants and donations. For both exterior and interior restorations, Montgomery's photographs were very useful. Also, in her journals, she describes in detail architectural features and the furnishings of the house. These photographs and descriptions were invaluable in restoring the property as authentically as possible to this period. Meanwhile, fundraising went on, everything from quilts and T-shirts to socials and teas.

Are there any artifacts or manuscripts housed at the Historic Leaskdale Manse and Church?
These properties do not have many original items, as Montgomery's son Stuart sold and donated most of the books in her library, scrapbooks, and photographs as well as the typescripts of her journals and other memorabilia to the University of Guelph's L.M. Montgomery Collection. On our properties, there are several original letters, postcards, and photos on display. We have books, donated by the Woster family of Minnesota, that replicate what Montgomery would have had in her library. The organ from Zephyr Church, dating from Montgomery's Leaskdale years, is now housed in the manse in the room that served as Montgomery's writing space. A few other items of interest have been obtained, such as the medical bag of Dr Mellow, who delivered Montgomery's sons, and a sewing machine and cedar chest donated by Montgomery's granddaughter, Kate Macdonald Butler. Another valued item is Arnold Hodgkins's painting *A Moment with Lucy Maud*

Montgomery, located in the entrance hallway of the manse. Tours of both sites are available by appointment throughout the year.

How many visitors do these sites attract annually? Where are they from and what are their interests? How do they hear about the properties?
We host a number of events year round – teas, tours, plays, open houses, a Christmas concert, an annual L.M. Montgomery Day in October with guest speakers – which attract visitors to Leaskdale. With its centenary celebration in November, 2011 was a banner year, and we had over five thousand visitors from as far east as Sweden and as far west as Japan. We currently see three to four thousand visitors a year. The LMMSO's website, Facebook, and other social media keep followers informed of current events. There is even a virtual tour of the manse on LMMSO's Facebook site.

How are the Leaskdale historic sites unique? How do they contribute to the appreciation of Montgomery?
We try to remain sensitive to the Leaskdale community; we are committed to the preservation of the site as a museum with historical and educational relevance. We are not a commercial enterprise; we apply for grants and fundraise, but because the site does not have regular funding from any one source, its sustainability must have a tourism component to remain open to the public. And these sites are the township's main attractions. Tourism is a by-product of these sites' literary and historical interest.

Leaskdale is not a site associated with any particular fictional character. It is the place where the author actually lived for fifteen years, as minister's wife and mother and neighbour, and where she wrote fifteen of her novels. Complementing our mandate to protect and preserve the two Leaskdale properties, our focus has always been educational and academic, that is, literary and historical. We provide the tools and resources for visitors to learn about the life and books – not just one book – of Montgomery.

We are not Anne of Green Gables; we are L.M. Montgomery.

Notes

ABBREVIATIONS USED IN NOTES

LMM: L.M. Montgomery

FICTION
AA: *Anne of Avonlea*
AHD: *Anne's House of Dreams*
BAQ: *The Blythes Are Quoted*
EC: *Emily Climbs*
EQ: *Emily's Quest*
MP: *Mistress Pat*
RI: *Rilla of Ingleside*

AGG: *Anne of Green Gables*
AIS: *Anne of the Island*
BC: *The Blue Castle*
ENM: *Emily of New Moon*
JLH: *Jane of Lantern Hill*
PSB: *Pat of Silver Bush*
RV: *Rainbow Valley*

LIFE-WRITING
AP: *Alpine Path*
CJ: *Collected Journals*
SJ: *Selected Journals*

All references from Montgomery's Prince Edward Island journal entries are to *The Collected Journals*, volumes 1 and 2 (CJ 1 and CJ 2); all references to Montgomery's Ontario journal entries are to *The Selected Journals*, volumes 2 through 5 (SJ 2, SJ 3, SJ 4, and SJ 5).

INTRODUCTION
1 LMM, SJ 2: 52.
2 Ibid., 52, 68, 61, 66.
3 Ibid., 81.
4 In the early years, after the line was opened in 1917, the train was well used; however, increased dependence on cars and the onset of the Depression forced its closure in 1932. Quaile, *L.M. Montgomery: The Norval Years, 1926–1935*, 85, 103.

5 LMM, *SJ* 2: 82.
6 LMM, *SJ* 3: 263, 265.
7 LMM, *SJ* 4: 358.
8 LMM, *JLH*, 163.
9 LMM, *SJ* 5: 5, 7.
10 Waterston, "Leaskdale: L.M. Montgomery's Rainbow Valley," 21; Cavert, "'To the Memory of,'" 52, 53; Steffler, "'Being a Christian,'" 72.
11 LMM, *SJ* 2: 64.
12 Her only collected volume of poems, *The Watchman and Other Poems*, was published in 1916.
13 LMM, *JLH*, 216.
14 Waterston, "Leaskdale: L.M. Montgomery's Rainbow Valley," 31.
15 Steffler, "'Being a Christian,'" 59.
16 Jones, "New Mother at Home," 92, 93.
17 Thompson, "Shadow on the House of Dreams," 113, 115, 116, 130.
18 Woster, "Old Years and Old Books," 151, 152; Forest, "(Re)Locating Montgomery," 168.
19 Rubio, *Lucy Maud Montgomery: The Gift of Wings*, 312.
20 LMM, *SJ* 3: 62.
21 Pike, "Propriety and the Proprietary," 188.
22 Rodenburg, "Bala and *The Blue Castle*," 220.
23 Clement, "Toronto's Cultural Scene," 238, 242, 259.
24 Butler, "Dear Grandmother Maud," 268.
25 Lefebvre, "Introduction: A Life in Print," 6.
26 Quoted in Rubio, *Lucy Maud Montgomery: The Gift of Wings*, 162–3.
27 "Beloved Writer Addresses Several Aurora Gatherings," *Aurora Era*, 22 February 1940, 1. In Lefebvre, *L.M. Montgomery Reader* 1: 356–8.
28 "L.M. Montgomery Rests beside the Sea," *Globe and Mail*, 30 April 1942, 11.

CHAPTER ONE
1 LMM, *SJ* 2: 246.
2 Ibid., 220, 223.
3 LMM, *RV*, 193.
4 LMM, *SJ* 2: 221.
5 Ibid., 207.
6 Ibid., 242.
7 Ibid., 253.
8 Ibid., 211.
9 Ibid., 206.
10 LMM, *RV*, 14–15.
11 LMM, *SJ* 2: 147, 221, 224.

CHAPTER TWO

1. Figure 2.1 is a composite of images: the photos of Lapp and Brooks were acquired from the Uxbridge Historical Centre (Uxbridge-Scott Museum & Archives) and the photo of Shier was provided by the Canadian Virtual War Memorial Photo Collection, Veterans Affairs Canada. Montgomery misspells Robert Brooks's name. She may have had the name of the war poet Rupert Brooke in mind when she added the dedication to the manuscript of *Rainbow Valley*.
2. This paper is an abbreviated version of "L.M. Montgomery and World War I" and other articles published in *The Shining Scroll* periodical (see under Cavert, bibliography), located on the website of the Lucy Maud Montgomery Literary Society. It is also part of an unpublished manuscript "L.M. Montgomery's Kindred Spirits: The Friends of Anne," which details Montgomery's friendships and book dedications in her published works from 1908 to 1939.
3. Mustard, *L.M. Montgomery as Mrs Ewan Macdonald*, 2–3.
4. Figure 2.2 is a composite of two 1895 maps of the township in McGillivray, *Decades of Harvest*, 50, 52.
5. Mustard, *L.M. Montgomery as Mrs Ewan Macdonald*, 7–8.
6. Information about Shier, Brooks, and Lapp was collected from their family records, resources in the Library and Archives of Canada, Veteran Affairs of Canada, Uxbridge Historical Centre (Uxbridge-Scott Museum & Archives), and Montgomery's journals.
7. McGillivray, *Decades of Harvest*, 235–6. Arnold Hodgkins's 1974 Leaskdale painting of Montgomery includes a plane in the lower left corner, adding this historical detail to represent the landing of a plane from Camp Borden in a Zephyr field at the end of October 1917.
8. LMM, *RI*, 211.
9. LMM, *After Green Gables*, 69; LMM, *RI*, 213.
10. Skeet, "RFC Pilot Training," 5, 7. See also Hugh A. Halliday and Laura Brandon, "Into the Blue: Pilot Training in Canada, 18," Canada War Museum, Government of Canada (http://www.warmuseum.ca/education/online-educational-resources/dispatches/into-the-blue-pilot-training-in-canada-1917-18/).
11. LMM, *RI*, 206–7.
12. Information on training and flying schools at this point in the war is found in Morley, *Earning Their Wings*, 104–7.
13. Boucher, "World War Aviation."
14. "From Colony to Country," Library and Archives Canada (Archival Material).
15. Lawson and Lawson, *First Air Campaign*, 123, 107.
16. Cashmore and Bews, "Fisherman's War," Highland Archives (Archival Material).

17 LMM, *SJ* 2: 267–8. This is also the film at which Rilla makes "an awful goose of [her]self" when, as she records in her diary of 1 September 1918, she becomes so engrossed in the film's reality that she responds, as Frede did, with a warning to the film's heroine. LMM, *RI*, 260–1.
18 "They Need Me Over There," Uxbridge Historical Centre (Uxbridge-Scott Museum & Archives).
19 "War Diary," Ontario Regiment (RCAC) Museum (Archival Material), and Nicholson, *Official History of the Canadian Army in First World War*, record the actions of the battalion.
20 "Picturing a Canadian Life," Virtual Museum Canada (Archival Material).
21 "They Need Me Over There," Uxbridge Historical Centre (Archival Material).
22 LMM, *RI*, 166.
23 McGillivray, *Decades of Harvest*, 237.
24 LMM, *RV*, 55.
25 Montgomery's loyalty is particularly apparent in her support of Effie over "some petty personal malice and spite among the [Red Cross Society] members" and gossip of her "diverting some of the money collected to her own purse": "And the woman against whom all this outburst of spite has been directed has had a son killed at the front. None of those who organized the cabal against her has anyone there." LMM, *SJ* 2: 238, 280.
26 Marilyn Rennie, "Lapp Family," email to author, 17 February 2009.
27 Mustard, *L.M. Montgomery as Mrs Ewan Macdonald*, 10.
28 LMM, *SJ* 2: 207. See Waterston, "Leaskdale," 25.
29 Marilyn Rennie, "Lapp Family," email to author, 17 February 2009.
30 LMM, *RI*, 187.
31 Jack Hutton, "Dog Monday," email to author, 3 April 2011. This story was told to Jack and Linda Hutton in the 1990s at the Bala Museum by a visitor who was in Montgomery's audience (Bala's Museum with Memories of Lucy Maud Montgomery).
32 LMM, *SJ* 3: 26. See Clement, "Toronto's Cultural Scene," 247.
33 Mustard, *L.M. Montgomery as Mrs Ewan Macdonald*, 14, 16.
34 Epperly, *Through Lover's Lane*, 37. See also Epperly's thorough description of the Frede "shrine," 78.
35 LMM, *SJ* 2: 217, 317–18.
36 Waterston, "Leaskdale," 32.
37 LMM, *SJ* 3: 265.
38 Raleigh, *Good Fairy Statuette*, 8.

CHAPTER THREE

1 LMM, *SJ* 3: 21.
2 Waterston, *Magic Island*, 113.

3   LMM, *SJ* 3: 21–2.
4   Ibid., 21–2.
5   Woster, "Old Years and Old Books," 159–60.
6   Smith and Watson, *Reading Autobiography*, 24, 22.
7   LMM, *After Green Gables*, 98–9.
8   Rubio, *Lucy Maud Montgomery: The Gift of Wings*, 274–5.
9   Rubio and Waterston, "Introduction," LMM, *CJ* 1: ix–x. I refer to the original diaries as the PEI diaries and the published book as the PEI journals.
10 Rubio, *Lucy Maud Montgomery: The Gift of Wings*, 290.
11 LMM, *SJ* 3: 22–3.
12 Woster, "Old Years and Old Books," 152.
13 LMM, *CJ* 1: 411.
14 LMM, *SJ* 2: 341–2.
15 Smith, *Poetics of Women's Autobiography*, 47.
16 LMM, *SJ* 3: 147.
17 Gilbert and Gubar, *Madwoman in the Attic*, 586.
18 Ibid., 587–8.
19 Montgomery senses that Ewan is jealous of her fame as a writer and believes that he views woman as "the plaything and servant of man" (LMM, *SJ* 3: 48).
20 LMM, *SJ* 2: 322.
21 Rubio, *Lucy Maud Montgomery: The Gift of Wings*, 292.
22 Clement, "Toronto's Cultural Scene," 243–4.
23 White, "Religious Thought of L.M. Montgomery," 84.
24 Rubio, "L.M. Montgomery: Scottish-Presbyterian Agency in Canadian Culture," 94–5.
25 Epperly, *Through Lover's Lane*, 75.
26 LMM, *SJ* 3: 170, 21.
27 Smith, *Poetics of Women's Autobiography*, 55.
28 Gammel, "Introduction: Life Writing as Masquerade," 8.
29 Waterston, *Magic Island*, 85.
30 Waterston, "Leaskdale," 22–4.
31 LMM, *RV*, 4.
32 Cavert, "'To the Memory of,'" 35–6.
33 LMM, *CJ* 1: 279, 439, 195, 278.
34 Ibid., 232, 236, 359, 161. In Montgomery's criticism of "high Anglicanism," she reveals her prejudice against Roman Catholicism. Rubio provides valuable background about the antagonism between Presbyterians and Roman Catholics in "L.M. Montgomery: Scottish-Presbyterian Agency in Canadian Culture."
35 LMM, *CJ* 1: 380–1.
36 Ibid., 65.

37 LMM, *CJ* 2: 262. In the earlier edition, "impressions" is "impression" (*SJ* 1: 378), which suggests that the doctrines have little if any influence.
38 LMM, *CJ* 1: 380–2.
39 Ibid., 347, 207.
40 Ibid., 354, 371.
41 Ibid., 324, 226, 111.
42 White, "Religious Thought of L.M. Montgomery," 85.
43 DuVernet, *Minding the Spirit*, 58.
44 LMM, *SJ* 2: 312.
45 Rubio, *Lucy Maud Montgomery: The Gift of Wings*, 277–8.
46 LMM, *SJ* 2: 322–3.
47 Rubio, *Lucy Maud Montgomery: The Gift of Wings*, 212.
48 LMM, *SJ* 3: 240, 260.
49 LMM, *SJ* 2: 340.
50 LMM, *SJ* 3: 39.
51 Rubio, *Lucy Maud Montgomery: The Gift of Wings*, 253–71.
52 LMM, *SJ* 2: 326, 334.
53 LMM, *SJ* 3: 44.
54 LMM, *SJ* 2: 351.
55 LMM, *SJ* 3: 44–5.
56 Ibid., 15.
57 LMM, *SJ* 4: 66, 235.
58 LMM, *SJ* 5: 21, 225.
59 LMM, *SJ* 2: 394.
60 LMM, *CJ* 1: 380.
61 *Canadian Oxford Dictionary*, 2004 ed., s.v. "Spiritual" (def.1).
62 Miller, "Transfiguring the Divine," 144, 147.
63 LMM, *SJ* 3: 132, 196.
64 Forest, "(Re)Locating Montgomery," 174.
65 LMM *CJ* 1: 440.
66 Ibid., 380.
67 LMM, *ENM*, 339; *EC*, 2.

CHAPTER FOUR
1 Kornfeld and Jackson, "Female *Bildungsroman*," 141.
2 LMM, *BC*, 17.
3 Kornfeld and Jackson, "Female *Bildungsroman*," 141–4.
4 Berg, "Sisterhood Is Fearful," 40.
5 Gubar, "'Where Is the Boy?'" 47.
6 Yeast, "Negotiating Friendships," 119.
7 Robinson, "'Sex Matters.'"
8 Faderman, *Surpassing the Love of Men*, 84.
9 Smith-Rosenberg, *Disorderly Conduct*, 74.

10 LMM, *AIs*, 37–8. It is worth noting for the discerning reader who might point out that *Anne of the Island* was written and published in the early twentieth century that it took some time into that century, perhaps particularly in Canada, for such attitudes to take hold.
11 Faderman, *Surpassing the Love of Men*, 174.
12 Ibid., 332.
13 Ellis, *Studies in the Psychology of Sex*, 199.
14 Tridon, *Psychoanalysis and Love*, 175, 187.
15 Faderman, *Odd Girls and Twilight Lovers*, 48, 238.
16 LMM, *SJ* 4: 34, 186.
17 Faderman, *Surpassing the Love of Men*, 171.
18 Marcus, *Between Women*, 29.
19 Duder, *Awfully Devoted Women*, 24.
20 Strong-Boag, *New Day Recalled*, 93
21 Cavanagh, "Heterosexualization of the Ontario Woman Teacher," 282. Cavanagh specifically discusses the period after the Second World War, well after the time I am examining; however, her argument highlights changing responses to women's growing independence. The backlash did not appear suddenly.
22 LMM, *BC*, 27.
23 LMM, *SJ* 3: 217.
24 Waterston, *Magic Island*, 139.
25 Epperly, *Fragrance of Sweet-Grass*, 238.
26 LMM, *AIs*, 5.
27 LMM, *BC*, 5.
28 LMM, *AIs*, 12, 13, 38, 172.
29 Ibid., 212.
30 Ibid., 73, 135.
31 LMM, *BC*, 1, 16.
32 Åhmansson, "Textual/Sexual Space in *The Blue Castle*," 151.
33 LMM, *BC*, 39.
34 Ibid., 86
35 Ibid., 128.
36 Ibid., 24, 38, 203.
37 Ibid., 218, 29, 115, 145, 128, 65, 183.
38 LMM, *AIs*, 243.
39 LMM, *BC*, 218.

CHAPTER FIVE

1 LMM, *SJ* 2: 82–90.
2 Ibid., 90.
3 Ruddick, "Maternal Thinking," 98, 99, 101, 102–3.
4 Bode, "Anguish of Mother Loss," 53.

5 Montgomery records in her journal the memory of seeing her mother in her coffin. See *CJ* 1: 390 (entry of 8 April 1898).
6 Devereux, "'Not One of Those Dreadful New Women,'" 120.
7 LMM, *AGG*, 12.
8 LMM, *CJ* 1: 26, 35.
9 Ibid., 42.
10 LMM, *AA*, 263.
11 LMM, *SJ* 2: 90, 97.
12 Steffler, "Performing Motherhood," 190.
13 LMM, *SJ* 2: 101.
14 Steffler, "Performing Motherhood," 191.
15 LMM, *SJ* 2: 112.
16 Ibid., 133, 139, 146–7, 151, 156.
17 LMM, *AIs*, 144–5. For Anne's imagined picture of this home, see *AGG*, 39.
18 Devereux, "'Not One of Those Dreadful New Women,'" 122.
19 LMM, *AHD*, 3, 44, 62.
20 Thompson, "Shadow on the House of Dreams," 113.
21 LMM, *SJ* 2: 173, 186, 193.
22 Ruddick, "Maternal Thinking," 99.
23 LMM, *SJ* 3: 180, 209.
24 LMM, *BC*, 45–6.
25 Robinson, "'Gift for Friendship,'" 87.
26 LMM, *BC*, 120.
27 Ibid., 45, 120–1.
28 Robinson, "'Gift for Friendship,'" 87.
29 Ruddick, "Maternal Thinking," 102–3.
30 LMM, *SJ* 4: 159 (n. 397), 178–80, 196.
31 Robinson, "'Sex Matters'"; Cavert, "Nora, Maud, and Isabel."
32 LMM, *SJ* 4: 178, 203, 229, 227.
33 LMM, *PSB*, chapter 39.
34 LMM, *MP*, 173–4.
35 See LMM, *SJ* 4: 251–2, 255.
36 Ibid., 257–72.
37 Ibid., 265, 282, 269, 278, 325, 327, 335.
38 Clement, "Toronto's Cultural Scene," 259.
39 Thompson, "Shadow on the House of Dreams," 123.
40 LMM, *SJ* 5: 67–147; ibid., 142.
41 Luepnitz, "Beyond the Phallus," 224.
42 O'Reilly, introduction to *Feminist Mothering*, 7.
43 Ruddick, "Maternal Thinking," 102.
44 LMM, *JLH*, 29.
45 Ibid., 41–3.
46 While Jane is not versed in psychoanalysis, Montgomery would likely

have enjoyed her own psychoanalysis of these characters and their relationships. In the previous chapter, Robinson notes Montgomery's familiarity with the work of sexologists of her time, and the author also sought out contemporary psychologists for her own enrichment.
47 Rubio, *Lucy Maud Montgomery: The Gift of Wings*, 502.
48 LMM, *JLH*, 217.

CHAPTER SIX

1 Bhadury, "Fictional Spaces," 214.
2 Czerny, "Return to the Wild," 149, 151.
3 Lensink, "Expanding the Boundaries," 41.
4 LMM, *SJ* 2: 180.
5 Clement, "Toronto's Cultural Scene," 240–1.
6 LMM, *AP*, 96.
7 Ibid., 45.
8 LMM, *AGG*, 92–3.
9 LMM, *AHD*, 3.
10 LMM, *CJ* 2: 249.
11 LMM, *AP*, 43.
12 LMM, *SJ* 2: 240.
13 Cowger, "From 'Pretty Nearly Perfectly Happy,'" 195.
14 LMM, *AHD*, 3.
15 LMM, *RI*, 134.
16 Epperly, *Fragrance of Sweet-Grass*, 118.
17 Gammel, "Safe Pleasures for Girls," 118.
18 Robinson, "'Sex Matters,'" 170.
19 LMM, *AHD*, 125.
20 Epperly, *Fragrance of Sweet-Grass*, 76.
21 LMM, *AHD*, 103–4
22 Waterston, *Magic Island*, 79.
23 LMM, *AHD*, 116.
24 Rubio, *Lucy Maud Montgomery: The Gift of Wings*, 184.
25 LMM, *SJ* 2: 152.
26 LMM, *AHD*, 117.
27 Ibid., 117–18.
28 Rubio, *Lucy Maud Montgomery: The Gift of Wings*, 205.
29 LMM, *AHD*, 189.
30 Ibid., 118–19.
31 Waterston, *Magic Island*, 110.
32 LMM, *SJ* 2: 185, 190.
33 Epperly, *Fragrance of Sweet-Grass*, 114–15.
34 Waterston, *Magic Island*, 106.
35 LMM, *RI*, 84–5.

36 Ibid., 171.
37 Ibid., 188–9, 206.
38 Epperly, *Fragrance of Sweet-Grass*, 115.

CHAPTER SEVEN

1 Bush, "'Broken Idols'"; Smith, *Shakespeare and Son*; Riegel, *Writing Grief*, 4–5. The quotation for this chapter's epigraph is from L.M. Montgomery's *Emily Climbs*, 22.
2 Paris, *Standing at Water's Edge*, 19.
3 Quoted in Riegel, *Writing Grief*, 11. Riegel cites Richard Stamelman, *Lost beyond Telling: Representations of Death and Absence in Modern French Poetry* (Ithaca: Cornell University Press, 1990), 19.
4 Zimmerman, *Writing to Heal the Soul*, 18.
5 Goldberg, *Writing Down the Bones*, 113–14.
6 LMM, *My Dear Mr M*, 17.
7 Goldberg, *Writing Down the Bones*, 114.
8 Lamott, *Bird by Bird*, 226.
9 Butler, *From Where You Dream*, 18.
10 LMM, *CJ* 1: 89.
11 LMM, *ENM*, 93.
12 Riegel, *Writing Grief*, 4–6.
13 LMM, *SJ* 2: 339.
14 Acton, *Grief in Wartime*, 7.
15 At first, the third-person narrator quotes from Rilla's journal; later, in chapters 21 ("'Love Affairs Are Horrible'"), 27 ("Waiting"), and 32 ("Word from Jem"), Rilla's journal becomes the primary narrative with excerpts beginning with date and place of writing.
16 LMM, *RI*, 43, 100.
17 Ibid., 127–8, 194.
18 Ibid., 169–70.
19 Ibid., 188–9
20 Ibid., 244, 190, 140–1.
21 Lefebvre, "Afterword/A Note on the Text," 521.
22 LMM, *SJ* 5: 350.
23 This is discussed most fully by Brown and Lefebvre, "Archival Adventures with L.M. Montgomery," and Rubio, *Lucy Maud Montgomery: The Gift of Wings*, 575–80.
24 LMM, *SJ* 5: 120–46, 309, 151, 290, 341.
25 LMM, *My Dear Mr M*, 190, 200.
26 LMM, *SJ* 5: 199.
27 Lefebvre, "'That Abominable War,'" 117.
28 Epperly, foreword, x, xiv.
29 LMM, *SJ* 2: 306, 309.

30 LMM, *BAQ*, 149.
31 Ibid., 3.
32 Ibid., 376, 401–2, 397–8, 439–40.
33 Ibid., 502–3.
34 Ibid., 509–10; LMM, *RI*, 153–4.
35 LMM, *BAQ*, 363, 370.
36 Ibid., 116–17, 480–1.
37 Epperly, foreword, xiv.

CHAPTER EIGHT

1 William Thompson's chapter in this volume calls *The Alpine Path* a "careful construction of Montgomery's early life" despite her many borrowings from her early journals. Thus, *The Alpine Path* and her journaling serve as evidence of Montgomery's multiple autobiographical impulses ("Shadow on the House of Dreams," 116).
2 LMM, *SJ* 3: 51.
3 LMM, *CJ* 2: 397.
4 Ibid., 367, 368–420; *SJ* 2: 64–83, 322, 295.
5 Flint, *Woman Reader*, 208.
6 Ibid., 10.
7 Kelley, "Crafting Subjectivities," 67.
8 Flint, *Woman Reader*, 187–8.
9 LMM, *SJ* 2: 357.
10 Ibid., 341.
11 Bloom, "'I Write for Myself and Strangers,'" 23.
12 LMM, *SJ* 3: 51.
13 LMM, *SJ* 2: 341.
14 Steffler, "'Being a Christian,'" 56.
15 LMM, *SJ* 2: 114.
16 Ibid., 143, 158.
17 Ibid., 189.
18 Ibid., 199.
19 Spacks, "Stages of Self," 48.
20 Flint, *Woman Reader*, 189.
21 Smith, *Poetics of Women's Autobiography*, 45.
22 LMM, *SJ* 2: 158, 199.
23 LMM, *SJ* 3: 166.
24 LMM, *SJ* 2: 350, 405.
25 Buss, *Mapping Our Selves*, 157.
26 LMM, *SJ* 3: 2, 5, 71.
27 LMM, *CJ* 1: 19.
28 LMM, *SJ* 3: 105.
29 In addition to the marginalia in her books and the reading records in her

journals, Montgomery's letters provide still further evidence of her projection of an image of self. Her epistolary relationships with George MacMillan and Ephraim Weber are marked by their literary interests and shared reading experiences. Many scholars of women's life writing have explored the nature of letters in autobiographical practice. Jennifer Cognard-Black and Elizabeth McLeod Walls's collection, *Kindred Hands: Letters on Writing by British and American Women Authors, 1865–1935*, deals at length with the nature of women's letters. Their collection emphasizes the ways in which letters are subject to some of the same time/space, public/private, and textual characteristics as scrapbooks and journals. Accordingly, Montgomery's many platforms and genres of autobiographical work all reflect her investment in self-presentation.

30 Montgomery's margin note in Wells's *Outline of History*, 508, Archival and Special Collections, University of Guelph Library.
31 LMM, *SJ* 2: 392, 393.
32 This unique reaction is complicated further when Montgomery sees Asquith speak in February 1922, as Clement discusses in "Toronto's Cultural Scene," 251–2.
33 Flint, *Woman Reader*, 187.
34 LMM, *SJ* 3: 362.
35 Thompson, "Shadow on the House of Dreams," 117.
36 LMM, *SJ* 3: 397.
37 LMM, *SJ* 5: 59.
38 Ibid., 202.
39 Ibid., 342.
40 Smith and Watson, *Reading Autobiography*, 73–5.
41 LMM, *SJ* 3: 21.
42 Turner, "'I Mean to Try,'" 94.

CHAPTER NINE

1 LMM, *SJ* 2: 368–70.
2 Gibson, "Timothy Findley," 138.
3 Botting, *Gothic*, 10.
4 Epperly, *Fragrance of Sweet-Grass*, 10, 3. See also MacLulich's criticism of Montgomery's version of the "real" in "L.M. Montgomery's Portraits of the Artist," 459–73.
5 Pike, "(Re)Producing Canadian Literature," 67, 71. See LMM, *SJ* 3: 387.
6 See also Lorna Drew, "Emily Connection"; Faye Hammill, *Literary Culture and Female Authorship*; Kate Lawson, "'Disappointed' House"; and Kathleen Ann Miller, "Haunted Heroines."
7 LMM, *SJ* 2: 370.
8 Lefebvre, "'That Abominable War!'"; Doody, "L.M. Montgomery: The Darker Side."

9 Woster, "Old Years and Old Books," 153.
10 Freud, *The Uncanny*, 155.
11 Sugars and Turcotte, "Introduction: Canadian Literature and the Postcolonial Gothic," ix.
12 Munro discusses Montgomery's influence in her afterword of the New Canadian Library edition of *Emily of New Moon*. For an account of interviews with Munro in regards to Montgomery and the *Emily* trilogy, see Rubio, "Subverting the Trite."
13 LMM, *SJ* 3: 147.
14 Hammill, *Literary Culture and Female Authorship*, 92.
15 Steffler, "Brian O'Connal and Emily Byrd Starr," 88.
16 Alexander, *Women in Romanticism*, 2–3.
17 LMM, *CJ* 2: 312.
18 Abrams, *Glossary of Literary Terms*, 187.
19 In *Survival*, Margaret Atwood comments on the consistency of "negative old women in Canadian fiction: diseased old women, like the mother in Alice Munro's 'The Peace of Ultrecht,' old ladies shut up in their sterile, life-denying houses, as in Anne Hébert's 'The House on the Esplanade' and P.K. Page's 'The Green Bird;' or, for fun (and treated somewhat more kindly by their authors) the wizened spinster Marilla in *Anne of Green Gables* and the raucous, blood-sucking, vital old grandmother in *Jalna*" (205).
20 LMM, *CJ* 2: 293.
21 Thompson, "Shadow on the House of Dreams," 115.
22 Alexander, *Women in Romanticism*, 78.
23 LMM, *ENM*, 29.
24 Munro, *Lives of Girls and Women*, 97.
25 Howells, *Alice Munro*, 15.
26 Munro, *Lives of Girls and Women*, 70.
27 LMM *SJ* 2: 79, 122, 124, 126, 127, 254, 251.
28 Lawson, "'Disappointed' House," 71, 73.
29 Atwood, *Survival*, 193.
30 Munro, *Lives of Girls and Women*, 80.
31 LMM, *ENM*, 1, 5, 52.
32 Ibid., 238.
33 Munro, afterword, 358.
34 Gammel, "Eros of Childhood and Early Adolescent Girl Series," 107.
35 LMM, *SJ* 2: 139, 95, 83, 139.
36 Steffler, "'Being a Christian,'" 61.
37 LMM, *SJ* 2: 370.
38 Steffler, "'Being a Christian,'" 67.
39 LMM, *SJ* 2: 322.
40 Rubio, "Subverting the Trite," 30.

41 LMM, *SJ* 2: 206.
42 Munro, "Authors on Their Writing," 254–5.
43 Rubio, "Subverting the Trite," 9.
44 Freud, *The Uncanny*, 155.
45 Woster, "Old Years and Old Books," 159.
46 LMM, *SJ* 2: 288.
47 Woster, "Old Years and Old Books," 157.
48 LMM, *ENM*, 120.
49 Wilmshurst, introduction to *Among the Shadows*, x.
50 LMM, "The Red Room," 159.
51 LMM, *SJ* 2: 402.
52 LMM, "Tryst of the White Lady," 248, 244, 247, 261.
53 See Epperly, *Fragrance of Sweet-Grass*, 146–8, 155–67, 178–81.
54 LMM, *ENM*, 142.
55 LMM, *SJ* 2: 368.
56 Alexander, *Women in Romanticism*, 5.
57 Munro, *Lives of Girls and Women*, 230–1.
58 Montgomery also attempts to capture her aesthetic perceptions and psychological experiences through her photography, as Epperly's *Through Lover's Lane* examines.
59 LMM, *ENM*, 333, 334, 337.

CHAPTER TEN

1 Johnston, "Landscape as Palimpsest, Pentimento, Epiphany," 15.
2 Epperly, *Through Lover's Lane*, 175–6.
3 LMM, *BC*, 21, 32, 33.
4 Lawson, "Victorian Sickroom," 238.
5 LMM, *BC*, 30, 12, 33, 36, 37, 11–12.
6 Hingston, "Montgomery's 'Imp,'" 199–201.
7 LMM, *BC*, 72, 66, 143, 138, 95.
8 Ibid., 116, 117, 115, 119, 123–4, 87.
9 Ibid., 30–1, 186.
10 Ibid., 186.
11 Hingston, "Montgomery's 'Imp,'" 204.
12 LMM, *BC*, 186, 193–4, 215, 25. The slogan "Try Purple Pills" is the one Anne Shirley dreams is painted on the school fence the night before she visits Judson Parker to try to persuade him not to rent his fence to a patent medicine company for advertising space (LMM, *AA*, 120).
13 LMM, *BC*, 30–1; Lawson, "Victorian Sickroom," 240.
14 LMM, *BC*, 9, 8.
15 Osborne, *Disturbances of the Heart*, n.p.
16 *Muskoka: Land of Health and Pleasure*, 6.
17 Wanderer, "Rest Cure in a Canoe," 619, 623.

18 *Muskoka: Land of Health and Pleasure*, 4.
19 Ibid., 11.
20 Jasen, 106, 107, 110–11, 126.
21 LMM, *BC*, 18; Wordsworth, *Poetical Works*, 93, 91.
22 Emerson, "Nature," 299, 295.
23 Carman, *Kinship of Nature*, 142, 250, 143.
24 LMM, *BC*, 9; Emerson, "Nature," 307.
25 LMM, *BC*, 18.
26 Ibid., 154.
27 Stephens, "Bliss Carman," 40.
28 LMM, *BC*, 203.
29 Stephens, "Bliss Carman," 43.
30 Epperly, *Through Lover's Lane*, 160, 158.
31 Carman, *Kinship of Nature*, 205–6; LMM, *BC*, 170.
32 Gundy, *Letters of Bliss Carman*, 543.
33 Carman hoped to be "all right financially before long" according to a letter written as *The Kinship of Nature* was being published. Gundy, *Letters of Bliss Carman*, 226.
34 LMM, *BC*, 132.
35 Ibid., 134.
36 Alaimo, *Undomesticated Ground*, 16.
37 Smith-Rosenberg, *Disorderly Conduct*, 252.
38 LMM, *BC*, 14.
39 Ibid., 109, 114, 152, 174, 213, 134.
40 Ibid., 157, 92, 130, 150.
41 Ibid., 150, 154, 161, 162, 169, 170, 175.
42 Ibid., 172, 173.
43 Rodenburg, "Bala and *The Blue Castle*," 213, 214.
44 LMM, *BC*, 163, 25, 121, 161–2, 170.
45 Ibid., 154, 160, 150.
46 Rodenburg, "Bala and *The Blue Castle*," 208.
47 LMM, *SJ* 3: 64, 62.
48 Ibid., 209, 222, 176–8, 54, 58, 62.
49 Ibid., 176, 177, 209.
50 Lawson, "Victorian Sickroom," 237, 238.
51 Clement, "Toronto's Cultural Scene," 258.
52 LMM, *BC*, 113; see also ibid., 168, 179, 183.
53 Ibid., 134, 216, 173.
55 Epperly, *Through Lover's Lane*, 176.

CHAPTER ELEVEN

1 LMM, *SJ* 3: 62–3, 65. The epigraph is from Roberson's introduction to *Defining Travel*, xi.

2. Rubio, "Subverting the Trite," 8.
3. The phrase "Spirit of Muskoka," quoted in this chapter's title, is how the painter Allan Tierney perceives Valancy and what he wants to capture in his proposed portrait of her. LMM, *BC*, 172.
4. LMM, *SJ* 3: 61, 62.
5. Tuan, *Space and Place*, 6.
6. LMM, *SJ* 3: 62.
7. Tuan, *Space and Place*, 6.
8. Woster, "Old Years and Old Books," 157.
9. Cavert, "Muskoka Dream," 6.
10. LMM, *SJ* 3: 63.
11. Ibid., 62.
12. Cavert, "Muskoka Dream," 6–7. Cavert quotes from LMM, *SJ* 3: 63, a phrase that Montgomery repeats in her letter of 24 September 1922 to G.B. MacMillan, who features in the dream. LMM, *My Dear Mr M*, 109.
13. Urry, *Tourist Gaze*, 12.
14. LMM, *SJ* 3: 63. Montgomery is referring to the lines from Robert Louis Stevenson's poem "Foreign Lands": "To where the roads on either hand / Lead onward into fairy land" (lines 17–18).
15. Ibid., 63.
16. Cohen, "Phenomenology of Tourist Experiences," 36.
17. Ibid., 33.
18. Ibid., 34, 42.
19. LMM, *SJ* 3: 65, 376.
20. Rubio, *Lucy Maud Montgomery: The Gift of Wings*, 327.
21. LMM, *SJ* 3: 222.
22. Rubio, *Lucy Maud Montgomery: The Gift of Wings*, 331.
23. LMM, *BC*, 1.
24. Ibid., 3–4.
25. Ibid., 4.
26. Urry, in *Tourist Gaze*, 1, asserts that the tourist gaze is "socially organised and systematised" because it draws on systems of knowledge and integrates the unknown into the known while searching for differences from established norms.
27. LMM, *BC*, 4, 5.
28. Ibid., 9.
29. Tuan, *Space and Place*, 6.
30. Tuan states, "If we think of space as that which allows movement, then place is pause; each pause in movement makes it possible for location to be transformed into place." Ibid., 4, 6.
31. Jones, "New Mother at Home," 102.
32. LMM, *BC*, 123–4, 87.

33 Robinson, "'Gift for Friendship,'" 80; Pike, "Propriety and the Proprietary," 189 passim.
34 LMM, BC, 70.
35 Cohen, "Phenomenology of Tourist Experiences," 32.
36 LMM, BC, 71, 81.
37 Baym, *Woman's Fiction*, 19.
38 Rubio, "Subverting the Trite," 16, 8.
39 LMM, BC, 218.
40 LMM, SJ 3: 62, emphasis added. After moving to Norval, Montgomery has an even more rapturous experience in the presence of the wind "singing" through "Russell's Pines" on the hill behind the manse. LMM, SJ 3: 385–6.
41 Pike, "Propriety and the Proprietary," 195.
42 Ibid., 191.
43 York, *Literary Celebrity in Canada*, 77.
44 A fuller examination of the specific material present in the museum is clearly warranted but goes beyond the scope of this paper. Both the Bala Museum website and the Huttons' book provide an indication of the breadth of memorabilia.
45 Bhadury, "Fictional Spaces, Contested Images," 214.
46 Bala Museum.
47 York, *Literary Celebrity in Canada*, 83.
48 Bhadury, "Fictional Spaces, Contested Images," 216.
49 Hutton and Jackson-Hutton, *Lucy Maud Montgomery and Bala*, 83.
50 Cohen, "Phenomenology of Tourist Experiences," 38.
51 MacCannell, "Sightseeing and Social Structure," 20–1.
52 The properties at Leaskdale, the Historic Church and Manse, have both national and provincial designations. For fuller discussion of these historical sites, see the interview in the appendix conducted with representatives of the L.M. Montgomery Society of Ontario by Kristina Eldridge and Chloe Verner.
53 This activity and others are described on the "Things to Do" link on the Bala Museum website.
54 MacCannell, "Sightseeing and Social Structure," 17, 18.
55 Lefebvre, "State," 64.
56 LMM, SJ 3: 63.
57 LMM, BC, 187.

CHAPTER TWELVE

1 Harrington, *Syllables of Recorded Time*, 19.
2 Vipond, "Canadian Authors' Association," 68.
3 Harrington, *Syllables of Recorded Time*, 23.

4 Ibid., 45–55.
5 Vipond, "Canadian Authors' Association," 69.
6 Parker, "Authors and Publishers on the Offensive," 162. See also Vipond, "Canadian Authors' Association," 70.
7 Harrington, *Syllables of Recorded Time*, 41.
8 Vipond, "Canadian Authors' Association," 71.
9 Rubio, *Lucy Maud Montgomery: The Gift of Wings*, 297.
10 LMM, *SJ* 3: 407.
11 LMM, *SJ* 2: 183, 286, 375.
12 Parker, "Authors and Publishers on the Offensive," 152.
13 Rubio, *Lucy Maud Montgomery: The Gift of Wings*, 295–6.
14 LMM, *SJ* 3: 24, 25. For a discussion of Montgomery's perception of the dinner in honour of Nellie McClung, see Clement, "Toronto's Cultural Scene," 250–1.
15 LMM, *SJ* 3: 128.
16 Ibid., 363, 380.
17 LMM, *SJ* 4: 107; LMM, *SJ* 3: 128; LMM, *SJ* 4: 221.
18 Rubio, *Lucy Maud Montgomery: The Gift of Wings*, 455, 457.
19 Canadian Authors Association, MS Coll 101, Box 3, Thomas Fisher Rare Book Library.
20 See, for example, LMM, *SJ* 5: 40, 59, 142, 163, 209–10.
21 Ibid., 142, 209–10.
22 Ibid., 206, 213, 37.
23 Rubio, *Lucy Maud Montgomery: The Gift of Wings*, 461, 535.
24 LMM, *SJ* 5: 37. Montgomery was less circumspect in her comments about Deacon in her private correspondence than in her (ultimately intended for public consumption) journals. See for example her commentary on Deacon in a 1930 letter to Ephraim Weber in LMM, *After Green Gables*, 180–2.
25 Deacon, *Poteen*, 169.
26 Rubio, *Lucy Maud Montgomery: The Gift of Wings*, 355.
27 Logan and French, *Highways of Canadian Literature*, 299–301.
28 LMM, *SJ* 5: 112.
29 Ibid., 45.
30 Rubio, *Lucy Maud Montgomery: The Gift of Wings*, 529.
31 LMM, *SJ* 5: 246–7.
32 Rubio, *Lucy Maud Montgomery: The Gift of Wings*, 529–30, 534–5, 568.
33 Ibid., 631.
34 Thomas and Lennox, *William Arthur Deacon*, 38, 47.
35 Deacon, *Dear Bill*, 66–7, 122–3, 210–15, 246.
36 Deacon's memorial to Emily Murphy included the following passage: "What did she do? Why, she showed the women of Canada, I think, that

the time has come for a new sort of pioneering; that the women must take hold of affairs, and use their minds, and make their wills felt, so that we can leave a better world than the man-made one into which we were born" (quoted in Thomas and Lennox, *William Arthur Deacon*, 67).

37 Gerson, "Canon between the Wars," 54.
38 Harrington, *Syllables of Recorded Time*, 22.
39 Curtis, *Life and Times of a Literary Chameleon*, 138–41.
40 Thomas and Lennox, *William Arthur Deacon*, 203.
41 Quoted in Gerson, "Canon between the Wars," 54.
42 Neijmann, "Fighting the Blunt Swords," 143–4.
43 Rubio and Waterston, introduction to LMM, *SJ* 5: xvii.
44 Gerson, "Canon between the Wars," 55.
45 Rubio, *Lucy Maud Montgomery: The Gift of Wings*, 463.
46 Gerson, "Canon between the Wars," 55. But see also Lefebvre, "Pigsties and Sunsets, 123–46, in which he argues that it is a myth that Montgomery wholly rejected modernism. And further, see Samara Walbohm, "Katherine Hale: 'But Now Another One Has Come,'" *Canadian Poetry* 56 (Spring/Summer 2005): 65–86, in which she uses the example of the poetry of Montgomery's contemporary Katherine Hale to deconstruct the binary between sentimentalism and modernism and thereby challenge the conception of Canadian modernism as primarily male.
47 Salverson rails against it all in a never-answered letter to Morley Callaghan: "The best chapter in *The Dove* was deleted when it was published as a serial, so were *all* the references to Steffania's birth which might have offended Mrs Prue. The only chapter I cared a hoot about in *The Viking Heart* was cut – it dealt with a man *who might* still be *alive* said the publisher, & so we could not offend. In Iceland we say what we like & often get hell for it but like the Irish we like a good fight. I've lost heart not so much from illness & poverty as from the sickening attitude of indifference & any progressive thought in the people here ... Now you can snub me again in Gods grace & good luck to ye" (quoted in Neijmann, "Fighting the Blunt Swords," 149).
48 Scott, *Leaving the Shade of the Middle Ground*, 33.
49 Gerson, "Canon between the Wars," 54.
50 Clement, "Toronto's Cultural Scene," 250–1. The incident Clement describes may also provide further evidence of sexism within the CAA, given that a number of male CAA members, including Deacon, were also active members of the Arts and Letters Club.
51 Thomas and Lennox, *William Arthur Deacon*, 200–1.
52 Canadian Authors Association, MS Coll 101, Box 2, File 2:5, Thomas Fisher Rare Book Library.
53 Thomas and Lennox, *William Arthur Deacon*, 37–8, 266, 215.
54 Rubio, *Lucy Maud Montgomery: The Gift of Wings*, 466.

CHAPTER THIRTEEN

1. LMM, *SJ* 2: 313.
2. LMM, *SJ* 4: 156.
3. Kipling, *Letters of Travel (1892–1913)*, 141.
4. Middleton, *Municipality of Toronto: A History*, 1: 405–6.
5. Hale, *Canadian Cities of Romance*, 112, 109, 120–1. The drawing (figure 13.1) is by Dorothy Stevens. Ibid., 113.
6. LMM, *SJ* 2: 137. The passage is quoted more fully in this chapter's epigraph.
7. York, *Literary Celebrity in Canada*, 30, 80, 82–5.
8. LMM, *My Dear Mr M*, 44.
9. York, *Literary Celebrity in Canada*, 84.
10. Ibid., 75, 4. York challenges the argument that Clarence Karr develops in chapter 8, "Lucy Maud Montgomery and Anne," *Authors and Audiences*.
11. LMM, *My Dear Mr M*, 44.
12. York, *Literary Celebrity in Canada*, 75.
13. LMM, *CJ* 2: 302; see ibid., 303–11, for a full description of Earl Grey's visit.
14. Ibid., 321, 326–32.
15. Rubio, *Lucy Maud Montgomery: The Gift of Wings*, 128.
16. Ibid., 175–6.
17. Ibid., 145, 166–7; see LMM, *SJ* 2: 81, for Montgomery's account of her arrival in Toronto.
18. LMM, *SJ* 2: 92–3.
19. Sandwell, "Annexation of our Stage," 23, 25.
20. LMM, *SJ* 2: 92–3.
21. Ibid., 137–8.
22. Rubio, *Lucy Maud Montgomery: The Gift of Wings*, 179.
23. LMM, *SJ* 2: 137–8.
24. "Woman at Work and Play" [Society Column], *Globe*, 21 March 1914, 10. Montgomery mistakenly reports that this was in Friday's *Globe* (20 March) rather than Saturday's. LMM, *SJ* 2: 144.
25. Davies, "Nineteenth-Century Repertoire," 107.
26. LMM, *SJ* 2: 144.
27. Ibid., 348.
28. LMM, *JLH*, 7, 144, 19, 29, 26. See Jones, "New Mother at Home," 107.
29. Conolly, "Man in the Green Goggles," n.p.
30. Plant, "Chronology: Theatre in Ontario to 1914," 346.
31. Davies, introduction to "Hope Deferred," 175.
32. LMM, *SJ* 3: 25.
33. Plant and Saddlemyer, introduction, 6.
34. LMM, *SJ* 3: 25.

35 York, *Literary Celebrity in Canada*, 94.
36 Bridle, "Gloom Like London Fog in the Little Theatre," *Toronto Daily Star*, 21 November 1921, 5.
37 LMM, *SJ* 3: 26–9. In chapter 2, "'To the Memory of,'" Cavert recounts Montgomery's emotionally wrought reading of the Dog Monday episode from *Rilla of Ingleside* to the girls at Jarvis Street Collegiate (45–6).
38 LMM, *SJ* 3: 28.
39 Ibid., 25.
40 Gwyn, *Private Capital*, 410.
41 M.O. Hammond Diary, microfilm, Archives of Ontario.
42 Ibid.
43 McBurney, *Great Adventure*, 49.
44 Arts and Letters Club Toronto Papers, 1923 file (1-68a), MS Coll 00315, Thomas Fisher Rare Book Library.
45 The Arts and Letters Club began admitting women to its membership in 1985. McBurney, *The Great Adventure*, provides a number of examples of Bridle's resistance to allowing women on the premises even as guests, despite the efforts of others, such as Hammond, to develop less discriminatory policies (5, 61, 65, 70).
46 LMM, *SJ* 3: 48, 25.
47 York, *Literary Celebrity in Canada*, 168,
48 LMM, *SJ* 3: 29.
49 Ibid., 39.
50 "Margot Talks 'Little Things': Amuses and Enlivens Audience with Intimacies of Great Folk," *Globe*, 28 February 1922, 11.
51 Kilbourn, *Intimate Grandeur*, 22, 15.
52 Lefebvre, "Introduction: A Life in Print," 5.
53 Rubio, *Lucy Maud Montgomery: The Gift of Wings*, 278–9. The journal entry she refers to is LMM, *SJ* 2: 391.
54 Woster, "Old Years and Old Books," 161–2.
55 Fairfield, "Theatres and Performance Halls," 279.
56 The phrase "Journeys End" or "Journey's End" is from, respectively, Shakespeare's *Twelfth Night* and the title of a 1928 play set in the trenches of the First World War and its movie adaptation that Montgomery saw in 1930. Rubio and Waterston, notes, LMM, *SJ* 5: 351–2.
57 Toronto journalist and film historian Eric Veillette has reposted information about and pictures of the Runnymede Theatre on the Heritage Toronto website (http://heritagetoronto.org/the-runnymede-theatre) from his own website (http://silenttoronto.com/).
58 LMM, *SJ* 5: 264. For similar examples, see ibid., 73, 208.
59 LMM, *SJ* 3: 244.
60 Scott, "Professional Performers and Companies," 32–3.

61 LMM, *SJ* 3: 389–90. The program for this production is in the Black Scrapbook, L.M. Montgomery Collection, Archival and Special Collections, University of Guelph Library. Other than Shaw's plays, the only plays that Montgomery mentions in her journals are *Three Live Ghosts*, a production of Charles Hamden's British Players, which she saw with Mary Beal at the Comedy Theatre late October 1925 – "It was the best comedy I ever saw and we laughed unceasingly all through it. How pleasant it would be to live where I could see a good play once a week – or even once a month" (ibid., 257) – and O'Casey's *Juno and the Paycock*, which she wrongly attributes to Shaw, an Abbey Players' production at the Royal Alexandra, attended with Miss Baskerville on 5 February 1938 – "It was very good too – but I was too obsessed to enjoy it" (LMM, *SJ* 5: 233).
62 LMM, *SJ* 3: 202.
63 Shaw, *Saint Joan*, 41, 97.
64 *Globe*, 11 April 1925, 9.
65 Salter, "At Home and Abroad," n.p.
66 Charlesworth, *More Candid Chronicles*, 386–7.
67 Salter, "At Home and Abroad," n.p.
68 This letter, from Robert McKown of Slinfold, Sussex, responds to Robert Prentis, probably the drama critic for *John o' London's Weekly*, a major London literary journal. In a letter to MacMillan of 15 March 1931, Montgomery thanks him for sending a bundle of these weeklies, which arrived just as she was leaving for her trip to the Prairie provinces: "They really saved my reason. And when I had read every word in them I worked the cross-word puzzles ... I had a real devilish orgy of it that day." LMM, *My Dear Mr M*, 157. This clipping in the Black Scrapbook is on a page with clippings, programs, and images from the early to mid 1930s.
69 Rubio and Waterston, *Writing a Life*, 13.
70 LMM, *SJ* 3: 202.
71 Thompson, "Shadow on the House of Dreams," 115.
72 LMM, *SJ* 3: 202–3. Although not describing her inaccurately as Montgomery does, the *Globe* reviewer also notes the discrepancy between Arthur's prettiness and Shaw's description: "Only once does she fail Shaw's description; she is pretty, and that gentleman insists that the original was not. Her voice is low and thrilling; her gestures seem unpremeditated; never once does she allow dramatic feeling to submerge her essential simplicity and sincerity" (*Globe*, 7 October 1924, 13). For examples of Montgomery's disdain of Hollywood "dolls" and "banal Hollywood love-making which never varies, no matter in what period or role," see LMM, *SJ* 3: 69, 306; LMM, *SJ* 5: 159, 164, 263.
73 Turner, "'I Mean to Try,'" 99.

74 LMM, *SJ* 3: 202–3; Cavert, "'To the Memory of,'" 49.
75 Charlesworth, "Music and Dance: Julia Arthur's Great 'Saint Joan,'" *Saturday Night*, 14 November 1925, 6.
76 "'The Universal Shaw': Timely Story of G.B. Shaw's Rise into World-Wide Fame, Told by One of his Biographers," *Globe*, 7 November 1925, 8.
77 LMM, *SJ* 4: 233, 89. For the other journal references to Shaw, see ibid., 91, 92. In the Nobel Prize presentation speech on 10 December 1926, Per Hallström, Chairman of the Nobel Committee of the Swedish Academy, claimed Shaw to be a modern Voltaire.
78 York, *Literary Celebrity in Canada*, 95.
79 Shaw, *Saint Joan*, 103.
80 Rubio and Waterston, *Writing a Life*, 120.
81 LMM, *EC*, 79.
82 LMM, *MP*, 270.
83 LMM, *EQ*, 5–6.

Bibliography

PRIMARY SOURCES

After Green Gables: L.M. Montgomery's Letters to Ephraim Weber, 1916–1941. Edited by Hildi Froese Tiessen and Paul Gerard Tiessen. Toronto: University of Toronto Press 2006.

The Complete Journals of L.M. Montgomery: The PEI Years, 1889–1911. Edited by Mary Rubio and Elizabeth Waterston. 2 vols. Toronto: Oxford University Press 2012–13.

Montgomery, L.M. *The Alpine Path: The Story of My Career.* 1917. Markham: Fitzhenry & Whiteside 1997.

– *Among the Shadows.* Edited by Rea Wilmshurst. New York: Bantam 1991.
– *Anne of Avonlea.* 1909. Toronto: Seal 1984.
– *Anne of Green Gables.* 1908. Toronto: Seal 1983.
– *Anne of the Island.* 1915. Toronto: Seal 1981.
– *Anne's House of Dreams.* 1917. Toronto: Seal 1983.
– *The Blue Castle.* 1926. Toronto: Seal 1988.
– *The Blythes Are Quoted.* Edited by Benjamin Lefebvre. Toronto: Viking Canada 2009.
– *Emily Climbs.* 1925. Toronto: Seal 1983.
– *Emily of New Moon.* 1923. Toronto: Seal 1983.
– *Emily's Quest.* 1927. Toronto: Seal 1983.
– "The Garden of Spices." In *Lucy Maud Montgomery Short Stories, 1909–1922,* 87–97. Newstead, Australia: Emereo Publishing 1991.
– *Jane of Lantern Hill.* 1937. Toronto: Seal 1988.
– *Mistress Pat.* 1935. Toronto: Seal 1989.
– "The Old Chest at Wyther Grange." In *Among the Shadows,* 141–54.
– *Pat of Silver Bush.* 1933. Toronto: Seal 1988.
– *Rainbow Valley.* 1919. Toronto: Seal 1996.
– "The Red Room." In *Among the Shadows,* 155–73.
– *Rilla of Ingleside.* 1921. Toronto: Seal 1987.
– *The Story Girl.* 1911. Toronto: Seal 1987.
– "The Tryst of the White Lady." In *Among the Shadows,* 242–61.

My Dear Mr M: Letters to G.B. MacMillan from L.M. Montgomery. Edited by Francis W.P. Bolger and Elizabeth R. Epperly. Toronto: McGraw-Hill Ryerson 1980.

The Selected Journals of L.M. Montgomery. Edited by Mary Rubio and Elizabeth Waterston. 5 vols. Toronto: Oxford University Press 1985–2004.

ARCHIVAL MATERIAL

Arts and Letters Club Toronto Papers. MS Coll 00315. Thomas Fisher Rare Book Library, University of Toronto Libraries, Toronto.

Canadian Authors Association Papers. MS Coll 101. Thomas Fisher Rare Book Library, University of Toronto Libraries, Toronto.

Cashmore, Stephen, and David Bews. "The Fisherman's War, 1914–1918." Highland Archive, Caithness. 1998. http://www.internet-promotions.co.uk/archives/caithness/sub2.htm.

Ephraim Weber Fonds. MG 30, D 53. National Archives of Canada, Ottawa.

"From Colony to Country: A Reader's Guide to Canadian Military History: The War in the Air." Library and Archives Canada. Government of Canada. 19 January 2006. http://www.collectionscanada.gc.ca/military/025002-6034-e.html.

George Boyd Macmillan Fonds. MG 30, D 185. National Archives of Canada, Ottawa.

Goldwin Lapp letter to Mr and Mrs George Lapp, 23 May 1915. Uxbridge Historical Centre, Uxbridge, Ontario.

L.M. Montgomery Collection. Archival and Special Collections, University of Guelph Library, Guelph, Ontario.

M.O. Hammond Diary (microfilm). Fonds F 1075. Archives of Ontario, Toronto.

"Picturing a Canadian Life: L.M. Montgomery's Personal Scrapbooks and Book Covers: L.M. Montgomery and the 116th Battalion." Virtual Museum Canada. 30 August 2002. Confederation Centre, Charlottetown, Prince Edward Island. http://lmm.confederationcentre.com/english/collecting/collecting-6-2d.html.

"They Need Me Over There and I've Got to Go." Clipping from unidentified Ontario newspaper. Zephyr, Ontario, 26 September 1918. Uxbridge Historical Centre, Uxbridge, Ontario.

Veteran Affairs Canada. "The First World War." Government of Canada, 30 July 2013. http://www.veterans.gc.ca/eng/feature/fww.

"War Diary: The Logistical Summary for the 116th (Ontario County) Canadian Infantry Battalion's Sojourn in France." The Ontario Regiment (RCAC) Museum. 2013. www.ontrmuseum.ca/history.htm.

SECONDARY SOURCES

Abrams, M.H. *A Glossary of Literary Terms*. 8th ed. Toronto: Thomson Wadsworth 2005.

Acton, Carol. *Grief in Wartime: Private Pain, Public Discourse*. New York: Palgrave Macmillan 2007.

Åhmansson, Gabriella. "Textual/Sexual Space in *The Blue Castle*: Valancy Stirling's 'Room of Her Own.'" In Rubio, *Harvesting Thistles*, 146–54.

Alaimo, Stacy. *Undomesticated Ground*. Ithaca, NY: Cornell University Press 2000.

Alexander, Meena. *Women in Romanticism*. Savage, MD: Barnes & Noble 1989.

Atwood, Margaret. *Survival: A Thematic Guide to Canadian Literature*. Toronto: Anansi 1972.

Bala Museum. "Bala's Museum: With Memories of Lucy Maud Montgomery." www.bala.net/museum.

Baym, Nina. *Woman's Fiction: A Guide to Novels by and about Women in America*. Ithaca, NY: Cornell University Press 1978.

Berg, Temma. "Sisterhood Is Fearful: Female Friendship in Montgomery." In Rubio, *Harvesting Thistles*, 36–49.

Bhadury, Poushali. "Fictional Spaces, Contested Images: Anne's 'Authentic' Afterlife." *Children's Literature Association Quarterly* 36, no. 2 (Summer 2011): 214–37.

Bloom, Lynn Z. "'I Write for Myself and Strangers': Private Diaries as Public Documents." In *Inscribing the Daily: Critical Essays on Women's Diaries*, edited by Suzanne L. Bunkers and Cynthia A. Huff, 23–37. Amherst: University of Massachusetts Press 1996.

Bode, Rita. "L.M. Montgomery and the Anguish of Mother Loss." In Mitchell, *Storm and Dissonance*, 50–66.

Botting, Fred. *Gothic*. New York: Routledge 1996.

Boucher, William Ira. "World War Aviation, British Two-Seaters 1916." *An Illustrated History of World War One*. 16 August 2011. http://www.wwiaviation.com/british2seaters1916.html.

Brown, Vanessa, and Benjamin Lefebvre. "Archival Adventures with L.M. Montgomery; or, 'As Long as the Leaves Hold Together.'" In *Basements and Attics, Closets and Cyberspace: Explorations in Canadian Women's Archives*, edited by Linda M. Morra and Jessica Schagerl, 233–48. Waterloo: Wilfrid Laurier University Press 2012.

Bush, Harold K., Jr. "'Broken Idols': Mark Twain's Elegies for Susy and a Critique of Freudian Grief Theory." *Nineteenth Century Literature* 57, no. 2 (September 2002): 237–68.

Buss, Helen M. *Mapping Our Selves: Canadian Women's Autobiography in English*. Montreal: McGill-Queen's University Press 1993.

Butler, Robert Olen. *From Where You Dream: The Process of Writing Fiction.* Edited by Janet Burroway. New York: Grove Press 2005.

Carman, Bliss. *The Kinship of Nature.* Boston: L.C. Page 1904.

Cavanagh, Sheila L. "The Heterosexualization of the Ontario Woman Teacher in the Postwar Period." In *Rethinking Canada: The Promise of Women's History.* 5th ed. Edited by Mona Gleason and Adele Perry, 278–86. Toronto: Oxford University Press 2006.

Cavert, Mary Beth. "Frede: More than Friend and Cousin." *The Shining Scroll* (2003): 5–8.

– "Images of Magic and Lament." *Kindred Spirits Chronicle* (November 2009): 2–3.

– "Lest We Forget: *Rainbow Valley.*" *The Shining Scroll* (2007): 14–15.

– "L.M. Montgomery and World War I in Leaskdale, Ontario: A Book Dedication to Goldwin D. Lapp." *The Shining Scroll* (December 2009): 1–15.

– "L.M. Montgomery's Book Dedications: Robert Brooks, 116th Battalion, C.E.F." *The Shining Scroll* (December 2008): 14–19.

– "Muskoka Dream." *The Shining Scroll* (Summer 1995): 6–7.

– "Nora, Maud, and Isabel: Summoning Voices in Diaries and Memories." In Gammel, *The Intimate Life of L.M. Montgomery,* 106–25.

– "'The Very Soul of the Universe Must Ache with Anguish': L.M. Montgomery, Leaskdale, and Loss in the Great War." *The Shining Scroll* (December 2011): 14–25.

Charlesworth, Hector. *More Candid Chronicles: Further Leaves from the Note Book of a Canadian Journalist.* Toronto: Macmillan 1928.

Cognard-Black, Jennifer, and Elizabeth McLeod Walls, eds. *Kindred Hands: Letters on Writing by British and American Women Authors, 1865–1935.* Iowa City: University of Iowa Press 2006.

Cohen, Erik. "Phenomenology and Tourist Experiences." In Roberson, *Defining Travel,* 29–55.

Conolly, L.W. "The Man in the Green Goggles: Clergymen and Theatre Censorship (Toronto, 1912–13)." *Theatre Research in Canada / Recherches Théâtrales au Canada* 1, no. 2 (Fall 1980): n.p.

Cowger, Ashley. "From 'Pretty Nearly Perfectly Happy' to 'the Depths of Despair': Mania and Depression in L.M. Montgomery's *Anne* Series." *The Lion and the Unicorn* 34, no. 2 (April 2010): 188–99.

Curtis, Tara Lee. "The Life and Times of a Literary Chameleon: Madge Hamilton Lyons MacBeth." Master's thesis, Department of English, University of Guelph 1996.

Czerny, Val. "A Return to the Wild or, Long-Lasting, Mystical 'Lunacy' in *Anne of Green Gables.*" *The Lion and the Unicorn* 34, no. 2 (April 2010): 148–66.

Davies, Robertson. Introduction (1980) to "Hope Deferred" (1948). In *Canada's Lost Plays.* Vol. 3, *The Developing Mosaic: English-Canadian*

Drama to Mid-Century, edited by Anton Wagner, 174–90. Toronto: Canada Theatre Review Publications 1980.
– "The Nineteenth-Century Repertoire." In Saddlemyer, *Early Stages*, 90–122.
Deacon, William Arthur. *Dear Bill: The Correspondence of William Arthur Deacon*. Edited by John Lennox and Michele Lacombe. Toronto: University of Toronto Press 1988.
– *Poteen: A Pot-Pourri of Canadian Essays*. Ottawa: Graphic Publishers Ltd 1926.
Devereux, Cecily. "'Not One of Those Dreadful New Women': Anne Shirley and the Culture of Imperial Motherhood." In Hudson and Cooper, *Windows and Words*, 119–30.
Doody, Margaret. "L.M. Montgomery: The Darker Side." In Mitchell, *Storm and Dissonance*, 25–49.
Drew, Lorna. "The Emily Connection: Ann Radcliffe, L.M. Montgomery and 'The Female Gothic.'" *Canadian Children's Literature / Littérature canadienne pour la jeunesse* 77 (Spring 1995): 19–32.
Duder, Cameron. *Awfully Devoted Women: Lesbian Lives in Canada, 1900–65*. Vancouver: University of British Columbia Press 2010.
DuVernet, Sylvia. *Minding the Spirit: Theosophical Thoughts Concerning L.M. Montgomery*. Toronto: DuVernet 1993.
Edwards, Owen, Dudley. "L.M. Montgomery's *Rilla of Ingleside*: Intention, Inclusion, Implosion." In Rubio, *Harvesting Thistles*, 126–36.
Ellis, Havelock. *Studies in the Psychology of Sex*. New York: Random House 1942.
Emerson, Ralph Waldo. "Nature." 1844. *Essays: First and Second Series*. London: J.M. Dent 1906.
Epperly, Elizabeth. Foreword to *The Blythes Are Quoted* by L.M. Montgomery, ix–xiv. Toronto: Viking Canada 2009.
– *The Fragrance of Sweet-Grass: L.M. Montgomery's Heroines and the Pursuit of Romance*. 1992. 2nd ed., Toronto: University of Toronto Press 2014.
– *Through Lover's Lane: L.M. Montgomery's Photography and Visual Imagination*. Toronto: University of Toronto Press 2007.
Faderman, Lillian. *Odd Girls and Twilight Lovers: A History of Lesbian Life in Twentieth-Century America*. New York: Penguin 1992.
– *Surpassing the Love of Men: Romantic Friendship and Love between Women from the Renaissance to the Present*. New York: William Morrow 1981.
Fairfield, Robert. "Theatres and Performance Halls." In Saddlemyer, *Early Stages*, 214–87.
Flint, Kate. *The Woman Reader, 1837–1914*. Oxford: Clarendon 1993.
Freud, Sigmund. *The Uncanny*. Translated by David McLintock. Toronto: Penguin 2003.
Gammel, Irene. "The Eros of Childhood and Early Adolescence in Girl Series:

L.M. Montgomery's *Emily* Trilogy." In Hudson and Cooper, *Windows and Words*, 97–118.
– ed. *The Intimate Life of L.M. Montgomery*. Toronto: University of Toronto Press 2005.
– "Introduction: Life Writing as Masquerade." In Gammel, *Intimate Life*, 3–15.
– ed. *Making Avonlea: L.M. Montgomery and Popular Culture*. Toronto: University of Toronto Press 2002.
– "Safe Pleasures for Girls: L.M. Montgomery's Erotic Landscapes." In Gammel, *Making Avonlea*, 114–27.
Gammel, Irene, and Elizabeth Epperly, eds. *L.M. Montgomery and Canadian Culture*. Toronto: University of Toronto Press 1999.
Gerson, Carole. "The Canon between the Wars: Field-Notes of a Feminist Literary Archaeologist." In *Canadian Canons: Essays in Literary Value*, edited by Robert Lecker, 46–56. Toronto: University of Toronto Press 1991.
Gibson, Graeme. "Timothy Findley." In *Eleven Canadian Novelists Interviewed by Graeme Gibson*, 115–50. Toronto: Anansi 1973.
Gilbert, Sandra M., and Susan Gubar. *The Madwoman in the Attic: The Woman Writer and the Nineteenth-Century Literary Imagination*. New Haven: Yale University Press 1979.
Goldberg, Natalie. *Writing Down the Bones: Freeing the Writer Within*. Boston: Shambhala 1986.
Gubar, Marah. "'Where Is the Boy?': The Pleasure of Postponement in the *Anne of Green Gables* Series." *The Lion and the Unicorn* 25, no. 1 (January 2001): 47–69.
Gundy, H. Pearson, ed. *Letters of Bliss Carman*. Montreal: McGill-Queen's University Press 1981.
Gwyn, Sandra. *The Private Capital: Ambition and Love in the Age of Macdonald and Laurier*. Toronto: McClelland & Stewart 1984.
Hale, Katherine. *Canadian Cities of Romance*. Toronto: McClelland & Stewart 1922.
Hammill, Faye. *Literary Culture and Female Authorship in Canada, 1760–2000*. New York: Rodopi 2003.
Harrington, Lyn. *Syllables of Recorded Time: The Story of the Canadian Authors Association, 1921–1981*. Toronto: Simon & Pierre 1981.
Hingston, Kylee-Anne. "Montgomery's 'Imp': Conflicting Representations of Illness in L.M. Montgomery's *The Blue Castle*." In Mitchell, *Storm and Dissonance*, 194–208.
Howells, Coral Ann. *Alice Munro*. Vancouver: University of British Columbia Press 1998.
Hudson, Aïda, and Susan-Ann Cooper, eds. *Windows and Words: A Look at Canadian Children's Literature in English*. Ottawa: University of Ottawa Press 1999.

Hutton, Jack, and Linda Jackson-Hutton. *Lucy Maud Montgomery and Bala: A Love Story of the North Woods.* Bala: Watts Printing 1998.

Jasen, Patricia. *Wild Things: Nature, Culture, and Tourism in Ontario, 1790–1914.* Toronto: University of Toronto Press 1990.

Johnston, Rosemary Ross. "Landscape as Palimpsest, Pentimento, Epiphany: Lucy Maud Montgomery's Interiorisation of the Exterior." CREArTA 5 (2005): 13–31.

Karr, Clarence. *Authors and Audiences: Popular Canadian Fiction in the Early Twentieth Century.* Toronto: McGill-Queen's University Press 2000.

Kelley, Mary. "Crafting Subjectivities: Women, Reading, and Self-Imagining." In *Reading Women: Literacy, Authorship, and Culture in the Atlantic World, 1500–1800,* edited by Heidi Brayman Hackel and Catherine E. Kelly, 55–71. Philadelphia: University of Pennsylvania Press 2008.

Kilbourn, William. *Intimate Grandeur: One Hundred Years at Massey Hall.* Toronto: Stoddart 1993.

Kipling, Rudyard. *Letters of Travel (1892–1913).* London: Macmillan 1920.

Kominars, Sheppard B. *Write for Life: Healing Body, Mind, and Spirit through Journal Writing.* New York: Kaplan 2010.

Kornfeld, Eve, and Susan Jackson. "The Female *Bildungsroman* in Nineteenth-Century America: Parameters of a Vision." In *Such a Simple Little Tale: Critical Responses to L.M. Montgomery's Anne of Green Gables,* edited by Mavis Reimer, 139–52. Metuchen, NJ: Scarecrow Press 1992.

Lamott, Anne. *Bird by Bird: Some Instructions on Writing and Life.* New York: Random House 1994.

Lawson, Eric, and Jane Lawson. *The First Air Campaign: August 1914 – November 1918.* Cambridge, MA: Da Capo Press 1996.

Lawson, Kate. "The 'Disappointed' House: Trance, Loss, and the Uncanny in L.M. Montgomery's Emily Trilogy." *Children's Literature* 29 (2001): 71–90.

– "The Victorian Sickroom in L.M. Montgomery's *The Blue Castle* and *Emily's Quest*: Sentimental Fiction and the Selling of Dreams." *The Lion and the Unicorn* 31, no. 3 (September 2007): 232–49.

Lefebvre, Benjamin. "Afterword/A Note on the Text." In *The Blythes Are Quoted,* by L.M. Montgomery, 511–22. Toronto: Viking Canada 2009.

– "Introduction: A Critical Heritage." In *The L.M. Montgomery Reader.* Vol. 2, *A Critical Heritage,* edited by Benjamin Lefebvre, 3–49. Toronto: Viking Press 2014.

– "Introduction: A Life in Print." In *The L.M. Montgomery Reader.* Vol. 1, *A Life in Print,* edited by Benjamin Lefebvre, 3–28. Toronto: University of Toronto Press 2013.

– "Pigsties and Sunsets: L.M. Montgomery, *A Tangled Web,* and a Modernism of Her Own." *ESC* 31, no. 4 (December 2005): 123–46.

– "'That Abominable War!': *The Blythes Are Quoted* and Thoughts on L.M. Montgomery's Late Style." In Mitchell, *Storm and Dissonance,* 109–30.

Lefebvre, Henri. "State." In *Henri Lefebvre: Key Writings*, edited by Stuart Elden, Elizabeth Lebas, and Eleonore Kofman, 61–4. New York: Continuum 2003.

Lensink, Judy Nolte. "Expanding the Boundaries of Criticism: The Diary as Female Autobiography." *Women's Studies* 14 (1987): 39–53.

Logan, J.D., and Donald G. French. *Highways of Canadian Literature: A Synoptic Introduction to the Literary History of Canada (English) from 1760 to 1924*. Toronto: McClelland & Stewart 1924.

Luepnitz, Deborah. "Beyond the Phallus: Lacan and Feminism." In *The Cambridge Companion to Lacan*, edited by Jean-Michel Rabaté, 221–37. Cambridge: Cambridge University Press 2003.

Lynes, Jeanette. "Consumable Avonlea: The Commodification of the Green Gables Mythology." In Gammel, *Making Avonlea*, 268–79.

MacCannell, Dean. "Sightseeing and Social Structure." In Roberson, *Defining Travel*, 13–28.

MacLulich, T.D. "L.M. Montgomery's Portraits of the Artist: Realism, Idealism, and the Domestic Imagination." *English Studies in Canada* 11, no. 4 (1985): 459–73.

Marcus, Sharon. *Between Women: Friendship, Desire, and Marriage in Victorian England*. Princeton: Princeton University Press 2007.

McBurney, Margaret. *The Great Adventure: 100 Years at the Arts & Letters Club*. Toronto: Arts and Letters Club of Toronto 2007.

McGillivray, Allan. *Decades of Harvest: A History of Scott Township, 1807–1973*. Uxbridge: Scott History Committee 1986.

McKenzie, Andrea. "Women at War: L.M. Montgomery, The Great War and Canadian Cultural Memory." In Mitchell, *Storm and Dissonance*, 83–108.

Middleton, Jesse Edgar. *The Municipality of Toronto: A History*. 2 vols. Toronto: Dominion Publishing Co. 1923.

Miller, Kathleen Ann. "Haunted Heroines: The Gothic Imagination and the Female *Bildungsromane* of Jane Austen, Charlotte Brontë, and L.M. Montgomery." *The Lion and the Unicorn* 34, no. 2 (April 2010): 125–47.

– "Transfiguring the Divine: L.M. Montgomery's *Emily* Trilogy and the Quest towards a Feminine Spirituality." CREArTA 5 (2005): 144–57.

Mitchell, Jean, ed. *Storm and Dissonance: L.M. Montgomery and Conflict*. Newcastle, UK: Cambridge Scholars Publishing 2008.

Morley, Robert. "Earning Their Wings: British Pilot Training, 1912–1918." Master's thesis, Department of History, University of Saskatchewan 2006.

Munro, Alice. Afterword to *Emily of New Moon*, by L.M. Montgomery, 357–61. New Canadian Library series. Toronto: McClelland & Stewart 1989.

– "The Authors on Their Writing." *Personal Fictions: Stories by Munro, Wiebe, Thomas, and Blaise*, edited by Michael Ondaatje, 224–30. Toronto: Oxford University Press 1977.

– *Lives of Girls and Women*. Toronto: Penguin Canada 1971.

Muskoka: Land of Health and Pleasure. 1897.
Mustard, Margaret H. *L.M. Montgomery as Mrs Ewan Macdonald of the Leaskdale Manse, 1911–1926*. Leaskdale: St Paul's Presbyterian Women's Association 1965.
Neijmann, Daisy. "Fighting the Blunt Swords: Laura Goodman Salverson and the Canadian Literary Canon." *Essays on Canadian Writing* 67 (Spring 1999): 138–73.
Nicholson, G.W.L. *Official History of the Canadian Army in the First World War: Canadian Expeditionary Force, 1914–1919*. Ottawa: Queen's Printer 1962. http://www.cmp-cpm.forces.gc.ca/dhh-dhp/his/oh-ho/index-eng.asp
O'Reilly, Andrea, ed. *Feminist Mothering: Essential Readings*. Albany: State University of New York Press 2008.
– Introduction to O'Reilly, *Feminist Mothering*, 1–22.
O'Reilly, Andrea, ed. *Maternal Theory: Essential Readings*. Toronto: Demeter Press 2007.
Osborne, Oliver T. *Disturbances of the Heart: Discussion of the Treatment of the Heart in Its Various Disorders, with a Chapter on Blood Pressure*. 2nd ed. Chicago: Journal of the American Medical Association 1916. http://www.gutenberg.org/ebooks/3731.
Paris, Anne. *Standing at Water's Edge: Moving Past Fear, Blocks, and Pitfalls to Discover the Power of Creative Immersion*. Novato, CA: New World Library 2008.
Parker, George L. "Authors and Publishers on the Offensive: The Canadian Copyright Act of 1921 and the Publishing Industry 1920–1930." *Papers of the Bibliographic Society of Canada* 50, no. 2 (Fall 2012): 131–85.
Pike, Holly. "(Re)Producing Canadian Literature." In Gammel and Epperly, *L.M. Montgomery and Canadian Culture*, 64–76.
Plant, Richard. "Chronology: Theatre in Ontario to 1914." In Saddlemyer, *Early Stages*, 288–346.
Plant, Richard, and Ann Saddlemyer. Introduction to Saddlemyer and Plant, *Later Stages*, 3–12.
Quaile, Deborah. *L.M. Montgomery: The Norval Years, 1926–1935*. Ontario: Wordbird Press 2006.
Raleigh, Jessie McCutcheon. *The Good Fairy Statuette*. Privately published brochure. Chicago, 1915.
Riegel, Christian. *Writing Grief: Margaret Laurence and the Work of Mourning*. Winnipeg: University of Manitoba Press 2003.
Roberson, Susan, ed. *Defining Travel: Diverse Visions*. Jackson: University of Mississippi Press 2001.
– Introduction to Roberson, *Defining Travel*, xi–xxvi.
Robinson, Laura. "'Sex Matters': L.M. Montgomery, Friendship, and Sexuality." *Children's Literature* 40 (2012): 167–90.

Rubio, Mary, ed. *Harvesting Thistles: The Textual Garden of L.M. Montgomery.* Guelph: Canadian Children's Press 1994.
– *Lucy Maud Montgomery: The Gift of Wings.* Toronto: Doubleday 2008.
– "L.M. Montgomery: Scottish-Presbyterian Agency in Canadian Culture." In Gammel and Epperly, *L.M. Montgomery and Canadian Culture,* 89–105.
– "Subverting the Trite: L.M. Montgomery's 'Room of her Own.'" *Canadian Children's Literature / Littérature canadienne pour la jeunesse* 64 (1992): 6–39.
Rubio, Mary, and Elizabeth Waterston. Introduction to *The Complete Journals of L.M. Montgomery: The PEI Years, 1889–1900,* vol. 1, edited by Mary Rubio and Elizabeth Waterston, ix–xi. Toronto: Oxford University Press 2012.
– *Writing a Life: L.M. Montgomery.* Toronto: ECW Press 1995.
Ruddick, Sara. "Maternal Thinking." In O'Reilly, *Maternal Theory,* 96–113.
Saddlemyer, Ann, ed. *Early Stages: Theatre in Ontario, 1800–1914.* Toronto: University of Toronto Press 1990.
Saddlemyer, Ann, and Richard Plant. eds. *Later Stages: Essays in Ontario Theatre from the First World War to the 1970s.* Toronto: University of Toronto Press 1997.
Salter, Denis. "At Home and Abroad: The Acting Career of Julia Arthur (1869–1950)." *Theatre Research in Canada / Recherches Théâtrales au Canada* 5, no. 1 (Spring 1984): n.p.
Sandwell, Bernard K. "The Annexation of our Stage." *Canadian Magazine* 38, no. 1 (November 1911): 22–6.
Scott, F.R. *Leaving the Shade of the Middle Ground: The Poetry of F.R. Scott.* Edited by Laura Moss. Waterloo: Wilfrid Laurier University Press 2011.
Scott, Robert B. "Professional Performers and Companies." In Saddlemyer and Plant, *Later Stages,* 13–120.
Shaw, George Bernard. *Saint Joan.* 1924. London: Constable 1925.
Skeet, Michael. "RFC Pilot Training." The Aerodrome Forum, December 1998. http://www.theaerodrome.com/forum/aviation-personnel/23225-rfc-pilot-training.html.
Smith, G. Oswald. *University of Toronto Roll of Service, 1914–1918.* Toronto: University of Toronto Press 1921. http://archive.org/details/torontoroll servicoounknuoft.
Smith, Keverne. *Shakespeare and Son: A Journey in Writing and Grieving.* Santa Barbara, CA: Praeger 2011.
Smith, Sidonie. *A Poetics of Women's Autobiography: Marginality and the Fictions of Self-Representation.* Bloomington: Indiana University Press 1987.
Smith, Sidonie, and Julia Watson. *Reading Autobiography: A Guide for Interpreting Life Narratives.* 2nd ed. Minneapolis: University of Minnesota Press 2010.

Smith-Rosenberg, Carroll. *Disorderly Conduct: Visions of Gender in Victorian America*. New York: Knopf 1985.
Spacks, Patricia Meyer. "Stages of Self: Notes on Autobiography and the Life Cycle." In *The American Autobiography: A Collection of Critical Essays*, edited by Albert E. Stone, 44–60. Englewood Cliffs, NJ: Prentice-Hall 1981.
Steffler, Margaret. "Brian O'Connal and Emily Byrd Starr: The Inheritors of Wordsworth's 'Gentle Breeze.'" In Hudson and Cooper, *Windows and Words*, 87–96.
– "Performing Motherhood: L.M. Montgomery's Display of Maternal Dissonance." In Mitchell, *Storm and Dissonance*, 178–93.
Stephens, Donald. "Bliss Carman." In *Canadian Writers, 1890–1920*, edited by William H. New, 38–44. *Dictionary of Literary Biography*. Vol. 92. Detroit: Gale Research 1990.
Strong-Boag, Veronica. *The New Day Recalled: Lives of Girls and Women in English Canada, 1919–1939*. Toronto: Copp Clark Pitman 1988.
Sugars, Cynthia, and Gerry Turcotte. "Introduction: Canadian Literature and the Postcolonial Gothic." In *Unsettled Remains: Canadian Literature and the Postcolonial Gothic*, edited by Cynthia Sugars and Gerry Turcotte, vii–xxvi. Waterloo: Wilfrid Laurier University Press 2009.
Thomas, Clara, and John Lennox. *William Arthur Deacon: A Canadian Literary Life*. Toronto: University of Toronto Press 1982.
Tridon, André. *Psychoanalysis and Love*. New York: Garden City Publishing 1922.
Tuan, Yi-Fu. *Space and Place: The Perspective of Experience*. Minneapolis: University of Minnesota Press 1977.
Turner, Margaret E. "'I Mean to Try, as Far as in Me Lies, to Paint My Life and Deeds Truthfully': Autobiographical Process in the L.M. Montgomery Journals." In Rubio, *Harvesting Thistles*, 93–100.
Urquhart, Jane. *L.M. Montgomery*. Extraordinary Canadians series. Toronto: Penguin Canada 2009.
Urry, John. *The Tourist Gaze*. 2nd ed. London: Sage 2002.
Vipond, Mary. "The Canadian Authors' Association in the 1920s: A Case Study in Cultural Nationalism." *Journal of Canadian Studies* 15, no. 1 (Spring 1980): 68–79.
Wanderer. "The Rest Cure in a Canoe." *Rod and Gun in Canada* 12, no. 5 (October 1910): 619–23.
Waterston, Elizabeth. *Magic Island: The Fictions of L.M. Montgomery*. Toronto: Oxford University Press 2008.
White, Gavin. "The Religious Thought of L.M. Montgomery." In Rubio, *Harvesting Thistles*, 84–8.
Wilmshurst, Rea. Introduction to *Among the Shadows*, by L.M. Montgomery, vii–xvi. New York: Bantam 1991.

Wordsworth, Dorothy. *Recollections of a Tour Made in Scotland A.D. 1803*. Edited by J.C. Shairp. 2009. www.gutenberg.org/ebooks/28880.
Wordsworth, William. *The Poetical Works of Wordsworth*. Edited by Paul D. Sheats. Boston: Houghton Mifflin 1982.
Yeast, Denyse. "Negotiating Friendships: The Reading and Writing of L.M. Montgomery." In Rubio, *Harvesting Thistles*, 113–25.
York, Lorraine. *Literary Celebrity in Canada*. Toronto: University of Toronto Press 2007.
Zimmerman, Susan. *Writing to Heal the Soul: Transforming Grief and Loss through Writing*. New York: Three Rivers Press 2002.

Contributors

RITA BODE is associate professor in the Department of English Literature at Trent University. Currently, her main research interest is in women writers of the nineteenth and early twentieth centuries, including their work in young adult literature and in transatlantic contexts. She has published on Joseph Conrad, George Eliot, Herman Melville, Harriet Prescott Spofford, and Harriet Beecher Stowe, among others. Her work on Montgomery has appeared in CREArTA and in *Storm and Dissonance: L.M. Montgomery and Conflict*.

KATE MACDONALD BUTLER, Montgomery's granddaughter and author of the *Anne of Green Gables Cookbook*, has a degree in food and nutrition. She is a board member of the Anne of Green Gables Licensing Authority, founded in 1994 and jointly owned by the Province of Prince Edward Island and the Heirs of L.M. Montgomery. She is president of Heirs of L.M. Montgomery Inc., a family-owned company that oversees all Montgomery-related inquiries and projects. She is also a patron of the L.M. Montgomery Society of Ontario.

KATHERINE (KAT) CAMERON has an MA in creative writing from the University of New Brunswick and teaches English and writing at Concordia University College in Edmonton. Her first collection of poetry, *Strange Labyrinth*, was published by Oolichan Books in 2014. Her poems, short stories, and essays have appeared in journals across Canada, including *FreeFall*, *Grain*, *Literary Review of Canada*, *Queen's Quarterly*, *Room*, PRISM *international*, and *Studies in Canadian Literature*.

MARY BETH CAVERT has an MA in educational administration. An independent Montgomery scholar, she specializes in the personal, historical, and literary context of Montgomery's kinship ties. She has articles in *The Intimate Life of L.M. Montgomery*, edited by Irene Gammel, and *The Lucy Maud Montgomery Album*, compiled by Kevin McCabe and edited by Alexandra Heilbron. She is the publisher and editor of the website of the L.M. Montgomery Literary Society and has published extensively in the society's periodical, *The Shining Scroll*, which she co-edits. Her current project is a study of Montgomery's book dedications, entitled "The Friends of Anne: L.M. Montgomery's Kindred Spirits."

LESLEY D. CLEMENT has held teaching and administrative positions in various Canadian universities and is currently at Lakehead University Orillia. She is the author of *Learning to Look: A Visual Response to Mavis Gallant's Fiction* and has published on (among others) Judith Thompson in the *Encyclopedia of Literature in Canada*, death in children's picture books in *Bookbird*, and L.M. Montgomery in *Studies in Canadian Literature*. She has co-edited *Global Perspectives on Death in Children's Literature* (Routledge, 2015) with Leyli Jamali and contributed a chapter on picture books on Emily Dickinson for that volume. Her most recent research explores visual literacy, the visual imagination, empathy, and death in children's and YA literature.

KRISTINA ELDRIDGE was born, raised, and educated in North York, Toronto. She is currently finishing her undergraduate degree in English with a minor in History at Trent University.

MELANIE FISHBANE holds an MFA in writing for children and young adults from the Vermont College of Fine Arts and an MA in history from Concordia University. With over seventeen years of experience in children's publishing, she lectures on children's literature and L.M. Montgomery. A freelance writer and social media consultant, she also teaches at Humber College. Her first novel, based on the teen life of Montgomery, will be published under the Razorbill imprint in 2016.

NATALIE FOREST holds an MA in public texts from Trent University. She has presented papers at various conferences, including the L.M. Montgomery Centennial Celebration, Leaskdale, Ontario, and the Popular Culture Association/American Culture Association National Conference. She is currently a PhD candidate in English at York University where her doctoral work focuses on early modern to current portrayals of Margaret of Anjou.

CAROLINE E. JONES teaches at Austin Community College, Austin, Texas. She has presented and published extensively on young adult literature in periodicals such as *The Lion and the Unicorn*, *Children's Literature in Education*, and *Children's Literature Association Quarterly*. She was a contributor to *The Cambridge Guide to Children's Books in English* and is on the editorial staff of *The Looking Glass: New Perspectives on Children's Literature*. She has an article in *Anne around the World: L.M. Montgomery and Her Classic*, edited by Jane Ledwell and Jean Mitchell.

E. HOLLY PIKE is associate professor of English at Grenfell Campus, Memorial University of Newfoundland. She has published on Montgomery in *Harvesting Thistles: The Textual Garden of L.M. Montgomery*; *L.M. Montgomery and Canadian Culture*; *Making Avonlea: L.M. Montgomery and Popular Culture*; *Storm and Dissonance: L.M. Montgomery and Conflict*; *100 Years of Anne with an 'e': The Centennial Study of Anne of Green Gables*; and the philosophy journal *Animus*.

LAURA M. ROBINSON, professor and interim dean of arts at Royal Military College, Kingston, has published articles about Canadian children's literature, Margaret Atwood, Ann-Marie MacDonald, *Pollyanna*, and the television show *The L-Word*, in addition to many articles on Montgomery's work, most recently in *Seriality and Texts for Young People*. Her current project examines Montgomery's depiction of friendship and sexuality, and as part of that, she curated the exhibit *The Canadian Home Front: L.M. Montgomery's Reflections on the First*

World War, which has been to France, Charlottetown, Kingston, Uxbridge, and Toronto and lives virtually at http://lmmontgomeryandwar.com/.

LINDA RODENBURG, a lecturer at Lakehead University Orillia, completed her PhD dissertation, "Alter/Native Spaces: Re/placing 'Aboriginal' in 'Canada' and 'Maori' in 'New Zealand' through the Novels of Thomas King and Patricia Grace," at the University of Otago in 2012. Most of her research focuses on Native Canadian and Maori literatures and their intersections with contemporary post-colonial theories. She is also interested in spatiality and place formation and travel-tourism and has presented at conferences on the ways in which identity and nationhood are constructed through stories in and about cultural sites created for tourists' consumption.

MARGARET STEFFLER is associate professor of English literature at Trent University. Her areas of research, publishing, and teaching include Canadian literature, post-colonial literature and theory, children's literature, Canadian women's life writing, and the construction of girlhood in Canadian fiction. Her work on Montgomery has appeared in *Anne's World: A New Century of Anne of Green Gables*; *Storm and Dissonance: L.M. Montgomery and Conflict*; *Windows and Words: A Look at Canadian Children's Literature*; *Making Avonlea: L.M. Montgomery and Popular Culture*; and the journal CREArTA.

KATE SUTHERLAND is associate professor at Osgoode Hall Law School, York University. She teaches and researches in the areas of law and literature and of tort law. She is the author of two short story collections, *Summer Reading* and *All In Together Girls*. She contributed a chapter to *Storm and Dissonance: L.M. Montgomery and Conflict* and has given papers on the courtroom battles of Harriet Beecher Stowe, Theodore Dreiser, and Montgomery. She is currently working on a book about lawsuits involving writers as litigants and literary texts as evidence.

CONTRIBUTORS

WILLIAM V. THOMPSON teaches children's literature at Grant MacEwan University in Edmonton, Alberta, and by distance for Athabasca University. He has a wide-ranging interest in young people's books and films, with a particular focus on dystopian writing and British fantasy. He has presented several conference papers at the L.M. Montgomery Institute conference on the *Emily* series. His current project is on monstrosity and rebellion in teen books for girls, and his most recent publication is "From Teenage Witch to Social Activist: Hermione Granger as the Female Locus in the Harry Potter Series" in *Hermione Granger Saves the World: Essays on the Feminist Heroine of Hogwarts*.

CHLOE VERNER is a fourth-year concurrent education student majoring in English at Lakehead University Orillia. She grew up in Toronto, attending Merle Levine Academy, where she realized her vocation for teaching students with special needs. Her love for reading inspired her decision to major in English while attaining teaching certification. Upon graduating in 2015, she hopes to further her studies with a master's degree in education and pursue a career as a special needs education teacher.

ELIZABETH WATERSTON is professor emerita at the University of Guelph. She is the author of many books, including *Magic Island: The Fictions of L.M. Montgomery*; *Rapt in Plaid: Canadian Literature and the Scottish Tradition*; and *Children's Literature in Canada*. She has also published extensively in scholarly journals and edited collections, and with Mary Rubio, is the editor of the multi-volume *The Selected Journals of L.M. Montgomery* and the recently published *The Complete Journals of L.M. Montgomery*.

EMILY WOSTER is an assistant professor in the Writing Studies Department at the University of Minnesota Duluth. She completed her PhD in English studies and children's literature at Illinois State University. Her scholarly interests include the reading and textual practices of L.M. Montgomery, the archival work of women's life writing, and intertextuality in children's literature. She has published on Montgomery and autobiographical texts and presented on these topics at a variety of conferences including those held by the Children's Literature Association and the International Association for Biography and Autobiography.

Index

Anderson, Isabel, 78–9, 102
Arthur, Julia, 255–7
Arts and Letters Club, 226, 235, 250–1
Asquith, Margot, 251–2; *An Autobiography*, 161
Aurora, ON: *Aurora Era*, 17. See also St Andrew's College (Aurora)
Authors League of America, 225
autobiography. *See* life writing

Bala, ON, 7, 13, 192, 199–200, 203–10, 214–20
Bala's Museum with Memories of Lucy Maud Montgomery, 13, 114, 130, 204, 215–20, 276
Beal, Mary, 245, 247–50
Benson, Nathaniel, 163
bildungsroman, 170
book dedications, 35, 62. *See also* Brooks, Robert; Campbell, Frederica (Frede); Lapp, Goldwin; Montgomery, L.M.: *Rainbow Valley*; Montgomery, L.M.: *Rilla of Ingleside*; Montgomery, L.M.: *The Story Girl*; Shier, Morley
Boston, 49, 242, 270
Bridle, Augustus, 247–8, 250–1
Brontë, Charlotte, 166; *Jane Eyre*, 175, 178, 180, 182
Brontë, Emily, 161; *Wuthering Heights*, 178, 180

Brooks, Robert, 35–6, 38, 41–2
Brooks family, 36, 42
Brown, George Douglas: *The House with the Green Shutters*, 164
Bulwer-Lytton, Edward: *Zanoni*, 157–8
Byron, Lord, 182; *Don Juan*, 152

Calderon, George: *The Little Stone House*, 247–8
Campbell, Frederica (Frede), 10, 40, 46–50, 53, 95, 247, 258; book dedications to, 10, 35, 46; death of, 10, 35, 46, 49–52, 58, 61, 70–1, 78, 83, 134, 138–40, 143–4, 147, 152–3, 168, 179; dreams about, 138, 179, 199–201; marriage of, 50
Canadian Authors Association (CAA), 14, 17, 223–37, 250–1
Canadian literary canon, 8, 14, 16, 223, 225–6, 228–31, 234–7
Carman, Bliss, 187, 194–5
Cavendish, PEI: burial, 17; commercialization, 114, 130, 216–17, 238, 247, 259–60; early years filtered through memory, 8, 26, 58, 60, 66, 71–3, 116–19, 155–60, 163, 174–5; as home, 6, 8, 72–3, 171–4; landscape, 31; leaving, 3–4, 6, 8, 95, 238; return visits, 72–3, 175. *See also* Prince Edward Island, return visits

INDEX

celebrity culture, 14, 116, 215–16, 241–2, 251, 252–3, 259–60
Charlesworth, Hector, 255, 258
children's magazine. *See Wide Awake.*
Church: Anglican, 63; Baptist, 62–5; Church Union, 72; evangelical, 55, 64–5; Methodist, 63, 246; Presbyterian, 56–7, 61, 63–4, 72–3; Roman Catholic, 63–4; United Church of Canada, 17, 42, 72. *See also* Leaskdale: St Paul's Presbyterian Church (Historic Leaskdale Church); Methodism/Methodist; Presbyterian/Presbyterianism
commodity/commodification, 8, 13–14, 116, 187–8, 192–3, 198, 201–2, 214–19, 241–2, 247. *See also* Cavendish: commercialization; Montgomery, L.M.: *The Blue Castle*, nature and tourism; Toronto, commercialism; tourism
consumerism. *See* commodity/commodification
copyright laws, 7, 223–7, 269
courtship/marriage plots. *See* domestic romance

Deacon, William Arthur, 229–34, 236–7
Dickinson, Emily, 58–9, 132, 144
domestic romance, 10, 30, 77–8, 83–4, 88–90, 98, 147, 166, 170, 181–3, 201, 203, 211–14, 234–5
du Maurier, George: *Trilby*, 159
Dumbells: *Biff-Bing-Bang*, 249–50

Edgar, Pelham, 223, 230–1, 233, 236
Emerson, Ralph Waldo, 66, 187, 193–4

female friendship, 10, 77–90, 120–3; and Lillian Faderman, 79–81
feminine utopia (Eve Kornfeld and Susan Jackson), 77–8
Findley, Timothy, 12, 167
First World War, 7–11, 17, 25–6, 30–2, 52–3, 77, 134, 139–41, 254–5; Canadian servicemen in, 10, 25, 35, 38–45. *See also* Leaskdale, and First World War; Montgomery, L.M.: and First World War; Montgomery, L.M.: as minister's wife during war
Fouqué, Friedrich de la Motte: *Undine*, 155, 162–3
Freud, Sigmund, 12, 81, 168, 178. *See also* uncanny

Glen Williams, ON, 4, 249, 254
gothic, 72, 141, 157, 166–70, 172–83. *See also* Southern Ontario Gothic
Great Depression, 82, 102
grief/grieving, and writing process, 131–4, 143–4; during war, 135. *See also* Montgomery, L.M.: mourning death of Frede; Montgomery, L.M.: mourning death of Hugh; Montgomery, L.M.: *Rilla of Ingleside*, and grief
Guelph, ON, 5; University of Guelph Library, Archival and Special Collections, 11–12, 138, 160, 245, 275–6, 279

Hamilton, ON, 249, 255
Hearts of the World, 40
Heirs of L.M. Montgomery, 151, 267–72, 279
Hemans, Felicia, 155, 157
home, 7, 238, 267; ancestral, 72, 173; church as, 72–3; Journey's End as, 6; Leaskdale as, 5, 47, 53, 72–3, 91–2, 243–4; Muskoka compared to Prince Edward Island, 203–5, 214; Norval as, 6; Ontario as, 4, 7, 72–3, 238, 60. *See also* Cavendish, as home
Hypatia Club, 41, 245

Irving, Washington: *The Alhambra*, 163

INDEX

journals (Montgomery), 15–16, 26, 151, 268–9, 276; commemorative journaling, 49–50; connection with fiction, 11, 16, 67, 115–16, 118–20, 123–4, 129–30, 134–5, 177–80, 183, 201, 219–20; final entries, 138–9; journal personae/selves, 12, 15, 56–9, 67–9, 72, 116, 151–5, 157–9, 161–5, 252, 257–9; retrospective journaling, 9, 54–9, 62–7, 70–3, 91, 116–18, 152–9, 165, 168, 176–7; writing it out, 61, 73, 115, 132, 139, 143, 147, 153–7, 172

Journey's End (Riverside Drive, Toronto), 5–6, 14, 70, 109, 253, 264–5, 275

Kailyard School, 164
Keith, Marian. *See* MacGregor, Mary Esther Miller
King, Basil, 247, 251
Kipling, Rudyard, 155–7, 239; *Kim*, 156–7
künstlerroman, 170, 172

Lacan, Jacques, 106–7
Lapp, Effie (née Wright), 36, 44–5
Lapp, Goldwin, 25, 35–8, 43–5
Lapp family, 36–7, 45
Laurence, Margaret, 131, 133
Leard, Herman, 67, 69, 176–8
Leaskdale, ON, 4–5, 7, 21, 239, 276–80; and First World War, 9–10, 26, 31, 52–3, 62, 127, 278; Guild, 155; landscape, 9, 31–2, 53; parish life, 21–2, 24–5, 30, 38, 91, 243, 278; Red Cross Society, 30, 43–4; and religion, 56–7, 66, 73; St Paul's Presbyterian Church (Historic Leaskdale Church), 4, 36, 59, 277–8; and writing, 8–10, 21, 30, 35, 52, 56, 59, 61–2, 72, 77, 174, 178–83; Young People's Association, 25, 30, 37–8. *See also* home, Leaskdale as
Leaskdale manse (Historic Leaskdale Manse), 3, 5, 15, 47, 59, 61–2, 91–2, 276–80; Gog and Magog, 51–2; Good Fairy statue, 50–3
legacy, 15, 260, 269, 275–7
life-writing, 115, 153–9, 162, 165. *See also* journals (Montgomery)
Livesay, Florence, 243
Lucky: death of, 106, 138, 228
Lucy Maud Montgomery Society of Ontario (LMMSO), 15, 277–80
Lundy, A.B.: "Men of the One-Sixteen," 42-3

Macbeth, Madge, 233–4
Macdonald, Chester (son): birth of, 5, 47, 70, 93, 95–9, 113, 120; as a child, 24–8, 31–2, 49, 53, 69–70, 83, 100; Norval years, 102–4, 106; problems, 6, 104, 106, 139, 228; religious upbringing, 56–7, 61
Macdonald, Ewan (husband): attitude to Montgomery's writing, 59; attitude to women, 251; engagement and marriage, 3–4; as Frede's friend, 46, 49; as husband, 22, 30, 53, 67–8, 91, 177, 242–3; melancholia (depression, mental illness), 6, 10, 22, 24, 39, 59–62, 67–70, 73, 83, 99–100, 104–5, 113, 139, 169, 176–7, 182, 200–1, 209, 228; as minister, 4–5, 22, 24, 36–8, 43, 61–2, 104, 176, 242–3; religious views, 60–1, 67–9, 71
Macdonald, Hugh (stillborn son), 43, 70, 94, 97–9, 105–6, 113, 116, 123–4, 133–4
Macdonald, Luella (née Reid; Chester's wife), 104
Macdonald, Ruth Eliza (née Steele; Stuart's wife), 265
Macdonald, Stuart, 15, 268–9, 279; birth of, 5, 99; as a child, 24–8, 53, 70, 100; as a father, 263–6; Norval years, 102–3, 105–6; religious upbringing, 55–7, 61; Toronto years, 228, 264–6

INDEX

MacFarlane, Cameron, 50
MacGregor, Mary Esther Miller (Marian Keith), 234, 243
Maclaren, Ian: *Beside the Bonnie Brier Bush*, 164
MacMillan, G.B., 66–7, 132, 138, 241
MacMurchy, Marjory, 243–4
Macneill, Alexander (grandfather): death of, 132–3
Macneill, Clara Woolner (mother), 92–4, 97, 109, 132–3
Macneill, Lucy Woolner (grandmother; surrogate mother), 30, 54, 61, 68–9, 92–3, 109, 170–1, 181, 263; death of, 3–4, 152, 172
McClung, Nellie, 226, 235, 250–1
McRae, Mary Ann. *See* Montgomery, Mary Ann McRae
Methodism/Methodist, 245–6, 252
Methodist Church. *See* Church: Methodist
Montgomery, Carl (half-brother), 40
Montgomery, Hugh John (father), 93–5, 147, 263
Montgomery, L.M.: attitudes to sex/sexuality, 54, 61, 63, 67–9, 78–9, 81, 121, 177; attitudes to women/women's roles/women's rights, 10, 26, 29–32, 251–2, 257; celebrity, 14, 17, 31, 58, 116, 215–16, 228, 238–42, 244–5, 248–9, 251–4, 256–60, 265–6; childhood reading, 155, 158–60; childhood, religious influences, 10, 54–6, 58–61, 64, 69–71, 73; childhood, rewriting, 58–9, 116–19, 162; childhood, vision of, 24–6, 118; concern over sons' religious upbringing, 56–7, 61; and cultural industry, 239, 241, 267–8, 271–2; death of, 17; depression, 7, 21, 70–1, 105–6, 126, 133, 138, 176; and domesticity, 30, 62, 91–2, 126, 166–71, 176–7, 179, 227–8; elocution, 242, 244, 249–52; and First World War, 11, 17, 25–6, 43–5, 52–3, 106, 109, 113, 123, 126, 156; funeral, 17; illness, 104, 113, 118–19, 126, 138–9, 201, 228; and lawsuits, 42, 49, 69, 83, 113, 225, 270–1; marriage, 3–4, 30–1, 67, 91–2, 95, 97, 129, 177; "Maudie," 56, 58, 69, 72; as minister's wife, 5, 14–15, 21–2, 24–6, 30–1, 54, 58, 60–2, 66, 72, 83, 116, 133, 169, 227, 244–6, 249, 280; as minister's wife during war, 25–6, 30–1, 43–4; motherhood, 10, 24, 26, 30–1, 43–4, 78, 83, 92–109, 120, 126, 129, 134; mourning death of Frede, 46, 49–50, 52, 58, 61, 70, 83, 134, 138–9, 143–4, 179–80; mourning death of Hugh, 43, 70, 94, 98–9, 106, 113, 123–4, 133–4; nervous breakdown (1910), 118–19; obituary, 17; photography, 16, 50, 152, 154, 267, 279; poetry, 8, 16, 43, 140–3; popularity/waning popularity, 17, 22, 114, 139, 225, 229–30, 236–7, 257, 265–7, 272; private versus public selves, 11, 56, 61, 106, 113–19, 123, 129, 241–2, 252–3, 258–60, 268; and religion, 10, 54–73; responsiveness to nature, 4, 6, 12–13, 31, 65–6, 187, 199, 201–2; scrapbooks, 16–17, 160, 245, 256, 275, 302n61, 302n68; self-construction/self-fashioning, 8, 12, 15, 115, 117–19, 151–5, 158, 161, 165, 168, 252–4, 257–8; self-dramatization, 8, 15, 245, 257; sense of displacement (homesickness), 3–8, 10, 57, 67, 72–3, 140, 155–7, 163, 169, 172–3, 179; and spirituality, 66, 71, 187. *See also* journals (Montgomery)
– *The Alpine Path*, 9, 11, 116–19, 151, 159
– *Among the Shadows*: "The Old Chest at Wyther Grange," 169,

326

180; "The Red Room," 169, 180; "The Tryst of the White Lady," 169, 180–2
- *Anne of Avonlea*, 31, 95, 294n12
- *Anne of Green Gables*, 31, 103, 117, 130; dark aspects of, 25, 119; depiction of childhood in, 24–5, 117; female friendship in, 78, 82–3; licensing and copyright, 269–72; popularity of, 229–30, 242, 266; significance of home and family, 94, 98; and tourism, 130, 216–19
- *Anne's House of Dreams*, 8, 31; darkening vision of, 11, 26, 109, 113, 117, 119–20, 122–9, 133; motherhood in, 26, 93–4, 98–9, 106, 260
- *Anne of Ingleside*, 9, 125, 129
- *Anne of the Island*, 8, 26, 31, 90, 113, 119; female friendship in, 10, 77, 79, 82–8, 90; mother-daughter relations in, 93–4, 97–8, 109
- *Anne of Windy Poplars*, 9, 125, 129
- *The Blue Castle*, 9, 260; female friendship in, 10, 77, 82–90; mother-daughter relations in, 10, 93, 99–102, 108–9; nature and tourism in, 12–13, 114, 187–202, 203–4, 209–20
- *The Blythes Are Quoted*, 9, 11, 132, 138–44, 260; "Fancy's Fool," 140
- *The Doctor's Sweetheart*, 269
- *Emily Climbs*, 9, 85, 131, 260
- *Emily of New Moon*, 9, 31, 61, 71–3, 102–3, 133, 230; adaptations of, 267, 276; autobiographical elements in, 10, 54, 56, 58–9, 69, 72–3, 85, 169–70, 174, 176–8; faith and spirituality in, 61, 71–2; and Southern Ontario Gothic, 12, 167–70, 172, 174–6, 178–83
- *Emily's Quest*, 9, 85, 177, 260
- "The Garden of Spices," 169, 180–1
- *The Golden Road*, 9
- *Jane of Lantern Hill*, 31, 260; mother-daughter relations in, 93, 106–9; and Toronto, 6, 9, 245–6
- *Kilmeny of the Orchard*, 31
- *Magic for Marigold*, 9, 31
- *Mistress Pat*, 9, 260; mother-daughter relations in, 93, 103–5, 109
- *Pat of Silver Bush*, 9, 31; mother-daughter relations in, 93, 102–5, 109
- *Rainbow Valley*: dedication of, 10, 25, 35, 38, 52; and First World War, 25–6, 38, 42–3, 49; and Leaskdale, 8–9, 21–32, 38, 52–3, 61–2; and religion, 21–2, 24, 61–2; role of Anne in, 125, 260
- *Rilla of Ingleside*, 8–9, 85; darkening vision of, 11, 113, 125–9; dedication of, 10, 35, 38, 46, 52, 135; and First World War, 38–9, 42, 45–6, 52, 120, 127–9, 134–8, 140–1, 260; and grief, 11, 52, 128–9, 132, 134–41, 143, 260
- *The Road to Yesterday*, 9, 269
- *The Story Girl*, 8–9, 21, 24; dedication of, 46
- *A Tangled Web*, 9, 227

Montgomery, Mary Ann (née McRae; stepmother), 92–4, 109, 263
Moodie, Susanna: *Roughing It in the Bush*, 168
motherhood, 10, 78, 92–4, 107; maternal thinking (Sara Ruddick), 92, 99, 101, 103. *See also* Montgomery, L.M.: motherhood
Munro, Alice, 12, 169, 172–8, 180, 182–3; *Lives of Girls and Women*, 172–4, 182–3; *Who Do You Think You Are?*, 173, 177
Muskoka, ON, 9, 12–14, 114, 187–8, 192–202, 203–10, 214–20
Mustard, John, 64, 206–7
Mustard, Margaret Leask, 36, 38, 45

North Bay, ON, 257
Norval, ON, 4–7, 9, 102–6, 109, 160, 223, 227, 239, 249, 264, 276; St Paul's Anglican Church Parish Hall, 276
Norval manse, 5

Ontario: gender roles, 82; landscapes, 7, 16, 21, 31, 192–3, 201; tourism, 13, 188, 192–3, 200–1. *See also* Aurora, Bala, Glen Williams, Guelph, Hamilton, Leaskdale, Muskoka, North Bay, Norval, Toronto, Uxbridge, Zephyr

Pankhurst, Emmeline, 249
Pickthall, Marjorie: *The Wood-Carver's Wife*, 247–8
place/space (Yi-Fu Tuan). *See* space/place (Yi-Fu Tuan)
Predestination, doctrine of, 60–2, 64, 67–8, 70–2
Presbyterian/Presbyterianism, 10, 56–7, 59–62, 64–7, 69–73, 176–7, 245–6
Presbyterian Church. *See* Church: Presbyterian
Press Club, 17, 230, 243, 247, 249
Prince Albert, SK, 64, 93–4, 206
Prince Edward Island, 4, 6–8, 152; gender roles, 82; religion, 60–6, 72; return visits, 12, 40, 102, 168, 173–4, 267. *See also* Cavendish; home, Muskoka compared to Prince Edward Island
Pritchard, Laura, 64, 164

Reid, Lily (Lillis Harrison), 39
Reid, Luella. *See* Macdonald, Luella
romanticism, 16, 157, 162, 166–7, 169–70, 178, 181–3, 234; and nature, 13, 187, 193–4, 197, 202
Ruskin, John, 166, 187

St Andrew's College (Aurora), 102
Scott, Walter: *The Betrothed*, 159

Second World War, 8, 17, 138–9, 141
The Sentimental Garden, 163
sexology/sexologists, 80–1, 89
Shakespeare, William: death of Hamnet, 131; *Macbeth*, 152–3; *Twelfth Night*, 301n56
Sharpe, Sam, 41–2
Shaw, George Bernard: *Androcles and the Lion*, 259; as celebrity, 255–6, 259; *John Bull's Other Island*, 254; *Saint Joan*, 15, 160, 254–60; *Three Live Ghosts*, 302n61
Shier, Morley, 35–6, 38–41
Shier family, 36–9, 41
Simpson, Edwin, 63, 65
Sinclair, Mary: *The Romantic*, 159
Smith, Edwin, 68–9
Southern Ontario Gothic, 12, 167–9, 173, 176–8, 182–3
space/place (Yi-Fu Tuan), 204–15, 219–20
spiritualism, 66–7
Stevenson, Robert Louis, 207

Tennyson, Alfred, 160
theosophy. *See* spiritualism
Toronto, ON, 4–7, 238; airfields during First World War, 39; commercialism, 239, 243, 247, 254, 259; cinemas, 239, 242, 253–4; cultural scene, 5, 14, 239, 241, 243, 246, 252; Hart House, 246–9, 254; Jarvis (Street) Collegiate, 45–6, 248; literary scene, 14, 223, 226–8, 237; Massey Hall, 251–2; move to, 5–7, 9; publishing industry, 5, 243; Royal Alexandra, 245, 254, 302n61; Runnymede 253; theatre censorship, 246; theatre scene, 239, 242–7, 254; University of Toronto (Knox College), 15, 264–5. *See also* Journey's End (Riverside Drive)
tourism: authenticity (Dean MacCannell), 218–20; literary, 114, 130, 204, 216–17, 280; tourist

experiences (Erik Cohen), 13, 204, 208–14, 216–17; tourist gaze (John Urry) 204, 207–9, 211–12, 215, 218–20. *See also* Bala's Museum with Memories of Lucy Maud Montgomery; Cavendish: commercialization; Ontario: tourism
Transcendentalism, 66, 71

uncanny, 12, 72, 168–70, 172–6, 178–9
Union, ON. *See* Glen Williams, ON
Uxbridge, ON, 4, 30–1, 36–7, 39, 41, 239, 276–8; *Uxbridge Journal*, 17. *See also* Hypatia Club

Weber, Ephraim, 39, 55–6, 67, 138
Wells, H.G.: *The Outline of History*, 160

Wide Awake, 156
woman reader (Kate Flint, Mary Kelley), 153, 162
Women's Canadian Club, 244, 252, 256
Women's Press Club. *See* Press Club
women's suffrage, 17, 26, 29, 31, 80, 82, 232
Wordsworth, Dorothy: *Recollections of a Tour Made in Scotland*, 171
Wordsworth, William, 21, 31, 59, 169–70, 187, 193

Zephyr, ON, 4, 36, 39, 41–2, 59, 176, 245–6, 249, 279

MAR 1 1 2016

CENTRAL LIBRARY